1001
Ways to be Your Own Boss

by
Vivo Bennett &
Cricket Clagett

WITH

PRENTICE-HALL, INC.
Englewood Cliffs, New Jersey

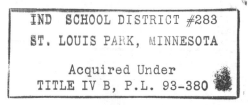
1001 Ways to Be Your Own Boss, by Vivo Bennett & Cricket Clagett
Copyright © 1976 by Vivo Bennett and Alice Clagett

Printed in the United States of America

Prentice-Hall International, Inc., London
Prentice-Hall of Australia, Pty. Ltd., Sydney
Prentice-Hall of Canada, Ltd., Toronto
Prentice-Hall of India Private Ltd., New Delhi
Prentice-Hall of Japan, Inc., Tokyo

10 9 8 7 6 5 4 3 2 1

Library of Congress Cataloging in Publication Data

Bennett,Vivo.
1001 ways to be your own boss.

Bibliography: p.
1. Small business. 2. Self-employed.
3. Small business—Management. I. Clagett,
Cricket. joint author. II. Title.
HD2341.B35   658'.022   75—38940
ISBN 0–13–636985–5
ISBN 0–13–636977–4 pbk.

To Peggy,
Kathy, Chip,
Betsy, Chuck, and Dawn—
May you always have 1001 ways to
be your own boss.

Acknowledgments

The authors would like to thank Mrs. Marion Mangion, Mrs. Dorothy Wilson, and Miss Margie Richardson—reference librarians at the Richland County Public Library, Columbia, South Carolina—for their valuable help in providing answers to innumerable questions. We also thank Mr. Calvert Thomas for his advice on Chapter 2.

Contents

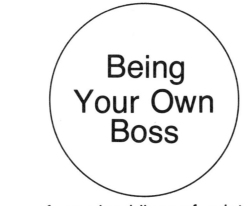

Being Your Own Boss

"The mass of men lead lives of quiet desperation."
—HENRY DAVID THOREAU

Every morning, across the United States, millions of alarm clocks vulgarly intrude upon the peaceful slumber of their masters.

In the murky light of a new day, a hand will reach out and silence the intruder for another twenty-four hours.

Perhaps the owner of the clock (or is he its slave?) will sit on the edge of his bed for a few minutes wondering: "If I *must* get up and go somewhere this morning, why must it be to a desk in an office, an assembly line in a factory, a counter in a store? Why must I be there exactly at nine in the morning and leave precisely at five in the afternoon? Why can't *I* be the boss and determine my own hours, my own activities, my own destiny?"

Well, my friend, the fact is that you *can* have things your way.

According to the U. S. Bureau of Labor, there are presently more than seven million self-employed people in the United States. Their activities range from raising earthworms to writing novels, from peddling trinkets door to door to buying and selling multimillion-dollar corporations.

You may say, "Well, these people have a *talent* for this. I couldn't do it." Nonsense. You may not have the ability (or the desire) to build and operate a national chain of department stores, but you certainly can start a small furniture refinishing business, a tool rental service, raise rats and mice for laboratories, or undertake and profit by any of the other 998 enterprises listed in this book.

Too many people in our society have relegated themselves to tasks which they think society, or fate, or "the gods," are forcing them to perform. The truth of the matter is that they are underestimating their worth as individuals, and it is just not necessary. In a sense, they have died before their time.

So you see, it's up to you. Just about anyone can get started in most of the businesses suggested in this book without any special skills or significant amount of capital. But regardless of which you may choose to tackle, the authors congratulate you on your adventurousness and wish you the best of success on your journey toward satisfaction and prosperity.

VIVO BENNETT
CRICKET CLAGETT

The Importance of
Advertising and Promotion

"No one can succeed at everything,
but everyone can succeed at something."

—ANON.

One of us has a distant cousin in southern California who started refinishing furniture for friends and neighbors as a teenager. Gradually, his services became more and more in demand, and today he heads one of the most prosperous furniture refinishing plants on the West Coast.

To us, the prospect of making a living refinishing other people's furniture seems about as glamorous as counting the grains of sand on a wind-swept beach. Chances are, if we tried to get started in this field, we'd fail just as sure as you're sitting there reading these words. On the other hand, if that successful and affluent cousin tried to sit down at our typewriter and bang out a book, he might not fare so well either.

The point is that each of us has certain aptitudes, talents, and desires that are unique to ourselves. We should allow these traits to decide how we're going to spend our days. The profit picture will then take care of itself.

According to Dun & Bradstreet, ten thousand businesses fail in our country every year. Such things as lack of sales, poor management, and insufficient capital are cited as reasons for the failures. What the statistics don't tell us, however, is how many of the people who started these collapsed enterprises were not suited to their chosen work to begin with.

Again, figure out what you enjoy doing and are able to do well—or would be able to do well after the proper training—and get started. It's as simple as that.

There is another ingredient, just as important, in the recipe for a successful business venture. That ingredient is *promotion*. Promotion of your product or service can easily mean the difference between success and failure.

Now we didn't say "advertising," we said "promotion." Although the line between the two is sometimes a thin one, there may be a vast difference.

Advertising is usually costly. Why? Because you're paying someone else to do a job for you. Although advertising sometimes pays off, it is a chore that in many cases you could just as well perform yourself. Furthermore, the consumer is so heavily bombarded with advertising from every nook and cranny that he has become somewhat desensitized to all but the most attention-getting appeals, which are usually extravagant Madison Avenue creations. Rather than attempting to overcome these overwhelming financial and competitive odds, it may be better to tackle the job yourself, applying your own creativity to your particular product or service.

You can take a product like a custom-made doghouse and put an ad in the paper, have a few spot announcements on the radio, even insert a large, expensive display ad in your local Yellow Pages. If your prices are right, you'll get a fair amount of business from these costly forms of advertising. However, if instead, you were to call the local newspaper or TV station and offer to be interviewed for a feature article or program, you would reach thousands of potential customers and it wouldn't cost you a dime!

But these are only two of many possible ways to promote your product effectively at little or no expense to yourself.

Present one of your doghouses to the mayor as a gift. Construct a giant model of your product, stock it with a half-dozen full-grown Great Danes or Saint Bernards, then get the local shopping center to allow you to display it in the center of their mall or in the parking lot. Put it on a flatbed truck and haul it through the center of town. Cooperate with a local pet shop and give away a few of your doghouses as raffle prizes to their customers. Award a doghouse every week to the husband or wife submitting the best reason why their spouse should be "in the doghouse." Hold a hot dog-eating contest for kids and award your product to the winner. You see, the possibilities for promoting your product or service are only as limited as your own imagination.

Of course, the type of promotions you undertake will depend upon the nature of your product or service as well as upon the vagaries of your own personality. The keys, however, to any successful promotion are *exposure* and *impression*. How large a mass of people will become aware of your product or service? How deeply are they amazed, titillated, motivated, shocked, intrigued, or otherwise impressed by your promotion?

Since most kinds of promotion depend on imagination and ingenuity, it is impossible to list them all. Nevertheless, here is a partial list of ways to advertise and promote whatever it is you want to sell. They run the gamut from the conventional to the ludicrous. Let them serve as a springboard to ideas for other aggressive means of motivating people to take advantage of what you have to offer.

TWENTY-FIVE WAYS TO ADVERTISE YOUR PRODUCT OR SERVICE

- Television spot announcements.
- Radio spot announcements.
- Newspaper display or classified ads.
- Yellow Pages advertising.

- Billboard advertising.

- Skywriting.

- Large display ads on buses or taxicabs.

- Display ads inside of buses and taxicabs.

- Direct mail advertising. For firms specializing in this, check your Yellow Pages under "Advertising—Direct Mail."

- Advertise in the local high school or college newspaper.

- Run a classified or display ad in a national magazine or newspaper.

- Run a classified or display ad in a trade magazine relevant to your product or service.

- Have a motion picture production house make a short film or slide presentation of you or your product and pay a local theater to run it between movies.

- Set up a "boiler room." In this operation you stock an office with telephones and hire cheap labor to call likely prospects in the area and offer your product or service. You can also hire people to call from their own home, which cuts down on your overhead. Employees usually work from "reverse directories," telephone directories which list by street rather than by name. These must be leased from the telephone company.

- Distribute leaflets. Thousands of these can be printed up cheaply. You can give them out yourself or hire high school kids to do it for you. In this case make sure, however, that they are distributed rather than thrown into the nearest trash can en masse. Leave them at front doors (mailboxes are a no-no, according to the Post Office) or on auto windshields. You could also stand in a congested area and hand them to people, or make a deal with your local newspaper to stuff them into their newspapers prior to delivery.

- Hire people to walk around in congested areas holding signs or with "sandwich boards" hung over their shoulders.

- Advertise on a vacant theater marquee.

- Imprint your name and product on unique specialty items and give them away. For ideas and services, check firms listed under "Advertising Specialties" in your Yellow Pages.

- Advertise on "shirt boards" (the cardboard slats contained inside men's shirts when they come back from the laundry). Buy a large quantity of these from a local paper supplier. Have advertisements printed on them and give them or sell them cheaply to local laundries.

- Locate your business on a busy street or next to a freeway where you could erect a large sign and/or display.

- Advertise on bus stop benches.

- Print your letterhead on your stationery.

- Print up business cards. These can sometimes be a detriment, however, as when a prospective customer, instead of saying "Yes," says, "Give me your card and I'll call you."

- Advertise on matchbooks and supply them free or at low cost to super-markets, drugstores—anywhere tobacco is sold. Make a deal with a cigarette machine vendor to distribute your matches in his machines.

- Have family and friends talk up your product or service.

THIRTY UNIQUE PROMOTIONAL IDEAS

- Notify the local TV or radio station of your business. Offer to be inter-viewed on one of their programs.

- Ask the local newspaper to send out a reporter to write a feature article on you and your business.

- Hold a shopping center promotion or exhibition.

- Cart your product around town on a flatbed truck for all to see.

- Hold a raffle.

- Get a famous personality to appear and be photographed with your product.

- Give away samples of your product.

- Hire 100 school kids to parade through congested areas carrying your product or signs advertising it.

- Have a contest and award your product or service as a prize.

- Get an authority or an institution to endorse your product.

- Offer an incentive for people just to come into your place of business.

- Sponsor a bowling team in your town. Supply the members with shirts imprinted with a picture of your product or with your company name on the back.

- Put on a free show with live music, comedians, magicians, etc.

- Drop 10,000 colored balloons—with a gift certificate inside or with your name imprinted on the outside—into the downtown area on a busy Saturday afternoon. Have a photographer there from the local news-paper. Be prepared to be fined for littering.

- Get arrested for one of many other possible inconsequential offenses, such as climbing up the city hall flagpole and throwing dollar bills to the people below, or holding a "spontaneous" midnight bonfire and wienie roast in the city square. Tip off the media beforehand and have your product prominently displayed at the time of arrest. Have money for bail.

- Hold classes in your home or store to generate interest in your product.

- Hold classes on your local TV or educational TV station in order to generate interest in your product.

- Display your product in shops that deal in related items. Other possible display sites are libraries, parks, museums, supermarkets—anywhere people congregate.

- Hire a balloonist to fly across town dropping samples or models of your product along the way.

- Sponsor a picnic during which people could try out your product.

- Donate your product to TV quiz shows in exchange for their mentioning your name.

- Ride a jackass with your signs on his sides through the downtown area. Tip off the media beforehand.

- Hire a group of costumed school kids to ride a string of jackasses, ponies, camels, or elephants through the center of town on a busy Saturday afternoon. Make sure your signs are prominently displayed. Since you'll probably cause a sizable traffic jam, you may get arrested for parading without a license. But the bail will probably be small and you'll end up being the talk of the town. Of course, the media won't want to miss this audacious display of promotional nonsense, so give them some warning.

- Wear an outlandish costume into town, prominently displaying your product.

- Have someone pole-sit with your product.

- Get a nude model to streak down the main drag carrying your product. Again, tip off the media beforehand. If this stunt is a bit "much" for you, you could simply have the lady stroll down the street in a bikini. This would be especially impressive in a snowy climate.

- Light up the night sky with spotlights in front of your place of business.

- Become a one-man beautification committee and get local school kids to plant a large quantity of trees and flowers around town. Be sure the media is given advance notice and that they know you are sponsoring the project.

- Sponsor a drive for a charity, again letting it be known that you are involved.

● Hold special holiday promotions. For instance, if you build rabbit hutches, have a bunny giveaway at Easter. If you're a candy maker, give a batch of candy to hospital patients just prior to Valentine's Day. And of course, anything and everything can be promoted at Christmastime.

Many of the business ideas in this book are accompanied by suggestions for pricing and indications of the possible profits to be made. However, many are not. These considerations depend a good deal on such things as competition in the area, availability and cost of raw materials, demand for the particular item or service, how well you do your job, and any extra services you may perform. The type of clientele will likewise influence price. You would certainly expect much greater remuneration for your time if you ran a posh "animal hotel" than if you simply operated a kennel. To the dog, both services are the same. But if the owner is affluent (and a little eccentric) he will be willing to pay a premium for the finer service.

Without exception, any of the 1001 businesses have a potential for operation on a grand scale. A part-time baby-sitter could open up a child care center which might, under the right management, be expanded into additional centers, eventually developing into a national chain.

In supplying home-grown worms to local fishermen, you might discover that a large sporting goods store in your area has a heavy demand for your type of worm. Or you might make a deal with a national sporting goods chain which would necessitate your developing a national "network" of growers who could supply you with the worms. On the other hand, you might invent a plastic replica that works even better than a live worm, and develop a lucrative mail order trade with the product. So if expansion is your desire, always keep your eyes and ears open for new horizons.

2

Business Organization and Legal Requirements

Before you have spent any significant amount of time, energy, or financial resources on your new business enterprise, there are a number of legal and administrative requirements to be considered. You should become thoroughly familiar with these, applying them not only to beginning your particular venture, but with an eye to expansion as well.

A few customers coming to your home each day for clothing alterations may pose no problems. However, should your business flourish and evolve into a bargain center for discounted fabrics or custom tailoring, you'll no doubt have parking problems and cause a hubbub of street activity. You'll then be required to conform to zoning and licensing laws pertaining to businesses in general, as well as to applicable deed restrictions on your property, and will probably have to move your enterprise into a more suitable area of town. Likewise, having a few egg-laying hens in the back yard of your suburban home *might* not disturb any of the neighbors, but try building and stocking a few rows of henhouses with a few hundred clucking, cackling inhabitants and see how fast the situation changes. Again, find out what the requirements are beforehand, and make provisions for all eventualities.

The following information will give you an outline of the legal requirements for small businesses, as well as help you decide on some important administrative policies. Keep in mind, however, that since regulations may vary greatly between communities, you should always check local requirements.

CHOOSING THE FORM OF YOUR BUSINESS

One of the first things you'll want to consider is the organizational form of your enterprise. There are three types of ownership in any business: sole proprietorship, partnership, and corporation. Each has its advantages and disadvantages, depending on such considerations as need for additional financing, implications of current tax laws, and amount of personal control desired.

Sole Proprietorship. The great majority of the approximately ten million businesses in the United States are run as sole proprietorships. Because of its simplicity and flexibility this is probably the best organizational form to use in starting most of the enterprises outlined in this book.

Under sole proprietorship you have complete control over your business, and all its profits are yours exclusively. Here, federal and state regulation are at a minimum, as compared with the corporative form, which is in most cases subjected to vigorous governmental control. As a sole proprietor, you pay income tax not on the business, but on your personal income. Business losses are, of course, deductible.

On the other side of the coin, as a sole proprietor the burden of all facets of the business, such as production, advertising and promotion, administration, and bookkeeping, falls entirely upon your shoulders. Financially, you have only your own personal assets to draw upon as capital. Because of this, lenders are not always as eager to oblige a sole proprietor as they are a partnership or a corporation.

Furthermore, you hold unlimited personal liability for your business debts. This means that, in case of business failure, all of your personal assets, such as your home, automobile, and real property, may be subject to claim by your creditors. When the sole proprietor dies, his business is automatically terminated.

Partnership. Like the sole proprietorship, the partnership enjoys relative freedom from governmental control. Here the organization may consist of two or more partners, who may or may not have equal investments in, and share equally in the profits of, the business.

In a partnership, the opportunity for growth may be enhanced for a number of reasons. Since, usually, two heads *are* better than one, a greater number of fruitful and creative business ideas may be generated. Also, personal abilities may be complemented, with each partner performing the duties for which he has the greater aptitude.

Financial resources may be pooled, making available more capital for the enterprise. This, in turn, will allow the business to rely less on borrowing. If borrowing becomes a necessity, however, the combined credit ratings of the partners may allow more money to be borrowed, and on more favorable terms.

There is no business tax. Each of the partners pays a personal income tax based on his share of the profits. Also, each may deduct his share of any losses during the tax year.

Just as all partners share in the profits of the venture, all are legally bound to share any liabilities the others may incur in the course of the business. There have been cases in which a partner went suddenly and unaccountably berserk, piling up debts by buying everything in sight. Unfortunately, by the time an activity like this is uncovered, the enterprise is usually doomed—with the other partners responsible for the outstanding debts.

Another disadvantage inherent in partnerships lies in the possibility of friction among those involved. More than one enterprise has been ruined through internal conflict.

Partnerships are automatically dissolved when any of the partners sells his interest, withdraws, dies, or is declared bankrupt. If the partners can't agree on dissolution, it can be effected through court action if it can be established that one of the partners is of unsound mind or otherwise incapable of carrying on his duties. A court will also order dissolution if it can be shown that the business can be carried on only at a loss.

As you can see, the partnership is somewhat more complex than the sole proprietorship. If you decide to organize your business as a partnership, it is advisable to draw up a partnership agreement through a competent attorney. This document will clearly define rights and responsibilities of each of the parties involved.

The Corporation. A corporation is a legal business entity, separate and distinct from those who share its ownership, and chartered under the laws of the state in which it is formed. Ownership is represented by shares of stock.

Because of the financial expense and legal complexities involved, most small businessmen do not initially organize their business along these lines. However, many enterprises that begin as sole proprietorships or partnerships eventually convert into corporations.

Of the three forms discussed, the corporation offers the best prospects for obtaining additional capital. Stock can be sold, loans made by issuing bonds, assets collateralized or exchanged, or profits reserved from the business. Furthermore, in case of lawsuits or business failure, the liability of the individual stockholders is limited to the amount of their investment in the stock. Unlike the sole proprietorship and the partnership, the continuation of the corporation is unaffected by the death of any of its owners.

On the negative side, legal and filing fees for incorporation start at several hundred dollars and range upward, depending on the complexity of the undertaking. The transaction of business is legally restricted to the state in which the corporation is chartered. This means that permission must be secured from each state in which the corporation desires to operate, entailing payment of additional license fees and conformity to existing regulations. Thus, expansion could be inhibited.

Although charter provisions can be broadly drawn, the activities of the corporation are usually limited to those specifically granted in the charter. This could place a heavy handicap on a company with diversification in mind. Corporations are subject to more control by the federal government than are the other organizational forms.

Taxes apply to corporate income, as well as to any dividends received by stockholders. In certain cases, however, individuals may avoid this "double tax" by electing to have the corporation taxed as though it were a partnership. That is, each of the partners pays only a personal income tax based on his share of the profits.

For further information:

Choosing a Form of Business Organization, Robert Davies and Kelwyn Lawrence. Durham, North Carolina, Duke University Press, 1963.

BUSINESS LICENSES

These are issued both as a means of regulating businesses and as a source of revenue for the community. A business license will be required by most municipalities prior to your being allowed to engage in any business within the city limits. Fees are usually based on a minimum figure and scaled upward depending on the estimated or established annual gross receipts of the business.

Before granting approval, the licensing authority determines whether the enterprise will conform to existing ordinances relating to such things as zoning, health, safety, and public morality. Generally speaking, a small, quiet business, run in a residential neighborhood but attracting little or no increased traffic to the area, may not be required to obtain a license—the authorities may not choose to enforce the regulations. However, any conspicuous display of commercial activity or large outdoor signs will surely, according to city hall, put you in the category of a full-fledged business and you'll probably be required to conform to all pertinent ordinances.

If you plan to hawk your wares on the street or solicit business door to door, a business or other special license may be required or these activities may be prohibited altogether. If in doubt, check with the licensing bureau at your city hall.

State Business and Professional Licenses. Most states require the passing of an examination and granting of a license in such fields as barbering and cosmetology, real estate and insurance sales, pharmacy, and public accounting. Of course, all states have adopted stringent licensing requirements for practicing physicians and attorneys. Stretching the point a bit, auto and encyclopedia salesmen fall under licensing requirements in some states. Check with the appropriate state agency to determine the regulations in your state.

Fictitious Name Statement. If you are going to open a business under any name other than your full legal name, you are generally required to file a document with your county clerk listing your legal name and the name of your business. The purpose of this statement is to prevent the running of two businesses under the same name within the county. It also serves as a legal record of who actually owns the business.

ZONING REGULATIONS

Zoning restrictions are in effect in almost all municipalities in the United States. These ordinances provide for the compatible coexistence of various businesses with each other and with the community as a whole.

Zoning laws effectively prohibit a noisy manufacturing plant from being located next to a hospital, for instance, or a malodorous rubber plant from opening up next to a restaurant.

Since zoning laws are a function of city government, a call to the zoning commission at city hall will answer any questions on the subject.

In addition, many residential subdivisions have enforceable deed restrictions running with the land, setting forth limitations on the use of the property. Any applicable restrictions should be noted and taken into consideration before beginning any home business venture.

HEALTH LAWS

Regulations protecting citizens from potential health hazards are in effect at all governmental levels. These laws apply to a broad range of products and activities such as food preparation and handling, animal slaughtering and processing, drug and patent medicine manufacture, and the preparation and sale of cosmetics.

Opening a small café in town normally comes under the sanitary code of the city health department. Starting the same type of business in an unincorporated area of the county, however, could conceivably lie in the domain of both the county and state health departments.

Most states have established meat and poultry inspection departments to supervise animal and poultry slaughter and processing. In addition, any or all of these activities could conceivably come under federal regulations as well, whether or not the products are shipped across state lines. Under the Food, Drug, and Cosmetic Act, for example, federal inspectors may enter and inspect any establishment where food, drugs, or cosmetic items are being stored or sold.

Before investing a sizable amount of time or finances in any venture that may possibly involve health laws, it's best to check all levels of government for any pertinent regulations.

SAFETY LAWS

Here we have another raft of regulations existing, again, on all levels, and governing everything from toy manufacture to building construction. If your business involves custom-tailoring of wearing apparel, for instance, and you send your finished product across state lines, you must abide by regulations under the Flammable Fabrics Act administered by the Federal Trade Commission. These regulations provide for the material to be made fire-resistant prior to shipment.

A state license is generally required prior to opening and operating a children's nursery. Before a license is granted, it must be demonstrated that stringent safety regulations have been, and will be, complied with.

On the county level, standards of building safety may take into consideration such things as design of the structure, building materials used, wiring, heating, plumbing, fixtures, store signs, and fire safety.

Cities, in addition to having still another set of standards, will usually require compliance with regulations on all governmental levels before issuing a business license.

As in the case of health laws, check applicable regulations thoroughly before getting involved in any venture.

LABOR LAWS

If you're even thinking of hiring people to help you in your business, you should be aware of federal and state legislation pertaining to employees of your firm. Such subjects as fair employment practices, regulation of wages, hours, and working conditions, social security contributions, and disability and unemployment compensation are all covered under a gaggle of federal and state regulations. Of course, if your enterprise is strictly a "family affair," you will for the most part escape these legislative complexities.

In some cases, you may hire help on an "independent contractor" basis. Under this arrangement, an individual signs a form stating that he has agreed to perform certain duties for you on a contractual basis, rather than as an employee. In such an instance you would not be required to adhere to the above regulations. However, because of abuses, the Internal Revenue Service (IRS) scrutinizes these arrangements very carefully. Any supervision and control exerted by you over the individual's time and activities would, according to the IRS, make him an employee, thereby making you subject to all applicable laws regarding employees, even though a statement might have been signed to the contrary. Outside commission salesmen are frequently taken on as independent contractors. If in doubt, ask your local IRS office to send you the pertinent information.

For other information on current labor laws, contact the U. S. Department of Labor in any large city or your state employment commission.

TAXES

Income Taxes. If you are a sole proprietor or a partner, your federal income tax returns are filed, and taxes paid, in substantially the same manner as if you were drawing a salary from an employer. Your profits, or share of the profits, are considered as personal income. Of course, in figuring your income taxes, all legitimate business expenses, such as license fees, office supplies, advertising, and wages paid to employees, may be deducted. In addition, if your business is in your home, you may deduct a proportionate amount of your home maintenance costs as business expenses. For instance, if you rent a six-room house and use one of the rooms as an office or workshop, you may deduct as a business expense up to one-sixth of your rent, insurance, utilities, and general maintenance costs. If you own your own home, you are entitled to take depreciation on that part which is converted to business use.

As mentioned previously, corporations are taxed on their income. You, as an officer or stockholder, would then pay an income tax on your salary and on dividends from your stock. Of course, a qualifying corporation could elect to be taxed as though it were a partnership, thus eliminating the double tax on dividends.

In states requiring the filing and payment of personal income taxes, the procedures for reporting business income are substantially the same as those established by the federal government.

Withholding of Tax. As an employer, you are responsible for withholding federal and, in some cases, state and local income taxes from the wages of each of your employees. For information contact the IRS or your state tax agency.

Social Security Taxes. Under the Social Security Act, you must make deductions from each employee's paycheck for Social Security taxes. In addition, you are required to pay a tax into this program for each of your employees. As a businessman, you must also pay funds into your own Social Security fund. This self-employment tax is applicable whether you work part-time or full-time. Social Security taxes are paid on a periodic basis along with other withheld taxes or with personal income taxes.

For further tax information consult your nearest IRS office or state income tax authority. Also, you may find the following publications helpful:

Tax Guide for Small Business, IRS Publication 334, Washington, D. C., Superintendent of Documents, U. S. Government Printing Office. Also available through your local District Director of Internal Revenue:

Getting the Facts for Income Tax Reporting, leaflet #144. Available from any Small Business Administration field office, or write Small Business Administration, Washington, D. C. 20416.

Prentice-Hall Federal Tax Service. Englewood Cliffs, New Jersey, Prentice-Hall.

State and Local Sales Taxes. Most states and municipalities levy taxes on retail items. Upon starting a retail business you are usually required to secure a retail tax license or permit from your state and, in some cases, your city. These documents allow you to collect taxes at the time of sale, which you must then periodically turn over to the licensing authority.

Check with your local state or municipal tax commission for regulations applicable to your particular business and locale.

For further information:

Prentice-Hall State and Local Tax Service, Englewood Cliffs, New Jersey, Prentice-Hall.

INSURANCE

The more deeply you become involved in your enterprise, the greater your potential loss in the event of injury to yourself, your employees, or your customers, the death of a partner, or damage to your property. Therefore, before hanging out your "shingle," you are advised to consult a competent insurance agent for an analysis of your insurance needs.

For further information:

Insurance Checklist for Small Business, Small Marketers' Aid #148. Available at any Small Business Administration field office, or write Small Business Administration, Washington, D. C. 20416.

Insurance and Risk Management for Small Business, SBA 1.12:30, Washington, D. C., Superintendent of Documents, Government Printing Office.

Risk Management in the Business Enterprise, Robert Mehr and Bob Hedges. New York, Richard D. Irwin, 1963.

FINANCING

The need for business capital may present itself during any or all of three different phases of your enterprise. Initial capital may be required for starting the business, working capital needed for continuing the operation, and expansion capital desired for growth.

First on the list of possible sources of capital are your own assets. Savings and checking accounts, stocks and bonds, real estate, insurance policies, jewelry, automobiles, and boats are just a few of the many items that can be converted into ready cash. Friends and relatives are likewise a possible source of capital. If you need additional help in running the business, a partner may be brought in, thus serving two purposes. Franchises, which give rights to others to distribute your product or perform your service, may be sold in your area or in other parts of the country.

Lending institutions such as banks and loan companies may extend funds on your signature, accounts receivable, equipment, or stock. If these methods of financing are not available to you, the Small Business Administration (SBA) is empowered to guarantee up to 90 percent of a bank loan or $350,000, whichever is less, to a small firm. The SBA may also advance funds, up to 75 percent or $100,000, whichever is less, on a participation basis with a bank. Failing these possibilities, this agency will consider granting a direct loan of $25,000. These maximums may fluctuate during any given period, depending upon congressional legislation and the agency's resources at the time.

Small Business Investment Companies (SBICs)—small, privately owned business investment companies licensed and regulated by the SBA—may grant long-term loans or finance a firm by purchasing its capital stock or debt securities or by purchasing debentures which are convertible into the stock of the business.

Credit is available through trade financing. This allows firms to take advantage of financing plans by equipment manufacturers and merchandise suppliers.

Special loans to minorities and economically disadvantaged businessmen are another possibility. These may be sponsored by the federal government, such as the Economic Opportunity loans granted through the SBA, or by various state governments which have made funds available to these groups.

For further information:

Loan Sources in the Federal Government, Management Aid #52. Available from any Small Business Administration field office, or write Small Business Administration, Washington, D. C. 20416.

The ABC's of Borrowing, Management Aid #170. Available from any Small Business Administration field office, or write Small Business Administration, Washington, D. C. 20416.

How to Finance a Growing Business, Royce Diener. New York, Frederick Fell, 1965.

How to Borrow Your Way to Great Fortune, Tyler Hicks. West Nyack, New York, Parker Publishing, 1970.

CREDIT

Virtually all the enterprises discussed in this book best lend themselves to a "cash and carry" trade. That is, the customer pays for the goods at the time he receives them. In cases involving pre-prepared or custom-made items, such as catered foods or custom draperies, a 10–50 percent deposit is not only appropriate but is considered wise business practice. If your product is of high quality, and a prospective customer is determined to have it, there's no reason for him to object to a partial advance payment.

If you are determined to extend credit to others in the form of trade credit (credit granted to a store or distributor to whom your product is sold), installment credit, or charge accounts, the publication listed below will help you decide on how to set up the system.

A fairly effortless, inexpensive, and nonrisk type of consumer credit is the honoring of bank or other credit cards, such as BankAmericard or American Express. Under these arrangements, the merchant records each transaction on a sales slip provided by the credit organization. Upon deposit in a special account, the full amount charged to the customer, as shown on the sales slip, is credited to the merchant's account. For this service, the merchant pays a fee of 2½–7 percent of the total amount charged, depending on his dollar volume and average sales slip total.

For further information:

Retail Credit Fundamentals, Clyde Phelps. St. Louis, International Consumer Credit Association, 1963.

RECORD KEEPING

Failure to keep adequate and accurate records can seriously handicap, even endanger, an otherwise successful business operation. Records involving such things as sales, profit and loss, expenses, and assets and liabilities must be kept in order for you to be constantly aware of your financial condition and the state of your business. This will enable you to foresee and correct any impending financial crisis before it happens.

The record-keeping process need not be elaborate. Simple forms and materials are available in any stationery store. You can also study the publications listed below. Many small businessmen hire a competent bookkeeper or accountant to set up the system initially, and then call him back periodically for any adjustments that may be needed and for advice on tax-saving measures.

It would be wise to open up a separate checking account for your business transactions, for tax purposes. Pay all your larger bills by check, getting receipts for any cash paid for out-of-pocket expenses. Pay yourself a regular salary by check.

For further information:

Financial Recordkeeping for Small Stores, SBA 1.12:32. Washington, D. C. Superindendent of Documents, Government Printing Office.

Recordkeeping Systems–Small Store and Service Trade, Small Business Bibliography 15. Available from any Small Business Administration field office, or write Small Business Administration, Washington, D. C. 20416.

THE SBA'S MANAGEMENT ASSISTANCE PROGRAMS

Aside from its provisions of financial assistance to the small businessman, which we have already discussed, the Small Business Administration offers valuable management assistance programs designed specifically to strengthen a person's managerial capabilities.

A wide range of programs is implemented through a network of local universities, colleges, trade and professional associations, chambers of commerce, retired executives, and the SBA's own counseling staff. For a nominal charge, courses, conferences, clinics, and workshops offer valuable instruction on such topics as marketing, accounting, product analysis, production methods, research and development, and general management guidance.

Contact your local SBA office for programs in your area.

The problems outlined in this chapter apply to small business as a whole. Obviously, as a greeting-card writer you wouldn't be concerned with zoning laws, nor would a small-appliance repairman be involved with health regulations. Selectively decide which of the rules and regulations apply to you and your situation, and ignore the rest. Don't let the seemingly ponderous mass of laws, regulations, restrictions, and ordinances summarized here dissuade you from beginning your chosen enterprise. Hundreds of thousands have succeeded, some to an extraordinary degree, in small businesses similar to those described in this book. You can, too.

3

The Small-Fry Bonanza

The world of children offers many opportunities for lucrative, rewarding enterprises. Since American parents traditionally are quick to indulge their inclinations to pamper their children, the field is a veritable gold mine.

Working directly with children, however, requires a genuine fondness for the younger set. We stress "genuine" here because children are sensitive enough to see through any pretension or affectation on your part. Of course, patience is a necessary virtue as well.

If the kids like you and what you have to offer, it's a pretty sure bet the parents will feel the same way—and they're the ones who hold the purse strings.

Of course, before embarking on any venture dealing with the care or transporting of children, you'll want to check out and comply with all existing licensing, zoning, safety, and health regulations, as well as obtain a good liability insurance policy designed to cover any and all eventualities.

Since children are everywhere, enterprises involving children lend themselves especially well to low-budget advertising. In many cases, telling a few friends and neighbors about your new product or service will be enough to get the ball rolling for you.

Use the following list, in addition to the tips given in Chapter 1, as a guide to possible ways of advertising your child-related enterprise. It is by no means complete in itself. As with all business ventures, the promotion of your particular enterprise will rely a great deal upon your own creativity and ingenuity.

- PTA groups
- Women's clubs
- Church groups
- Civic organizations
- Community recreation departments
- Toy shops
- Maternity shops
- Children's apparel shops
- Notices on supermarket and school bulletin boards

- Distribution of leaflets in suburban neighborhoods and on windshields of cars parked in suburban shopping centers
- Distribution of leaflets through (or obtaining names from) local diaper services

Entertainment

PARTY ENTERTAINMENT BUREAU

This service consists of providing novel entertainment for children's parties. As a talent scout, you would seek out entertainers such as clowns, jugglers, musicians, ventriloquists, puppeteers—even trained dog and chimp acts. As a booking agent, your task would be to promote these acts to parents.

Find your talent through nightclubs, street performers, colleges and universities, and through ads in the local newspaper. For animal acts, contact local kennel clubs or veterinarians.

Book your acts into the "better" homes in town, charging a high enough fee for you to pay them and come out with a good profit for yourself.

CHILDREN'S MAGICIAN

Here your job is to amaze and astonish children with your magical skills.

To learn the tricks study books such as those listed below and visit magic and novelty stores in your area for free demonstrations.

After you've gained enough confidence in your abilities, distribute leaflets around your neighborhood advertising a show in your garage or living room. Charge fifty cents or so per child.

For further information:

The Amateur Magician's Handbook, Henry Hay. New York, Thomas Y. Crowell, 1972.

Magic Tricks for Amateurs, W. Dexter. Hackensack, New Jersey, Wehman Brothers.

Professional Magic for Amateurs, Walter Gibson. New York, Dover, 1974.

RUN A TALENT AGENCY

This enterprise involves accumulating a "stable" of children fitting a variety of character parts. Seek out these kids through schools or children's beauty pageants.

After getting written permission from the parents, arm yourself with a portfolio of "your" children's photos, making the rounds of motion picture casting offices and TV commercial producers. If they happen to like some of your kids and want to sign them to a contract, you'll get an agent's fee of 10–20 percent. A few fat contracts every month can net you a comfortable income.

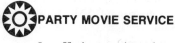
PARTY PLANNER

Many parents would jump at the chance to have a professional party planner take over all the details of their children's birthday parties. Your work would involve everything from buying or baking the cake to cleaning up the crumbs. The parties could be held either in your home or in the client's. You would be responsible for sending out the invitations, planning the games and activities, shopping for party favors, and decorating the party area.

Charge the parents a set fee, three to five dollars per child attending.

For further information:

Successful Parties and How to Give Them, Lillian Graham and Marjorie Wackerbarth. Grand Rapids, Michigan, Baker Book House, 1974.

Betty Crocker's Parties for Children, Louis Freeman, ed. Racine, Wisconsin, Western Publishing, 1964.

PARTY MOVIE SERVICE

In offering motion picture cartoons at children's birthday parties, your initial expense will be buying or renting a projector and screen. Reliable equipment can be purchased, used, at a camera or pawnshop, or rented from a camera store or audiovisual supply house.

You can rent old cartoons cheaply through a film library, found in just about every large city in the country. Look up the one nearest you in the Yellow Pages, and write for its catalogue.

BE A PUPPETEER

Visit a large toy store in your town, where a variety of puppets can be found. Next, design and build a minitheater for your shows. It can be made from sturdy cardboard or wooden cartons, painted brightly and shaped to your own needs. You'll have to create some sort of "plot" for your characters to enact.

Then let the world know that you're available for children's birthday parties. In addition, your community department of recreation might be interested in hiring you to entertain throughout the summer.

For further information:

You Can Be a Puppeteer, Carolyn London. Chicago, Moody Press, 1972.

How to Be a Puppeteer, Eleanor Boylan. New York, Saturday Review (orders to E. P. Dutton), 1970.

Sports and Recreation

KIDNICS

What's a kidnic? Why, it's a kids' picnic. Provide a service of escorting mobs of small-fry on picnics. Have the parents pack a picnic lunch for each child. If your group consists of more than five or six children, better arrange for a friend to come along to help watch the kids. Charge two or three dollars per child plus any transportation expenses.

MOBILE NATURE SHOW

This enterprise requires the modification and use of a large mobile trailer. On the inside you build display cases housing such animals as gophers, rabbits, porcupines, mice and rats, and snakes. Fish can be displayed, too, either in aquariums or mounted. Have pictures or samples of various plants.

Get permission to set up your trailer in shopping centers, parks, and schools. Charge fifty cents admission per child, with a special discount to groups.

 ROLLER-SKATING RINK

On an outside lot lay a smooth wooden floor or pave it with a smooth concrete finish. Put a few benches around the sides, and build a small concession stand for dispensing hot dogs and soda pop. You'll need an inventory of skates in various sizes, for rental.

Before getting started, check local zoning and licensing requirements.

RECREATIONAL DAY TRIPS

Pick up a group of kids on a Saturday or Sunday morning—or on a weekday during the summer months—and transport them to places where they can go swimming, horseback riding, skating, skiing, hiking, or participate in other fun activities. An amusement park or zoo would also be enjoyable.

Charge three to five dollars per child for the day, plus any admission fees involved. Have the parents pack a box lunch for each child.

For further information:

> *Recreation Program Guide: Organizing Activities for School, Camp, Park, Playground, or Children's Club*, Jean Kujoth. Metuchen, New Jersey, Scarecrow Press, 1972.

> *How to Fly a Kite, Catch a Fish, Hatch a Cocoon, & Other Activities for You & Your Child*, Alvin Schwartz. New York, Macmillan, 1965.

 MOBILE MERRY-GO-ROUND

Rent or buy a portable, motor-driven merry-go-round from a carnival supply house. Then, after permission has been obtained, set yourself up in a shopping center, public park, group picnic area—anywhere there are kids. Charge each child twenty-five to fifty cents per ride.

You can also rent your service out to church bazaars and birthday parties for a set fee.

HAYRIDES

Make a deal with a farmer to rent a horse and a large, hay-filled wagon for a specified number of afternoons and evenings each week. Then, offer an hour-and-a-half or two-hour hayride for two or three dollars, with special discounts for groups.

Arrange to have your "kiddie rides" on weekend afternoons, with an assistant in the wagon to watch over the kids. Teenagers would enjoy rides during mild, moonlit evenings, for obvious reasons.

MOVIE ESCORT SERVICE

Haul busloads or carloads of kids to and from weekend afternoon movie matinees.

Charge a dollar or so per child. Be sure to have adequate automobile insurance, and plenty of tranquilizers and bubble gum-remover on hand for the occasion.

BE A SPORT!

Parents are eager for their kids to pick up as many skills as possible. If you're proficient in activities such as swimming, tennis, golf, or karate, give classes in one or more of these sports.

If you don't have your own swimming pool or tennis court, use public facilities or make an agreement with friends to use theirs. Also, teaching opportunities may exist with your local recreation department, YMCA, or evening adult school.

For further information:

> *Complete Book of Sport*, Euan Sutherland and Kate Sutherland. New York, International Publications Service, 1969.

Major Sports Techniques Illustrated, Ethan Allen *et al.* New York, Ronald Press, 1954.

ICE-SKATING RINK

Flood a lot with water, let it freeze over, and you have an ice-skating rink. Add a few frills by putting some benches around the outside and opening up a snack bar and a heated shack where the skaters can thaw out.

Buy a variety of different sizes of ice skates and rent these out to your customers. A fair price might be $1.75 admission and 75 cents skate rental.

Before starting, check local zoning and licensing regulations.

RECREATION DIRECTOR

If you live in a town where no recreation department exists, persuade the city fathers to put you on the payroll as a recreation director.

Organize sports and activities of all kinds, and encourage local citizens to participate. Your programs could include everything from sidewalk chalk-drawing contests for the kiddies to domino and horseshoe tournaments for the oldsters.

For further information:

Creative Leadership in Recreation, Howard Danford and Max Shirley, eds. Boston, Allyn & Bacon, 1970.

Recreation Today: Program Planning and Leadership, Richard Kraus. New York, Appleton-Century-Crofts.

Playground and Recreation Director's Handbook, David R. Turner. New York, Arco, 1967.

EDUCATIONAL FIELD TRIPS

Take groups of children to museums, observatories, mountains, the desert, the seashore—just about anywhere that would prove interesting and educational to the child. These trips can be made in your car, but of course a station wagon or minibus would be best. Before each trip, brush up on the subject matter of each place, and be prepared to talk and answer questions about it.

Charge four or five dollars per trip per child, and have the children bring their lunches along.

TEEN DANCES

Teenagers are always good customers for Friday and Saturday night dances, so why not rent a hall, play some records, and let them have fun?

Arrange to have a different DJ spin the records each week, perhaps one of the local teenagers. You'll also want to change the decorations each week so the kids won't get bored. Giving away door prizes will likewise create some steady customers. Make extra profits by selling hot dogs and soda pop.

SWIMMING SCHOOL

You'll need your own swimming pool, plus the ability to swim well and a knowledge of lifesaving techniques.

Specialize in the under-five group, for it is here that children gain confidence in their aquatic ability as a base for later learning.

To get your business off the ground (or into the water) notify pediatricians of your service. Once you get going, call the local newspaper offering to be interviewed for a feature article.

For further information:

Teaching an Infant to Swim, Virginia Newman. New York, Harcourt Brace Jovanovich, 1971.

Teaching Your Tot to Swim, Lucile Cowle. New York, Vantage Press, 1970.

Shoot Kids!

Of all the businesses involving children, photography is one of the surest money-makers. Pictures provide parents with a vivid visual record of their children. The person who becomes adept at "shooting" kids for posterity is certain to be in demand.

For other tips on using your camera for profit, see Chapter 9.

PONY MAN

This gimmick has been around for years but still continues to make money for its operators.

Buy or rent a pony. Cover it with a colorful blanket and lead it through suburban neighborhoods, ringing a bell to attract attention. Wear a cowboy outfit and carry a sign saying "Portrait of Your Child on Pony—only $2."

You can either shoot the kids with a conventional camera, sending the prints to the parents when you get them, or use a Polaroid and produce the pictures on the spot.

For further information:

How to Make Better Polaroid Instant Pictures: Complete Guide to the Successful Use of the Polaroid Land Camera, Paul Giambarba. Garden City, New York, Doubleday, 1970.

Polaroid Photography, Kalton Lahue. Los Angeles, Petersen, 1974.

MOTORCYCLE PHOTOG

Here's a variation on the previous idea. Use a motorcycle instead of a pony. Wear a leather jacket and goggles. Instead of ringing a bell, honk your horn.

Should be a big hit with the motor-minded youngsters of today—and you won't have to carry around a shovel and bag!

A CHILD'S DAY

Offer parents a portfolio of pictures documenting a day in the life of their child.

Your job would be to take forty or fifty shots of the child from the time he gets up till the time he goes to bed. Show him going to school, sitting in class, walking home, eating dinner, and falling off to sleep at night.

Package twenty-five to thirty pictures in an attractive album and don't be afraid to charge fifty to one hundred dollars for your day's work.

For further information:

Child Photography Simplified, Edna Bennett. New York, American Photographic Book Publishing, 1964.

INFANT I.D. PHOTOS

Offer hospitals in your area a service whereby you set up and maintain a camera in their delivery rooms, to make a photographic record of each baby as soon as it is born.

After permission has been obtained, set up your equipment so that the infant can be placed on its back under the camera, together with an identifying label.

STORE STUDIO

Contact merchants of stores with adequate floor space for picture taking. Tell them you'll put on a one- or two-day "children's photo promotion" which will cost them nothing.

Place a display ad in the local newspaper to appear the day before the promotion. Offer to give away a free 8 by 10 of each child to the parents. Make arrangements for them to return and see their proofs a week or ten days later. Of course at that time you'll sell them whatever additional prints you can.

For further information:

Child Photography Made Easy, J. Schneider. New York, American Photographic Book Publishing, 1957.

SCHOOL PHOTOGRAPHY

Most schools already have a photographer who comes in prior to the end of each semester and takes individual shots of each student. Although prices are low, it's a relative windfall for the photographer. Each child brings his proof home in an envelope and the parents, if they're pleased with the outcome, order additional prints.

Because most school photographers are rather well-entrenched, this field may be tough to crack. But if you can squeeze yourself in, you've got it made. A good way to start would be to watch for new suburban schools opening up and apply for the job before anyone else does.

For further information:

> *Photographing Children,* Time-Life Books Editors. Dobbs Ferry, New York, Morgan & Morgan, 1972.

SANTA CLAUS PORTRAITS

Approach a store owner a few months before Christmas. Offer to supply a Santa Claus for the season if he will let you take and sell pictures of the kids on Santa's knee.

When the appointed day rolls around, have on hand an assistant dressed as Santa's helper. As each child approaches Santa, ask the mother if she'd like a picture of her child on Santa's knee. After permission has been given, snap the picture and collect a deposit on prints to be delivered later. If you're using a Polaroid you can collect for, and deliver, the prints on the spot.

For further information:

> *How to Make Better Polaroid Instant Pictures: Complete Guide to Successful Use of the Polaroid Land Camera,* Paul Giambarba. Garden City, New York, Doubleday, 1970.
>
> *How I Photograph Children,* Suzanne Szasz. New York, American Photographic Book Publishing, 1972.
>
> *Polaroid Photography,* Kalton Lahue. Los Angeles, Petersen, 1974.

Child Care

CHILD CARE CENTER

Child care facilities are much in demand by working mothers, and a well-run operation can make top dollar.

Since most of your charges will be in the under-five category, you'll need such items as toys, games, cribs, cots, playpens, high chairs, and some simple playground equipment for the backyard. Since you'll be required to serve hot lunches and midafternoon snacks, you'll need a fairly large kitchen and a spacious eating area.

Check prevailing rates in your area, and set your fees accordingly.

For further information:

> *Day Care: How to Plan, Develop and Operate a Day Care Center,* E. Belle Evans *et al.* Boston, Beacon Press, 1973.
>
> *How to Start and Operate a Day Care Home,* Al Griffin. Chicago, Regnery, 1973.

BABY-SITTING BUREAU

Locate twenty or more senior citizens, retired nurses or teachers, students, and anyone else willing to be "on call" for baby-sitting assignments. Interview and personally check the references of each applicant. Honesty and dependability are musts.

Find out what the prevailing baby-sitting rate is in your town and tack on one-third for your profit.

For further information:

> *The Baby Sitter's Guide,* Mary Moore. New York, Barnes & Noble (orders through Harper & Row), 1973.
>
> *The Franklin Watts Concise Guide to Baby Sitting,* Rubie Saunders. New York, Franklin Watts, 1972.

CHILDREN'S HOTEL

The perfect solution for parents who want to escape domestic cares for a weekend, or a week, your "hotel" would take in children of all ages.

Of course, you must maintain a variety of facilities such as a nursery, game room, TV lounge, and large dining room for meals. A large, fenced-in yard with simple playground equipment would be an asset.

Charge by the night, with reduced weekly rates.

AFTER-SCHOOL CHILD CARE

Many mothers work during the day and don't get home till the dinner hour. Instead of leaving their children alone at home after school, they would feel more comfortable if the children were with another adult.

The kids would walk to your home from school and be looked after until picked up by the mother or father at dinner time. Again, you'll need diversions for the children while they're in your care. Charge, and collect from, the parents by the week at the prevailing baby-sitting rate.

CHILDREN'S DUDE RANCH

If you own some land in the country, have some city kids vacation with you a few days a week. Offer them swimming, fishing, horseback riding, handicrafts, and, in addition, they might get a kick out of milking the cows and feeding the chickens.

Charge the parents a set fee per day.

TRAVELING GOVERNESS

Many parents in foreign lands want their children to learn fluent English and they realize the best way is to have an English-speaking governess (or her male counterpart) living with, and helping to care for, their children.

Get initial information from the embassy or consulate of the country you're interested in. You may land an overseas job — and have your transportation costs paid as well!

CHILD BANK

A mother can "deposit" her offspring in your "bank" for a few hours while she tends to her shopping. Afterwards she can "withdraw" them. Have some toys and games for the children to play with. If the weather is nice and you own a fenced yard, so much the better.

Keep track of the amount of time each child stays with you and charge the mothers by the hour at the prevailing baby-sitting rate.

Products

BYE-BYE BABY

Find used cribs, playpens, strollers, high chairs, and other infant paraphernalia at garage sales, flea markets, and in the classified ads. Repair and paint them and you've got a salable, profit-making item.

Sell them through the same sources and, in addition, distribute leaflets throughout new suburban housing developments.

CUSTOM-MADE CLOTHES

The best way to get started designing, making, and selling your own line of children's wearing apparel is to make up some unique samples.

Take your samples to children's apparel shops and department stores in your area and get them to take on your line. If they don't want to buy your creations outright, offer to leave them on consignment — anything to get your product into the stores. If sales go well, you can name your own price later on.

For further information:

Sewing Children's Clothes: A Golden Hands Pattern Book. New York, Random House, 1973.

Children's Wear Design, Hilda Jaffe. New York, Fairchild, 1972.

Making Children's Clothes, Joan Moloney. New York, Drake Publishers, 1970.

RECYCLE THE BICYCLE

Scour flea markets, garage sales, and the newspaper classifieds for used bikes and parts. Encourage local bike and sporting goods stores to take in used bikes as trade-ins from their new bike customers.

Buy these used bikes from the stores, painting and fixing them up. They can be sold at a moderate profit through the same sources.

For further information:

> *Glenn's Complete Bicycle Repair Manual: Selection, Maintenance, Repair,* Clarence Coles & Harold Glenn. New York, Crown, 1973.

> *Bicycle Repair,* Irene Kleeberg. New York, Franklin Watts, 1973.

> *The Super Handyman's Big Bike Book,* Al Carrell. Englewood Cliffs, New Jersey, Prentice-Hall, 1973.

CHILDREN'S FURNITURE

There are scores of children's furniture items that you can make, which will appeal to parents and grandparents, aunts and uncles. Cribs, dressers, rocking chairs, small sofas, clothes racks, bookcases, headboards for beds, desks, and nightstands are just a few.

Sell your products outright, or on consignment, if you must, to furniture and department stores. You can also open up your own small shop.

For further information:

> *How to Make Children's Furniture and Play Equipment,* Mario Fabbro. New York, McGraw-Hill, 1975.

> *Making Children's Furniture and Play Structures,* Bruce Palmer. New York, Workman, 1974.

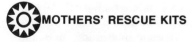

MOTHERS' RESCUE KITS

These are play kits designed especially for children to use while sick in bed, on rainy days, and during traveling. They may include such items as scissors, scraps of colored paper, glue, rubber bands, a harmonica, balloons, colored beads, miniature figures, colored clay—anything a child can amuse him-

self with. Vary the items in the different kits and label them "Rainy Day Kit," "Travel Kit," and so on.

Sell your kits to toy stores, children's shops, hospital gift shops, drugstores, and supermarkets.

For futher information:

> *The Rainy Day Book,* Alvin Schwartz. New York, Simon & Schuster, 1973.

> *838 Ways to Amuse a Child,* June Johnson. New York, Macmillan, 1970.

GAME INVENTOR

Children's game manufacturers are always in the market for new ideas, and pay handsomely for them. At toy shops, look over the current games and then try to come up with other ideas utilizing the same basic principles, but different in format.

If you think you've latched on to an exceptional concept, apply for a patent in order to protect yourself, and send your idea to a large game manufacturer. Names of these can be found in the *Thomas Register of American Manufacturers,* available at your local library.

RECYCLE CHILDREN'S CLOTHING

Obtain used children's apparel from church rummage sales, flea markets, garage sales, and from friends and neighbors. After washing, ironing, and mending the clothes, display them attractively in a rented shop or in a spare room of your home.

Place a small classified ad in the "merchandise for sale" column of your local paper. Print up and distribute leaflets throughout town giving a few examples of your bargains.

MAKE CHARACTER DOLLS

Try creating unique ethnic and character dolls. In addition to representing various ethnic groups, your creations might resemble clowns, cowboys, hoboes, hippies, surfers, sailors . . . There are loads of possibilities.

Sell them door to door and to toy shops and children's apparel shops.

For further information:

Making Costume Dolls, Jean Greenhowe. New York, Watson-Guptill, 1973.

Costume Dolls and How to Make Them, Winifred Craven. Plainfield, New Jersey, Textile Book Service, 1968.

CHILDREN'S SAVINGS BANKS

These can be made in all sizes, shapes, colors, and designs. Your banks could resemble animals, dolls, houses, boats, flying saucers, monsters — anything that might delight the imagination of a child.

They can be made to hang on a wall or from the ceiling, stand on a table, or — in the case of a wind-up version — walk around the floor.

Take orders from toy, variety, and department stores. In addition, your more novel creations should sell well through mail order.

TONS OF TOYS

Collect secondhand toys by going door to door, offering five or ten cents a pound. Have a small scale with you, and weigh and pay for the toys at the door. Have a wagon or cart on the sidewalk and a car or truck nearby to use for hauling your booty home. You can also pick up old toys cheaply at flea markets, garage sales, and secondhand stores. Repair and paint them in your garage or workshop.

Hold garage sales to dispose of the toys and let it be known throughout the neighborhood that you have a large inventory.

For further information:

How to Hold a Garage Sale, James Ullman. New York, Scribner's, 1973.

The Better Garage Sale Book, Jean Young and Jim Young. New York, Bantam, 1974.

Services

TOY HOSPITAL

Start a toy repair service. The skill required is minimal, and what you can't figure out yourself can be gleaned from repair manuals distributed by the various toy manufacturers. Get their names and addresses from local toy stores or from the *Thomas Register of American Manufacturers* at your library.

DIAPER SERVICE

All you need initially is a washer and dryer, some covered plastic hampers, a car, and — of course — a thousand or so diapers, which you can buy wholesale.

Commercial diaper services presently exist in most large cities, but you can beat the competition by offering potential customers personalized service at a more economical rate.

CHILDREN'S ROOM DECORATOR

As a children's room decorator, concentrate on selling your services to wealthy parents. If you can come up with such novel ideas as a revolving merry-go-round chandelier or a cuckoo bird that sings operatic arias, you'll be the talk of the upper crust.

In addition to conventional forms of advertising and promotion, fix up one of your own children's rooms in some outrageous manner. Then invite photographers from your local newspaper and home magazines into your home for some interesting shots and free publicity.

For further information:

Family Handyman's Book of Children's Room Ideas, Family Handyman Magazine Editors. New York, Universal Publishing and Distributing, 1971.

For Children, Claire Rayner. New York, International Publications Service, 1967.

Children's Rooms and Play Yards, Editors, *Sunset* magazine, Menlo Park, California, Lane, 1970.

DOLL HOSPITAL

Many children, and even adults, own dolls in need of repairs. As a "doll doctor," repair and restore these items by performing such "operations" as sewing, gluing, and re-shaping.

For additional income, acquire a line of new dolls and have them on display for your customers.

For further information:

How to Successfully Start and Operate a Doll Hospital, Riverdale, Maryland, Edel Torngren. Hobby House Press, 1969.

Doll Repair, Evelyn Gaylin. Riverdale, Maryland, Hobby House Press, 1967.

CHILDREN'S MAGAZINE SUBSCRIPTIONS

A subscription to a children's magazine in the child's name can solve a gift problem for birthdays, Christmas, and graduation.

Write to the children's publications listed below. (A more comprehensive list can be found in the *Writer's Market,* available at your local library or bookstore.) Tell them you wish to become their agent, and they will send you forms to fill out for each new customer. You'll get a commission on each subscription sold.

Children's Playmate and *Jack and Jill,* P. O. Box 567B, Indianapolis, Indiana, 46206.

Highlights for Children, 803 Church Street, Honesdale, Pennsylvania, 18431.

Humpty Dumpty's Magazine, 52 Vanderbilt Avenue, New York, New York, 10017.

Cricket, P. O. Box 100, La Salle, Illinois, 61301.

LETTERS TO LITTLE ONES

A lucrative business can be built up by answering children's letters to Santa Claus, the Easter Bunny, the Sand Man, the Tooth Fairy or Uncle Sam.

Charge the parents two dollars per letter for the service, which they can slip inside the child's letter before mailing.

Advertise in the classifieds of national publications, as well as locally.

CHILDREN'S TONSORIAL PARLOR

As you know, a tonsorial parlor is simply a barbershop with a fancy name. Catering to the under-twelve set exclusively, you'll feature such innovations as animal-patterned barber chairs, a play corner, colorfully dressed barbers, and free trinkets with every haircut.

Once Junior sets foot in your hair-trimming heaven he'll want to return again and again.

THE BRONZE-PLATING BOOM

Anything with a sentimental value is a candidate for bronze-plating, whether it be baby's first shoes or that golf ball that made the hole in one. The technique is easy to learn and the process is equally uncomplicated.

The best customers are mothers wanting infant items preserved. Aside from promoting your service locally, advertise in the classified sections of national women's magazines such as *Good Housekeeping* and *Parents' Magazine.*

For further information:

"Electroplating Baby Shoes," *Mechanics Illustrated,* Vol. 27 (March 1942), page 126.

"Electroplating Leather, Wood, Plaster, and Other Nonconductors," *Popular Mechanics,* Vol. 65 (January 1936), pp. 146–151.

MUSIC SCHOOL

The best way to start a music school is to begin giving lessons in your home, or at your local YMCA or evening adult school.

Make a deal with a local music store to send your new students to them for instruments in exchange for their recommending you to prospective students. You may eventually decide to take on your own line of instruments.

For further information:

Teaching Instrumental Music, George Duerksen. Washington, D. C., Music Educators National Conference, 1972.

Playing Social and Recreational Instruments, Robert John and Charles Douglas. Englewood Cliffs, New Jersey, Prentice-Hall, 1972.

CHILDBIRTH, NATURALLY!

These classes are taught in the home, usually once a week for six weeks, during the last three months of pregnancy. There are several natural childbirth methods, the most popular being the Lamaze.

You can be trained, and accredited, through a chapter of The American Society for Psychoprophylaxis in Obstetrics, Inc., 1165 Fifth Avenue, New York, New York, 10029.

For further information:

Painless Childbirth: The Lamaze Method, Fernand Lamaze. New York, Pocket Books, 1970.

A Way to Natural Childbirth: A Manual for Physiotherapists and Parents-to-Be, Helen Heardman. New York, Longman, 1974.

OPERATE A TUTORING AGENCY

The best way to begin a tutoring agency, or registry, is to start taking on students who are having difficulty in school, or high school students needing help in preparing for college.

When you find you've got more business than you can handle, advertise for other qualified tutors. Hire them and take a percentage of the fees they bring in.

A BICYCLE DOCTOR

You can run a bicycle repair business in your own workshop or garage, starting with just a few simple tools.

You'll be competing with the bike shops in town so you'll have to offer somewhat lower prices, or a free set of handlebar grips or inexpensive bike horn with each repair job.

For further information:

It's Easy to Fix Your Bike, John McFarlane. Chicago, Follett, 1973.

Simple Bicycle Repair and Maintenance, Ross Olney. Garden City, New York, Doubleday, 1973.

4
The Great Animal Windfall

Working with animals or animal products can be a great source of satisfaction — and income — for you. Pet owners spend millions annually for everything from basic items such as food and medicine to such frivolities as diamond-studded cat collars and canine fur coats.

The one requisite in dealing directly with animals, especially domestic pets, is that you like them and enjoy working with them. Owners — and especially the animals themselves — are usually sensitive enough to detect any antipathy or disdain on your part, diminishing the prospects for favorable results from the animals involved.

If you're primarily interested in working with smaller animals, a distinct advantage here is that a minimum of space is required. Rabbits and guinea pigs can be raised in a corner of the backyard (in mild climates), rats and mice in a garage or shed, and tropical fish in a spare room of your house — or even in a small apartment!

In promoting products and services relating to animals, you can contact pet shops, grooming salons, veterinarians, breeders — anyone who will buy or help you to sell your product. Of course, you'll always want to be on the lookout for possible free publicity in the form of news releases, feature articles, and radio and TV talk show interviews.

If you're interested in a particular enterprise and want to get some inside information on how the business is run, visit a like business, posing as an interested customer. Don't be afraid to ask questions regarding its operation. Usually, owners are so taken aback by such direct questioning that they will come up with honest answers, not fully realizing your motives until after you've left.

You'll find the following list of enterprises dealing with animals to be fairly comprehensive. However, don't eliminate the possibility of expanding on any of these ideas: starting an animal "jungleland" from the animals you've found in opening up an animal talent agency, for instance; or expanding your worm-raising business into the manufacture of plastic "see-through" worm houses as an educational toy. The possibilities are endless.

Always be looking in all directions and you're sure to progress toward greater fulfillment as well as a burgeoning income.

In the City . . .

WALKIN' THE DOG

After a hard day's work at the office, many apartment-dwellers don't have the get-up-and-go to take their dogs out walking every day. Yet they realize that the animals require exercise.

Charge a dog owner ten dollars a week for walking his dog. You can walk as many as five or six dogs at a time!

Make arrangements to pick up the animals at specified times, thus creating a regular route for yourself.

PET-GO-ROUND

This job consists of calling on the pet at home, feeding it, and cleaning up after it while the owners are away. Dogs, cats, birds, guinea pigs, and fish are some of the pets you'll be caring for. Charge each customer a few dollars a day and try to build up a regular clientele through being dependable.

CANINE AND FELINE I.D. TAGS

Supply pet owners with small, engraved metal tags bearing the owner's name, address, and phone number.

Get the tags from a metal products company, which can be found through your Yellow Pages. Look under "Engraving Equipment" to find an inexpensive engraving tool.

Make up attractive display stands with a dozen blank tags on each and leave them in area pet shops and grooming salons. Price the tags to include the engraving. Give the store owner a discount on the merchandise. The customer can bring or mail the tags to you for engraving.

EXTERMINATOR

Get initial information by writing to the Bureau of Entomology and Plant Quarantine, U. S. Department of Agriculture, Washington, D. C. They will supply a list of publications on the subject.

After you've studied up and you're ready to go, the quickest way to get new business is to spend a few hours a day going door to door. Introduce yourself and your service and leave a card. If you don't like pounding the pavement, you might try direct-mail advertising.

For further information:

Pest Control: Biological, Physical and Selected Chemical Methods, Wendell Kilgore and Richard Doutt. New York, Academic Press, 1967.

Chemicals for Pest Control, G. S. Hartley & T. F. West. Elmsford, New York, Pergamon Press, 1969.

PET LOST AND FOUND

Provide a telephone number for the owners of lost pets to call day or night. They will hear a recording instructing them to give the pet's description, the area in which it was lost and their name and telephone number. Also instruct them to send a few dollars for the service.

Provide a separate line, also with a recording, for people who have found pets. They'll be instructed to give a description of the animal and their name and phone number.

After you've received your money from the pet owner, call and give him the name and phone number of the person who found his pet letting him make arrangements for the pet's return.

DOG AND CAT TOYS

Pet owners spend millions every year attempting to keep Fido and Tabby entertained by providing them with such items as rubber bones and mice. Cash in by creating new—and even more elaborate—animal toys. For refined dogs and cats, your toys could be made to emit stains from Beethoven's Fifth Symphony or Tchaikovsky's *Nutcracker Suite.*

DELIVER DOGGIE DINNERS

Deliver freshly ground government-inspected meat to dogs several times each week.

The authors realize that it might be stretching the reader's credulity a bit to suggest that it's possible to make a living at this. Nevertheless, we've seen it operate successfully in New York City, and can only assume it will, if promoted properly, pay off in any large metropolitan area.

PETUETTES

You won't find the word in the dictionary, but a "petuette" is a small statue, or statuette, with a photo of an individual's pet on the front and carved in the shape of that pet. A small brace allows the figure to stand upright on a desk or table.

Make up some samples using your own pets as models. Take them around to pet shops, grooming salons, veterinarians, and photo and art stores.

In addition to making the figures you'll have to photograph each pet yourself, probably in the customer's home.

CUT-RATE PET SHOP

If you enjoy working with pets and feel for the plight of the thousands of unwanted pets killed every month by the "animal shelters" of large cities, why not open a cut-rate pet shop stocked with give-aways and strays?

Needless to say, your loveable mutts, kitties, hamsters, guinea pigs, mice, and birds will cost far less than the purebreds found in most pet stores. You'll be saving animal lives, making money, and providing pets for children who otherwise could not afford to have an animal friend.

PET PORTRAITS

Offer veterinarians and the owners of pet shops, grooming salons, and kennels a free portrait of their dog or cat, if they will display it prominently on their wall. You'll want to make these portraits so outstanding that any pet owner who sees them will want one made of their own pet.

Combine this program with the promotional ideas given in Chapter 1, and word will spread. You may even become the "Prince [or Princess] of Pet Portraits."

For further information:

How to Photograph Cats, Dogs, and Other Animals (AC-38), Walter Chandoha. New York, American Photographic Book Publishing, 1973.

Animal and Pet Photography, Mildred Stagg. New York, American Photographic Book Publishing, 1969.

CLIPPIN' AND CLEANIN'

Many dog owners, especially those with poodles, like to have Fido clipped and trimmed regularly. Baths are also a service they would rather pay someone else to do.

Fees usually start at ten dollars and can range sharply upward, depending on the breed and the neighborhood. Check the going rates and price your services competitively.

You might also consider offering a pickup and delivery service, charging accordingly.

To get started, attend classes on dog grooming. Pet shops or veterinarians can tell you who offers these in your area. Practice on your own or a friend's dog, till you get the process down pat. Then hang our your "shingle."

For further information:

All Breed Dog Grooming Guide, Sam Kohl and Catherine Goldstein. New York, Arco, 1973.

Dogs: Modern Grooming Techniques, Hilary Harmar. New York, Arco, 1970.

In the Country . . .

CHILDREN'S ZOO

If you like children and animals and live a little way out of town, fence off a half-acre or so and stock it with farm animals: a pony, a cow, some rabbits, goats, chickens, piglets—whatever else you can think of. Put up a sign out front and distribute leaflets in town advertising a children's zoo. Families love to have a place to escape to on weekends. Charge fifty cents or a dollar per child.

SQUAB FARMING

Raise squab, supplying them to restaurants and supermarkets in your area.

First check with these establishments and see what they'll pay you. You'll be responsible for slaughtering, processing, and delivering the birds, so you'll want to take this into consideration before agreeing on a price.

Before committing any time or expense to this enterprise, however, you'd best check local licensing, zoning, and health laws.

For further information:

Pigeons for Pleasure and Profit, Charles Foy. Moline, Illinois, Swanson Publishing, 1972.

Making Pigeons Pay, Wendell Levi. Sumter, South Carolina, Levi Publishing, 1972.

National Pigeon Association, Route 4, Watertown, Wisconsin 53094.

BE A LEPIDOPTERIST

In case you don't know it, a lepidopterist is a butterfly collector.

Museums and colleges buy thousands of specimens yearly for their collections. An extremely rare specimen may command up to $200! These colorful creatures can be mounted or pressed in glass and framed, encased in plastic and used for paperweights, or put into hollow cubes or spheres and sold to gift shops and department stores as decorative items.

You must live near a pasture or wild area and do your catching during the warm months.

A net is available at any pet shop. Buy or make a board on which to mount your specimens.

For additional information:

Butterflies of the World, H. L. Lewis. Chicago, Follett, 1973.

Butterflies and Moths, Alfred Werner and Josef Bijok. New York, Viking, 1970.

PHEASANT PHARMING

This is no "yoke": Pheasant eggs as well as the birds themselves are in demand by restaurants everywhere.

Build an enclosure for the pheasants and stock it with a dozen or so. You will find suppliers in the classified ads of outdoor magazines such as *Outdoor Life* and *Field & Stream.*

Advertise in restaurant trade magazines such as: *Nation's Restaurant News,* 2 Park Avenue, New York, 10016 or *Food Executive,* 508 IBM Building, Fort Wayne, Indiana 46805.

For further information:

Pheasant Breeding and Care, Jean Delacour. Neptune City, New Jersey, T. F. H. Publications, 1970.

Pheasants: Including Their Care in the Aviary. New York, International Publications Service, 1971.

Game Bird Breeders, Pheasant Fanciers and Aviculturists' Gazette, Salt Lake City, Utah, Allen Publishing (a monthly publication).

TROUT POND

If you have a large pond on your property, or the possibility of creating one, you've got an almost effortless way of capitalizing on it.

Stock the pond with trout or bass, which you can buy wholesale from a fish hatchery. Then buy a large quantity of worms and some used fishing tackle.

Leave some leaflets advertising your pond with sporting goods stores.

Charge customers fifty cents or a dollar for each fish caught. You can either supply them with the bait and tackle or charge extra for it.

You might also consider having some picnic benches and a small concession stand.

GAME FARM

This enterprise requires that you have access to a relatively large piece of fenced property.

Stock your property with game birds such as pheasant, quail and partridge. Hunters will welcome the chance to have a place to go for year-round hunting.

Charge them for each bird taken. Make extra profits by dressing the birds, providing bird dogs, and selling shotgun shells.

Be sure to provide adequate water and vegetation for your birds. Also, a good liability insurance policy is a must, just in case one of your customers gets mistaken for a quail.

For further information:

Game Bird Breeders, Pheasant Fanciers, and Aviculturists' Gazette, Salt Lake City, Utah, Allen Publishing (a monthly publication).

EGGING YOU ON

Come feast or famine, count on the egg market to consistently provide a profit to thousands of egg farmers throughout the country.

Selling the eggs is no problem. In any rural area there are cooperatives that will gladly assist you in getting started and guarantee to buy your eggs from you.

They can be found in the Yellow Pages under "Eggs." Or you can get information from your state or federal Department of Agriculture.

For further information:

> *Egg Science and Technology*, William Stadelman and Owen Cotterill. Westport, Connecticut, Avi Publishing, 1973.

BOARDING KENNEL

Every summer thousands of pet owners face the dilemma of what to do with their pets at vacation time.

Open up a boarding kennel for dogs, cats, birds, fish, and any other critter the customer may want to leave with you.

You'll have to have adequate space, shelter, and patience to deal with what we hope will be the large volume of pets you'll te taking in —and cleanliness is a must!

To get an idea of what's involved, visit some kennels in your area. Notice how the facilities are laid out. Inquire about such things as the heating system, meals, and rates.

For further information:

> *Successful Kennel Management,* Mark Taynton. Juno, Florida, Beech Tree Farm, 1971.

HORSE RENTAL SERVICE

Acquire some riding horses and rent them out to the city folk. Usually these animals rent at two to three dollars per hour, or about ten dollars for a half-day.

If you're proficient in riding give lessons, either privately or in classes. Extra revenue can be obtained by boarding other people's horses.

Don't forget to get a good liability insurance policy before starting, however, to protect yourself in case of an accident.

FROGS INC.

If you live near a pond or creek you can profit from these jumpy creatures by catching and selling them to restaurants which serve frogs' legs. There is also a demand for frogs in medical schools and laboratories.

If your pond has no frog population, stock it with a dozen or so from a nearby creek or from another breeder. Get the colony fattened up by feeding them bugs, which you can attract by rigging up an electric light over the pond. Frogs breed fast, and soon you'll be able to start harvesting your "crop."

RAISE RABBITS

There are at least two ways to make money with rabbits. One is by raising Angoras for their fur. The fur is sheared periodically and sold to garment manufacturers, who use it as lining in coats and gloves.

The other way is to raise rabbits for food. You would then have to slaughter, process, and market them.

Check with your state Department of Agriculture, the U. S. Department of Agriculture, and local health departments. Stringent requirements usually apply to animal slaughtering and processing and you should be aware of them before getting involved.

Then, try to make a deal with the chain stores in your area to buy your slaughtered rabbits.

For further information:

> *Raising Rabbits for Fun and Profit,* Milton Faivre. Chicago, Nelson-Hall, 1973.

> *Rabbit Raising,* Paul Sawin. Columbus, Ohio, Fur-Fish-Game.

> *Fur Trade Journal.* Bewdley, Ontario, Canada (a monthly trade magazine).

> *Official Guide to Raising Better Rabbits.* Pittsburgh, American Rabbit Breeders Association, 1972.

BE A BEEKEEPER

Apiculture, as the beekeeping business is called, seldom makes headlines, but if you're at all bee-oriented there are several different ways to make money with these frightening little insects. You probably know that bees are valuable as a source of honey and wax, as well as for their ability to cross-pollinate. But did you know that their venom has been found to have medicinal properties and that, in some parts of the world, toasted honeybees are considered a gastronomic delicacy?

For further information:

Beekeeping: A Beginner's Guide to Profitable Honey and Beeswax Production, Francis Smith. New York, Oxford University Press, 1963.

The Complete Guide to Beekeeping, Roger Morse, ed. New York, E.P. Dutton, 1974.

Gleanings in Bee Culture, 623 West Liberty Street, Medina, Ohio 44256 (a monthly publication).

SINGING CANARIES

There's big money here, and very little competition—especially if you can get away from the big-city breeders.

As a breeder of singing canaries, your best bet is to make the rounds of pet shops with your feathered friends. But don't turn down any retail customers, as canaries sell for $40 up to over $100 on the retail market! Also, mail order could be a source of potential profits.

For the most part, it's the males that do the singing. But they must be given the proper vitamins, minerals, and feed. So study up first on the basics, then let these birds feather your nest!

For further information:

Canaries, Their Care and Breeding. Alhambra, California, Borden Publishing.

Canaries for Pleasure and Profit, Neptune City, New Jersey, T. F. H. Publications, 1965.

Care and Breeding of Budgerigars, Canaries, and Foreign Finches, Reginald Bennett. New York, Arco, 1961.

HORSE PHOTOG

If you like to bomb around in the boondocks with your camera, shooting horses (photographically, of course) may be the ideal job for you.

Personally call on horse breeders at their ranches and offer them a package deal on enlargements of photos of their animals.

Get a deposit, take the picture, then mail the prints out C.O.D.

TROUT HATCHERY

If you have a few acres of land and a good water supply it's possible to start your own fish hatchery.

First check any applicable federal, state, and local regulations. Study up thoroughly on the subject. When you're ready, get your eggs from another hatchery.

Sell your trout to fishing clubs for stock, and to fish preserves, private pond owners, and restaurants.

For further information:

The Farming of Fish, C. F. Hickling. Elmsford, New York, Pergamon Press, 1968.

Nutrient Requirements of Trout, Salmon, and Catfish, Agricultural Board. Washington, D. C., National Academy of Sciences, 1973.

City and Country . . .

TAKE A CRACK AT CRICKETS

More families live in apartments and condominiums these days than ever before. In such quarters, keeping a dog or cat is often impractical, or downright forbidden. How to satisfy the cravings of the pet lover and the regulations of the landlord at the same time? Introduce a hobby that has intrigued the space-cramped Japanese for centuries: the pet cricket.

Needless to say, crickets are free for the taking in the countryside. Cricket cages can be purchased from an Oriental import wholesaler, or you can manufacture them yourself. Sell your unique pets through local pet stores, and fill the homes of countless city dwellers with the reassuring cricket night-songs of the country.

CUSTOM-MADE DOGHOUSES

Americans spend millions of dollars a year pampering their pets. Some of it can be yours by designing and building unusual doghouses.

Your doghouses can be collapsible, so that owners can take them on trips or otherwise move them easily. They can have removable roofs for easy cleaning, and two-way doors so Fido can walk in and out at will and still be protected from the elements. Naturally they'll be painted and decorated attractively.

Make up a few samples and try to sell them to pet shops. Because of their uniqueness, collapsible, lightweight versions of this product have met with much success in the mail-order business.

For further information:

How to Build a Doghouse, Cat Shelter and Duck-Inn, Donald Brann. Briarcliff Manor, New York, Directions Simplified, Inc., 1975.

BOUDOIRS FOR BEASTS

Create beds for dogs and cats in various sizes, shapes, and designs. Use baby mattresses for average-sized dogs and twin-size mattresses for the Great Dane variety. Surround the bed itself with wickerwork, or upholstered side- and headboards. Try creating four-poster canopied versions.

Market your creations through pet shops and better department stores. Your motto might be "Creative comforts for all creatures."

GUINEA PIGS

Guinea pigs, or cavies, can be sold to pet shops and hospital and university laboratories. The animals are relatively easy to care for and provide good initial training for those individuals wishing to progress to the more exotic types of caged animals.

To start your "guinea pig farm" buy a male and a few females from a local pet shop, where you can also get tips and booklets on how to raise and care for them.

For further information:

Know Your Guinea Pigs, William Ritter. Garden City, New York, Doubleday, 1973.

Guinea Pigs, C. H. Keeling. New York, Arco Publishing, 1972.

MOUSE AND RAT FARM

University and hospital laboratories have need for mice and rats for experimental purposes, and the demand far exceeds the supply!

The animals are easy to care for and they reproduce quickly. You can expect to get about a dollar each for the more common strains. An extremely rare type will command a price in excess of twenty dollars. It's best to start out with a relatively hearty strain and gradually progress to the rarer types after you've learned the ropes.

Contact the lab of a local hospital or university and ask about their requirements. They can also recommend a supplier who will provide you with initial breeding stock.

For further information:

All About Rats, Howard Hirschhorn. Neptune City, New Jersey, T. F. H. Publications, 1974.

All about Mice, Howard Hirschhorn. Neptune City, New Jersey, T. F. H. Publications, 1974.

Standards and Guidelines for the Breeding, Care and Management of Laboratory Animals, Institute of Laboratory Animal Resources. Washington, D. C., National Academy of Sciences Printing and Publishing Office, 1969.

✸TIE FLIES

If you're a fly fisherman, you no doubt have some favorite flies you've rigged up that consistently bring in the big ones. Why keep them a secret?

Sell them through sporting goods stores and tackle shops. If your creations are really hot, the fishermen will be biting.

For further information:

Fly-tying Problems and Their Answers, John Veniard and Donald Downs. New York, Crown, 1972.

Fly-Tying Materials — Tools — Technique, Helen Shaw. New York, Ronald Press, 1963.

✸BOOTS FOR BOWSER

Now we wouldn't want to imply that you could make a living designing shoes for *average* dogs, but by making tough little boots for *hunting* dogs—maybe.

A busy hunting dog will cover miles and miles of rough terrain—sharp rocks and prickly shrubs—in a day's work. Hunters who care about their dogs will want to order your boots for all their hunting dogs—in sets of four!

Endow your product with a catchy name such as "bowser boots" or "paw protectors." Make them out of a durable material such as leather. Dye them in attractive colors, perhaps even monogramming them for the discriminating pooch.

✸PONY-GO-ROUND

Set yourself up in a shopping center, zoo, public park, beach, amusement park, carnival, fair—anywhere there are children.

Rent or buy six or eight ponies from a local farmer and attach them to a circular rotating frame, which you can have made relatively inexpensively.

Charge each child fifty cents for a five-minute ride. If you promote your business properly, during the summer months you can gross twenty to twenty-five dollars per hour. If you live in Florida or southern California, where summer is a year-round season, so much the better.

Make sure every child is harnessed securely to the pony. Also, best protect yourself with a good liability insurance policy. In spite of precautions, animals are unpredictable and accidents can happen.

✸DOG PENS AND KENNELS

With a little know-how and some fencing you can custom-build outdoor dog pens and kennels. Pens are usually about 6 feet by 6 feet and surrounded by wire fencing. An owner may desire a roof or tarp across the top to shelter the animal from the rain.

Kennels are usually longer, allowing the animal to run back and forth within the enclosure.

To learn the basics of construction, visit a few kennels and ask questions.

✸TROPICAL FISH

Aquariums take up little space, and this is one venture you can enjoy right in a corner of your own living room. Most neophyte breeders start with one of the more common species of fish, such as guppies, then progress to the rarer types. Extremely rare fish may command prices of up to $150. Check with local pet shops to see what their needs are.

Set up five tanks for an initial investment of about $200, and expand from there. To obtain direct customers, advertise in the newspaper and Yellow Pages.

For further information:

Breeding Aquarium Fishes, Herbert Axelrod and Susan Shaw. Neptune City, New Jersey,T. F. H. Publications, 1968.

Tropical Fish Hobbyist, 211 West Sylvania Avenue, Neptune City, New Jersey 07753 (a monthly publication).

How to Keep and Breed Tropical Fish, Clifford Emmens. Neptune City, New Jersey, T. F. H. Publications, 1974.

HOW LOW CAN YOU GET?

Believe it or not, there are companies that make large profits supplying worms to nurseries and as bait to sporting goods stores and bait shops. These firms buy millions of worms annually through independent growers.

Start out by supplying worms to one of these companies—they will sell you initial stock and give you complete instructions on breeding—and then gradually find your own markets, hire your own worm growers, and, who knows, maybe worm your way into something big!

You can find the names of bait wholesalers in the classified ads of national magazines or by asking at your local sporting goods store. Be wary, however, of any companies that ask for large sums of money.

For further information:

ABC's of the Earthworm Business, Ruth Myers. Elgin, Illinois, Shields, 1973.

Raising Earthworms for Profit, Earl Shields. Elgin, Illinois, Shields, 1973.

MINING MINNOWS

Minnows are another popular fishermen's bait. They can be raised almost as effortlessly as worms, requiring only a few small tanks in your backyard, garage or house. They breed rapidly and cost next to nothing to maintain.

For initial stock and information on marketing them, contact bait wholesalers or sporting goods stores.

DOG BREEDING

You'll need a moderately sized bundle to break into this business. A pedigreed bitch will cost anywhere from $150 up, and a rare breed may go as high as $200. Stud fees also start at about $150 and up. Then you'll have

veterinary and license fees and, of course, food costs and overhead.

If you're unfamiliar with the field, the best reference is the official publication of the American Kennel Club, *The Complete Dog Book.* This publication contains a wealth of information on such things as the care, training, breeding, and whelping of all the various breeds of dog. Another way to learn is to attend dog shows. Study the breeds you're interested in and don't be afraid to ask questions of the owners.

For further information:

How to Make Money in Dogs, Kurt Unkelbach. New York, Dodd, Mead, 1974.

How to Breed and Whelp Dogs, Joseph Hansen. Springfield, Illinois, Charles C. Thomas, 1973.

BE A TAXIDERMIST

Anyone, after learning a few basic techniques, can practice taxidermy. However, as in all skills, experience is the best teacher.

Once in business, you'll be asked to mount everything from beavers to bears, minnows to marlin. Prices can range from twenty-five or thirty dollars for a small fish into the hundreds of dollars for a sailfish or bear.

Pick up a few of the reference books listed below. Get some practice, then spread the word through local sporting goods stores, boat landings, and lodges where hunters congregate.

For further information:

The Amateur Taxidermist, Jean Labrie. New York, Hart, 1972.

Home Book of Taxidermy and Tanning, Gerald Grantz. Harrisburg, Pennsylvania, Stackpole Books, 1970.

DECORATIVE BIRDHOUSES

If you're handy with simple woodworking and feel good about providing housing for our feathered friends, you might enjoy—and profit by—creating decorative birdhouses.

You can either design them yourself or consult the reference books listed below. There are loads of possible designs. The houses can be made in the shape of churches, barns, tepees—even automobiles and airplanes. Then they can be painted bright colors and mounted on a pole or in a tree.

You can sell them to pet shops or direct to the consumer. With some really unique designs, you might consider mail order advertising in national nature magazines.

For further information:

> *How to Have Fun Making Bird Feeders and Bird Houses.* Mankato, Minnesota, Creative Educational Society, 1973.

> *How to Attract, House, and Feed Birds: Forty-eight Plans for Bird Feeders and Houses You Can Make,* Walter Schultz. Macmillan, New York, 1974.

CASH FROM CHINCHILLAS

To get started in this lucrative field you'll have to invest several hundred dollars in a male and three or four females, the most efficient production ratio. To find breeders who'll provide you with your initial stock, look in the Yellow Pages of any big-city telephone directory.

A word of warning. The chinchilla industry has recently been invaded by bands of disreputable, fast-talking promoters who promise the moon but deliver nothing. So before buying any of these animals or signing any contracts to do so, check the breeder out thoroughly.

For further information:

> *Fur Trade Journal.* Bewdley, Ontario, Canada (a monthly trade magazine).

> *Modern Chinchilla Farming,* John Clarke. Toronto, Fur Trade Journal of Canada, 1961.

GUARD DOG SERVICE

For most businesses, guard dogs are a relatively cheap and efficient form of protection against theft and vandalism. You would deliver your dogs, which can be obtained from a local trainer, to the business after working hours and pick them up just prior to the start of the workday. Naturally, you'll need a caged truck for transportation.

Offer your service to used car lots, retail stores, warehouses, and industrial and manufacturing plants. Charge a monthly fee, working on a contractual basis.

For further information:

> *Guard Dogs,* Jerold Mundis. New York, McKay, 1970.

SIAMESE CATS

There's something majestic, almost human, about Siamese cats. Perhaps that's the reason breeders can command—and get—up to $200 for these fancy felines.

Start by boning up on the care and feeding of Siamese cats. Get your initial stock from a pet shop or breeder, making sure the animals have pedigrees from the Cat Fanciers Association.

For further information:

> *Cat Breeding and Showing: A Guide for the Novice,* Meredith Wilson. Cranbury, New Jersey, A. S. Barnes, 1972.

> *Complete Book of Cat Care,* Leon Whitney. Garden City, New York, Doubleday, 1953.

> *Cat Fancy,* 11558 Sorrento Valley Road, San Diego, California 92121 (published every two months).

> *Cats Magazine,* P. O. Box 4106, Pittsburgh, Pennsylvania 15301 (a monthly magazine).

DOG AND CAT SHOW PHOTOG

Dog and cat shows offer an excellent opportunity for the photographer looking for new and unique outlets for his work.

Make up an attractive portfolio of your work. Then approach pet owners at these shows, asking for business.

Rather than one picture, you'll want to sell a package consisting of color prints of the animals in the various standard poses, perhaps included in an album.

For further information:

How to Photograph Cats, Dogs, and Other Animals (AC-38), Walter Chandoha. New York, American Photographic Book Publishing, 1973.

Animal and Pet Photography, Mildred Stagg. New York, American Photographic Book Publishing, 1969.

MAKE TWO-WAY PET DOORS

A great convenience for pet-owning homeowners would be a private entrance-exit for their dog or cat. This would enable the animal to come and go as he pleased without disturbing his master.

These devices usually involve cutting a small hole, just big enough for the animal, in the house's side or front door. Then hinged, swinging doors or flexible plastic vents are inserted in the hole.

Pick up a copy of *Outdoor life* or *Field & Stream.* In the back you'll find illustrated ads relating to these products. Write to these companies to get an idea of their designs and prices.

RABBIT HUTCHES

One good basic hutch plan is all you need to enter this business. If you're at all handy with wood and chicken wire you'll be able to turn them out fairly fast. Make them attractive by painting them bright colors. Then you can either sell your hutches to pet shops or leave them on consignment. You'll want to sell direct to the consumer as well.

Since an empty hutch is worthless, offer customers a package deal consisting of a hutch, rabbits, feed, and an instruction manual.

For further information:

Rabbit Raising, Paul Sawin. Columbus, Ohio, Fur-Fish-Game.

All About Rabbits as Pets, Kay Cooper. New York, Julian Messner, 1974.

Raising Rabbits for Fun and Profit, Milton Faivre. Chicago, Nelson-Hall, 1973.

CHICK HATCHERS

Chick hatchers are very easy to make. They're simply composed of a round plastic dome on a base, about a foot in diameter, with a small electric light bulb mounted in a socket inside the dome. Ordinary electric wire connects the socket to a plug.

Fertilized chicken eggs are placed inside the dome, where the bulb keeps them warm. The whole family can then watch the hatching process.

Provide eggs and an instruction book with your hatchers. The sets usually sell for five to ten dollars each and are especially popular at Easter and Christmas.

DOG TRAINING

You can operate a dog-training business in one of two ways. Either you can hold regular classes in a large yard or rented hall, or you can offer individualized training in the customer's home.

We once wrote a newspaper article on a man in South Carolina who specialized in training dogs in the home. He called on each dog twice a week for six weeks, spending an hour at each session. His rates ranged from $150–$250 per dog, depending on the breed and what the owner wanted. When we met him, his business was just getting off the ground and he had sixteen customers. According to our mathematics, this man was earning over $2,000 per month.

If the subject is unfamiliar to you, the best way to break into the field is to go to work for a kennel or trainer for at least a few months in order to learn the ropes before branching out on your own.

For further information:

Dog Obedience Training, Gust Kessopulos. Cranbury, New Jersey, A. S. Barnes, 1974.

Dog Psychology: The Basis of Dog Training, Leon Whitney. New York, Howell Book House, 1971.

PET ADOPTION AGENCY

Here's an occupation for the pet lover who wants to help ease the unwanted-pet crisis. Set up a pet adoption agency, in which you will care for pets whose owners are no longer able to keep them. Charge the owners the going kennel rate until you are able to place the pets. In return for this weekly or monthly fee, you will promise never to do away with any pets placed in your care.

Make the public aware of your service, and solicit new owners for your pets through ads in the newspaper classifieds and in the Yellow Pages. Make sure that your location is zoned for such an operation, but fairly close to the city.

5

A Festival of Food

The food field offers an extremely wide range of potentially lucrative enterprises. Whether your interest lies in growing a few mushrooms in your basement for sale to local food stores or in establishing a national chain of gourmet restaurants, you're sure to find something here that appeals to you.

Of course, before involving yourself in this field it's necessary to check and comply with all federal, state, and local regulations pertaining to health, zoning, and licensing. Also, if you deal directly with the public, you'll want to secure a good liability insurance policy.

More than in any other field, the attractive packaging and labeling of food products is of the utmost importance. In packaged foods a decorative basket, a colorful wrapper, a few ribbons can make the difference between success and failure. In the pie and cake category, a dab of whipped cream or a few colorful embellishments can induce a purchase.

In the food field, as in any commercial enterprise, aggressive promotion and exploitation of your product is necessary to ensure high profits. The following is only a partial list of the many possible outlets available to you. Use this in combination with the advertising and promotional ideas outlined in Chapter 1 and you may just find your success exceeding your greatest expectations.

Sell your food product or service to or through:

- Supermarkets
- Convenience stores
- Specialty food shops
- Food brokers
- Restaurants
- Cafeterias
- Bakeries
- Variety chains
- Gift shops
- Roadside stands
- Vending machines
- Party supply stores
- Party rental agencies
- Fund-raising organizations
- Social clubs
- Women's and men's clubs
- PTA groups
- Church groups
- Sporting events
- Festivals, fairs, carnivals
- Door-to-door sales crews
- Mail order

Food Preparation

The field of food preparation can encompass everything from apple sauce pudding to zucchini casserole—and anything in between! For most of the specialties listed we've included references for you to consult.

In addition, here is a list of some of the better-known and more highly regarded *general* cookbooks on the market:

Betty Crocker's Cookbook. New York, Bantam Books, 1974.

The Good Housekeeping Cookbook, Hazel Schoenburg. New York, Hearst, 1973.

Joy of Cooking, Irma Rombauer and Marion Becker. Indianapolis, Bobbs-Merrill, 1951.

Amy Vanderbilt's Complete Cookbook, Amy Vanderbilt. Garden City, New York, Doubleday.

MICHELANGELO IN BREAD

We've all seen cookies shaped in the form of hearts, houses, and gingerbread men, but how about sculptured loaves of bread resembling *Venus de Milo, The Thinker,* and the *Pietà*? If you're artistically inclined, you can make permanent molds of these and other items, which can be used over and over again.

Only a lack of creativity can limit one in this field. Aside from fashioning unique bread designs for cocktail parties, wedding receptions, and Bar Mitzvahs, you can exploit the lucrative convention banquet field: Bread houses for a construction industry convention, bread shoes for a meeting of shoe manufacturers, and for the whisky industry—you guessed it—a loaf of rye.

BASKET LUNCHES

If you live in San Francisco you can forget this idea, as it's already being done there successfully. However, we doubt that it's been exploited in any other large city.

This enterprise involves making hordes of good-quality sandwiches and stocking them in large, old-fashioned picnic baskets. Each basket is sent out into the business district during the lunch hour on—you guessed it —the arm of a pretty girl frocked out in an old-fashioned granny dress.

When we were in San Francisco last year, the sandwiches were selling for $1.50 each. A truck was kept nearby where the ladies could replenish their stock when needed.

For further information:

> *Make Me a Different Kind of Sandwich Book,* Richard Harrison and Albert Adler. New York, Essandess Specials (orders to Simon & Schuster), 1969.

> *Good Sandwiches and Picnic Dishes,* Ambrose Heath. Levittown, New York, Transatlantic Arts, 1949.

HAWK HORSERADISH!

If you've ever tried to find a flavorful, potent bottle of horseradish in a supermarket, you know that it's next to impossible. The major brands are all mass-produced—watered down and stored for long periods until the flavor is diluted to a kind of tasteless pulp.

Any good cookbook will give you the basic

ingredients, which you can improve upon. Then bottle and label your creation and sell it to food outlets. If your product begins to generate a demand, you might try getting a large food broker to distribute it for you.

CATERING SERVICE

As a caterer you'll be called upon to provide edibles from appetizers to full-course meals, for occasions such as wedding receptions, birthday parties, and bar mitzvahs. You'll prepare the food at home, bringing it to the function just before it begins.

Assuming you're already proficient in the culinary arts, the best way to start is to spread the word through high class neighborhoods and social clubs. Also, you can pay a small commission to bridal shops, delicatessens, and bakeries for referring clients to you.

For further information:

> *Profitable Catering,* Bruce Axler. Indianapolis, Bobbs-Merrill, 1974.

> *Catering Handbook,* Hal Weiss and E. Weiss. Rochelle Park, New Jersey, Hayden, 1971.

PARTY COOK

This enterprise differs from the preceding in that all the cooking is done in the customer's kitchen. One advantage here is that the food can be served to the guests piping hot. Also, the need for your transporting large quantities of cooked food is eliminated.

A complete service consists of first going over the food requirements with the hostess, then, on the day of the party, doing the necessary marketing, transporting the groceries to the house, and arriving early enough to complete the necessary preparations in time for the party.

SMOKING CAN BE HEALTHY!

Ham, bacon, sausage, Cornish hens, and fish are just a few of the many food items that can be smoked and successfully sold to food markets, delicatessens, and tourist shops.

You'll need to build or buy your own smokehouse, which you can set up in your backyard if regulations permit. For smoking, use any hardwood such as hickory, oak, or walnut.

Get complete information on the process, as well as on any applicable regulations, from your state Department of Agriculture.

For further information:

> *The Art of Curing, Pickling, and Smoking Meat and Fish,* James Robinson. New York, Gordon Press, 1973.

PICNIC LUNCHES

Here you may want to specialize in haute cuisine, preparing such delicacies as shrimp cocktail, crabmeat salad, or lobster and avocado sandwiches. French bread, wine, gourmet cheeses, and exotic desserts are additional possibilities. Pack your lunches in attractive, disposable baskets.

A good way to start promoting your service would be to distribute leaflets to "singles" apartment complexes. Also, you might interest civic and fund-raising organizations in your service.

For further information:

> *Make Me a Different Kind of Sandwich Book,* Richard Harrison and Albert Adler. New York, Essandess Specials (orders to Simon & Schuster), 1969.

> *Good Sandwiches and Picnic Dishes,* Ambrose Heath. Levittown, New York, Transatlantic Arts, 1949.

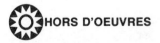

HORS D'OEUVRES

Hors d'oeuvres, canapés, and the like are regularly served at social functions from teas to wedding receptions. They may consist of simple, inexpensive fare such as deviled eggs, or exotic delicacies such as caviar on melba rounds or quiche Lorraine.

There are many fine books available on the preparation of these tasty morsels. Experiment at home till you get the knack, then let social clubs, civic organizations, and future brides know that your service is available.

For further information:

> *Snacks and Appetizers,* Editors. *Better Homes & Gardens.* Des Moines, Iowa, Meredith Corp., 1974.

> *Appetizers and Canapes,* William Kaufman. Garden City, New York, Doubleday, 1968.

A SALAD DRESSING MOGUL

Experiment with salad dressing recipes found in a general cookbook or in the reference below, adding some ingredients of your own, until you come up with the perfect concoction. Perhaps you can invent a savory herb dressing, using fresh herbs, or a new onion-cheese combination. The possibilities are only as limited as your own imagination.

Be sure to package your masterpiece attractively before making the rounds of possible buyers. In addition to the normal outlets, a truly unique mixture, if it's promoted properly, should sell very well via mail order.

For further information:

> *Salads and Salad Dressings,* Eulalia Blair. Boston, Cahners, 1974.

HOMEMADE BREAD

In this day of mass-produced packaged foods, good home-baked bread is a rarity. You can capitalize on this unfortunate situation by baking and selling this item directly from your home, if regulations permit, or by opening a small shop in town. Market your product also through food stores and restaurants.

Have several different varieties and shapes to choose from. Aside from the standard types, offer specialties such as honey bread, cheese twirl, and cinnamon loaf. Then sit back and rake in the dough!

For further information:

The Complete Book of Breads, Bernard Clayton. New York, Simon & Schuster, 1973.

Sunset Cookbook of Breads, Editors, *Sunset* magazine, Menlo Park, California, Lane, 1966.

 **A SPECIALTY COOK**

If you have a flair for creating a particular dish, such as stuffed grape leaves or paella, supply restaurants with these dishes on a regular basis.

Visit local restaurant owners and let them sample your specialty. Offer to deliver to them daily, at a reasonable price.

BOX LUNCHES

If you like the idea of making and selling simple lunches, you should consider opening a small shop near a school, factory, or large office building.

Offer a variety of packed lunches, keeping the contents simple and inexpensive. You might include a sandwich, an apple, and a few cookies. Or a sandwich, small container of cole slaw, and piece of cake. Lunches may be sold to include the price of a drink, or you may want to charge extra for it.

For further information:

Good Sandwiches and Picnic Dishes, Ambrose Heath. Levittown, New York, Transatlantic Arts, 1949.

Lunchbox Cookbook, Beverly Nemiro and Marie Von Allman. Chicago, Swallow.

The Sandwich Book, The Modern Art of Sandwich Making for All Occasions, Ann Seranne and Eileen Gaden. Garden City, New York, Doubleday, 1964.

 **HOME CANNING**

There is always a demand for "down home" preserves or canned foods, whether they be jams and jellies, fruits and vegetables, syrups and sauces, or meats and fish. If you've never canned before, be sure to research the subject thoroughly and take all necessary precautions against spoilage.

Label and package your products attractively before attempting to market them. Just about any food outlet is a good place to sell such goods.

For further information:

A Guide to Canning and Preserving, Calvin Hold and Patch Caradine. New York, Pyramid, 1974.

Complete Guide to Home Canning, Preserving, and Freezing, U. S. Department of Agriculture. New York, Dover, 1973.

CREAMED HERRING

If you can come up with a quality creamed herring product it can be sold to friends, neighbors, party caterers, supermarkets, and specialty food shops.

Get yourself some good cookbooks and experiment, using their recipes as a base. Add some of your own ingredients until you have a unique, savory taste. Try flavoring your herring with wine or some other tasty ingredient.

Bottle your product and label it attractively. Then take some free samples around to the above-mentioned outlets to promote your specialty.

DEHYDRATED FOODS

In this venture a dehydrating oven is necessary. This will require an investment of about $200. Manufacturer's instructions come with each oven.

Arrange with local farmers, supermarkets, and dairies to buy their surplus fruits, vegetables, and dairy products. After dehydrating them, you can package the products and sell them to supermarkets, convenience stores, and sporting goods and camping supply stores, which in turn will sell them to campers and hikers.

For further information:

Dry It You'll Like it, Gen MacManiman. Seattle, Montana Books, 1974.

Home Food-Dehydrating: Economical "Do-It-Yourself" Methods for Preserving, Storing, and Cooking, Jay Bills and Shirley Bills. Bountiful, Utah, Horizon Publishers, 1974.

BARBECUE CHEF

Promote your services to schools, church groups, civic organizations, large companies—anyone interested in throwing a good old-fashioned barbecue picnic.

You must have at least a few acres suitable for outings. Build a barbecue oven by placing large grates over cement blocks.

In addition to rounding up interested groups, organize the entire affair, including shopping for the chicken, steak, spare ribs, or hamburger, providing the utensils and condiments, and supervising the cooking.

For further information:

The Better Homes and Gardens Barbecue Book, Editors, *Better Homes & Gardens.* New York, Bantam, 1974.

Sunset Barbecue Book, Editors, *Sunset* magazine. Menlo Park, California, Lane, 1972.

FRESH FRUIT JUICES

Years ago, before the invention of frozen foods, a person could walk into any restaurant and order a glass of fresh orange or grapefruit juice with his ham and eggs. The waitress would squeeze the juice directly from the fruit, right before his eyes.

You can help bring about a fresh-juice revival by making a deal with a local citrus rancher to buy large quantities of his fruit at reasonable prices. Then extract the juice by use of a machine which can be purchased at any health food store. Bottle the juice by the gallon and sell it to individual restaurants.

VERY BRITISH

If you've ever visited a pub in jolly old England, you know that meat pies are a constant solace to the hungry ale drinker. Why not make a platterful of these tasty treats and try selling them to your neighborhood bars?

Make each one about the size of an apple turnover and sell them for whatever price you must charge in order to pay for the ingredients and your time. Later on you can expand your food line to include other snacks such as pickled tomatoes, pigs' feet, hard-boiled eggs, hors d'oeuvres, etc.

Any English cookbook will tell you how to make meat pies and, in addition, will provide you with ideas for other possible products.

HEALTH BAKERY

There are about a half-dozen health food grocery stores in my town. They all sell health breads but, since there is no local baker of these goods, this product must be shipped in from distant cities. What better opportunity for a bakery specializing in such breads as whole wheat, whole rye, soy, gluten, and pure honey?

Check to see whether this need exists in your area. If it does, you can be rolling in dough in no time.

For further information:

Home Bakebook of Natural Breads and Goodies, Bruce Sandler and Sandra Sandler, New York, Bantam, 1974.

TALK TURKEY!

If you have, or can get access to, some large ovens, you can provide customers with cooked, stuffed, and seasoned turkeys—any time of the year.

Buy your turkeys wholesale from a turkey rancher. Spread the word of your turkey-roasting business throughout your neighborhood, to PTA groups, social and civic organizations—even small restaurants and cafés might want to take advantage of your service.

For further information:

All Poultry Cookbook, Michele Evans. New York, Dell, 1974.

The American Illustrated Cookbook of Turkey, Chicken, and Other Fowl, Anne Tynte. Garden City, New York, Doubleday, 1973.

 **A KITCHEN COACH**

Many brides-to-be—and long-married women, for that matter—have never mastered the art of cooking to their satisfaction. Why not hold cooking classes in your home, or at a YWCA or evening adult school?

You could start out with basic dishes such as omelettes and progress to such specialties as cheese fondue and boeuf Bourguignon.

Advertise your classes in bridal salons, through PTA groups, and in the Yellow Pages.

Growing and Selling

 **SELL SEAWEED**

Edible varieties of this product grow free for the taking along both the East and West Coast of the United States. First learn to identify the kind you'll be selling. Then gather, pulverize, and sell it in bulk to health food stores.

This valuable supplier of trace minerals retails at over $1 a pound, and is a tasty addition to soups, salads, and baby formulas. Because of its keeping qualities, this product makes a good mail order item. Advertise it in national health food magazines.

For further information:

Seaweeds and Their Uses, V. J. Chapman. New York, Halsted Press, 1970.

MUSHROOM MADNESS

Mushrooms are a delicacy and can be grown easily in a dark, ventilated cellar at a

regulated temperature of 60–70 degrees. The soil must be rich and a high-grade fertilizer rich in phosphates must be used.

Sell your mushrooms to food stores, specialty food shops, and large restaurants.

For further information:

Mushroom Growing, Arthur Simons. New York, Drake, 1972.

Mushroom Growing for Everyone, Roy Genders. Levittown, New York, Transatlantic Arts, 1970.

 **TEA TREATS**

An overwhelming variety of natural far-out teas can be made from wild or garden plants. Some of the better known of these talented plants: alfalfa, sassafras, anise, birch, wild mint, and wild cabbage rose. Then there are the many tasty combinations of the above.

From trimmings in wilderness areas and your neighbors' gardens, you can come up with a unique line of teas, to be sold in bulk to health food stores and restaurants. By all means approach the buyers for grocery store chains as well. It's about time these stores stocked something more imaginative than orange pekoe.

CRAWLING THINGS

If you live near the seashore, make a deal with some local fishermen to supply you with live lobsters or crabs. Set up a stand consisting of a tank and stove near a public beach.

Offer your creatures either cooked (with a container of sauce or condiments), for beach picnicgoers, or uncooked, for those on their way home.

For further information:

Lobsters, Crabs, Etc., Andre Simon. Hackensack, New Jersey, Wehman, 1957.

 **PROMOTE PEANUTS**

Buy yourself some roasting ovens and make arrangements to buy some large quantities of peanuts through a local farmer or food broker.

You can promote your peanut business in a variety of ways. In addition to having a small stand or store, you can hire students to sell your goobers on the street, at bus stops, or in parks; at fairs, carnivals, and sporting events. Sell them at a discount to scouting and fund-raising organizations, encouraging them to have peanut sales. And, of course, food stores and roadside stands are always good outlets.

FOR LAZY PEANUT LOVERS

Just about everyone loves peanuts, but many people don't like the task of shelling them before eating them.

For a few hundred dollars, you can buy a roasting oven and a peanut-shelling machine. Then pack your "nude" peanuts in small plastic bags and sell them wholesale to local food stores. Your product will be fresher and cheaper than the canned variety.

Get your raw nuts direct from the farm or from a local food broker.

SPROUT SUPPLIER

Chinese restaurants use soybean sprouts and mung bean sprouts abundantly in food preparation. Supermarkets also sell them.

You can profit by growing and selling this crispy, tasty vegetable. Buy a supply of beans at a health food store or wholesale seed outlet. These firms will also provide you with growing instructions. Generally, all the beans need in order to start sprouting is water and a few days of tender, loving care—then they're ready to be turned into cash.

A FARMERS' BROKER

Contact nut and fruit growers, as well as producers of honey, olives, dates, preserves—anything that can be sold in town. Offer to act as agent for these people, charging a 10 percent commission. Then actively promote these products to food outlets in your area.

If you're suited to the work, you'll soon be established as a food broker, and you'll find both sellers and buyers seeking out your services.

GROW AND SELL HERBS

Grow a variety of herbs in old egg cartons or containers of similar shape. Label each section as to which herb it contains.

When the herbs begin to sprout, sell them to nurseries and food stores. Herbs also sell well through mail order, if promoted properly.

For further information:

How to Grow Herbs, Editors, *Sunset* magazine. Menlo Park, California, Lane, 1972.

How to Grow Herbs for Gourmet Cooking, Frederick Anderson. New York, Hawthorn, 1967.

ROADSIDE STAND

Fruits, vegetables, nuts, honey, olives, pickles, pastries, fruit and vegetable juices, sugar cane, and sides of bacon and ham are just a few of the innumerable goodies that can be sold at roadside stands. One man in California sells frozen buffalo meat from his stand, while an enterprising businessman in Illinois sells cans of chocolate-covered ants from his.

Of course, the more unique your products are (and the larger and more numerous your signs are), the greater the chance that motorists will stop and make a purchase.

For further information:

Profitable Roadside Marketing, R. B. Donaldson and W. F. Johnstone. State College, Pennslyvania, College Science Publishers.

Farm Roadside Marketing in the United States, James Milmoe. Newark, Delaware, Food Business Institute, University of Delaware, 1965.

ORGANIC GARDENING

The demand for organically grown fruits and vegetables, which are free of chemical fertilizers or pesticides, is growing greater every year.

Organic crops are mulched with rich humus which has been composted from dead leaves, grass, weed clippings, kitchen garbage, and other organic material.

Sell your organic produce to health food stores, at roadside stands or farmers' markets, house to house, or even through operation of your own concession in the produce section of a supermarket.

For further information:

Everything You Want to Know About Organic Gardening, G. J. Binding. New York, Pyramid, 1973.

Growing Food the Natural Way: A How-to Workbook, Ken Kraft and Pat Kraft. Garden City, New York, Doubleday, 1973.

FLAVOR WOODS

Woods such as apple, oak, hickory, and maple, when used in barbecuing, impart a unique flavor to the food being cooked. This fact opens up the possibility of starting an enterprise in which you'd sell packaged chips of these woods to the public as well as to various retail outlets.

Since, in the food business, image is almost as important as the product itself, promote your "flavor chips" heavily, perhaps by supplying some to the better-known barbecue restaurants in town free of charge, in exchange for their putting your product's name on their menus.

AN EGG SALESMAN

Most eggs purchased in supermarkets are days old and, compared to fresh eggs, taste like it. And this is the eggs-act truth.

Make a deal with a farmer in the area to buy large batches of his eggs at wholesale prices.

Then get in your car and start calling on housewives at the door. Carry your eggs in an old basket, for atmosphere.

Work toward building up a regular route for yourself, calling on each neighborhood the same day of the week, so your steady customers will know when to expect you.

HYDROPONIC FARMING

Hydroponics, or soilless gardening, involves the growing of crops without soil in water to which nutrients have been added. Using the proper equipment and nutrients, an individual can grow any crop, regardless of the season—even in his basement!

The cost of the equipment is high, however, and special training is required.

For further information:

Beginner's Guide to Hydroponics, James Douglas. New York, Drake, 1973.

Hydroponic Gardening: The Magic of Hydroponics for the Home Gardener, Raymond Bridwell. Loma Linda, California, Woodbridge, 1972.

GIFT PACKS

This enterprise involves attractively packaging a variety of specialty foods and selling them to food and variety stores, gourmet food shops, drugstores, and hospital gift shops.

One package might contain imported cheese, crackers, nuts, and fruits. Another might consist of stuffed olives, a fruitcake, canned herring balls, and preserves. Pack the items in a large basket and cover with colored cellophane or wrap with wide, colorful ribbons.

Services

BE AN APPLE PEELER

Believe it or not, there are people in this world who make money peeling apples.

Restaurants, hotels, and bakeries have varying demands for peeled and sliced apples. You can even turn the peels themselves into dollars by making jelly out of them, and then selling the jelly to bakeries and canneries.

The apples are purchased through local farmers. Machinery does all the work and can be found through the Yellow Pages or by contacting food brokers in your area.

WRITE A COOKBOOK!

First let me warn you that attempting to get a cookbook published is a most difficult endeavor. Hundreds, perhaps thousands, of cookbook manuscripts pass over editors' desks every year, only to be summarily rejected.

However, if you have some truly unique slant on a book of this type—and some dynamite recipes, to boot—give it a try.

First get your ideas together, put them down on paper, and submit them in the form of a query letter to a book publisher. Details on how to do this are outlined in the *Writer's Market*. Get a copy at your library or bookstore.

BARTENDING SCHOOL

If you're proficient at mixing drinks and can convince men and women to enter the bartending profession, you can successfully open and operate a bartending school.

One of the fastest ways to get started is to spread the word and leave leaflets at local taverns. Bar owners are continually looking for dependable help, so they'll be cooperative in sending prospective students to you.

BE A FREE-LANCE BARTENDER

If you're an expert mixologist, you might consider renting out your services for wedding and bar mitzvah receptions, conventions, cocktail parties, and other social functions.

In addition to mixing the drinks, you would be responsible for supplying the liquor, mixes, ice, and related necessities. Also, for large affairs, you would have to hire and supervise extra help.

To get started, promote your services through social and civic organizations, bridal salons, and places where the well-to-do congregate, such as yacht and country clubs.

For further information:

Everything You Always Wanted to Know About Bartending, George Perikli. New York, Vantage, 1972.

Bartender's Guide: How to Mix Drinks—for Home and Professional Use. Chicago, Stein.

Trader Vic's Bartender's Guide, Trader Vic. Garden City, New York, Doubleday, 1972.

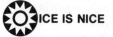
START A DINER'S CLUB

This idea involves making arrangements with owners of some of the better-class restaurants in town. Get them to agree to serve coupon holders one free meal for each meal bought.

Of course, you will be responsible for printing up the coupon books. You'll make your money when you sell the books for $10–$20 each to individuals who will then be able to obtain free meals worth $200 or more by using the coupons. The restaurant owner will have his restaurant promoted inexpensively, since new customers will be brought in by the coupons.

ICE IS NICE

The ice business, of course, works best in a hot climate. Here you'll need at least a half-dozen dependable ice-vending machines, requiring an initial investment of several thousand dollars, in order to make any appreciable amount of profit. To find machines, look in the Yellow Pages of any big-city phone directory under "Vending machines."

When you're ready, line up your locations at service stations, supermarkets, convenience stores, and anywhere else a traveler or shopper might have a need for your product.

STUDENT SURVIVAL KITS

This novel enterprise involves making arrangements with out-of-town parents of local college students to provide their sons and daughters, at final exam time, with packages of goodies, in order that they may survive the "ordeal."

Get parents' names from college records and student directories. Mail the letters six weeks or so before exam time, offering to send the students assorted packages of cheese and crackers, candy, dried fruits, nuts, canned gourmet foods, and the like.

Of course, you'll be responsible for shopping, packaging, and delivery, so you'll want to charge enough to cover expenses and a sizable profit for your efforts.

START A GOOD-EATING GUIDE

Make it your business to discover some of the more unique eateries in your town, then publish a booklet giving descriptive information about each establishment. Call it "The Underground Gourmet Guide" or some such catchy title.

After you've written up your guidebook, take it around to a few local printers for estimates. If a printer thinks you have a hot item, he may even foot part of the printing costs himself, in exchange for a percentage of the profits on the sale of the book.

Very important: Don't forget to get a copyright on your work.

BE A MENU PLANNER

Many small restaurants lack business or fail because their menus are nor varied enough. People get tired of the same old fare and start patronizing other establishments.

You can rescue these sinking enterprises by offering your services as a menu planner. Make up an assortment of appetizing dinner ideas that a restauranteur can add to his menu.

Charge five dollars or so per month, and every month submit a new batch of ideas to each restaurant. With 100 or more restaurants on your list, you can pick up a nice bit of change for your efforts.

For further information:

> *Menu Planning,* Eleanor Eckstein. Westport, Connecticut, Avi, 1973.

> *Menu Planning: A Blueprint for Better Profits,* Peter Vankleek and H. E. Visick. New York, McGraw-Hill, 1973.

RECYCLE YOUR RECIPES

Sell your unique family recipes to housewives for twenty-five or fifty cents each. Offer only your best recipes, giving each an attractive name.

Recipes can be sold through newspaper ads or through the classified sections of magazines such as *Sunset* or *Gourmet.* Also, students of cooking classes are excellent prospects.

Your service might also include typing, on file cards, and categorizing the recipes of others.

COFFEE SERVICE

This enterprise consists of providing businesses, mainly offices, with coffee-making equipment and supplies. After installing the equipment, you would have to call on each firm weekly to replenish needed supplies.

First, contact a coffee equipment distributor in your area. He'll help you get started, as he'll be supplying you with the merchandise.

Then call on offices, stores, factories—any place your service might be needed—and sell them on the idea of using your service.

For the Sweet Tooth

FRUITCAKES—NOT SUCH A NUTTY BUSINESS

Fruitcakes can be sold by literally scores of methods. They can be sold to bakeries, restaurants, gift shops, drugstores, supermarkets, department stores, schools, fund-raising organizations such as the Boy Scouts or Little League, or to business executives for use as gifts. They can be sold through mail order, roadside stands, or wrapped into gift packs. They can be made into wedding cakes, birthday cakes, and cupcakes. The cupcake size would sell to vending machine operators and snack bars.

To get started, experiment with various recipes until you come up with a high-quality product. Then give it a fancy wrapper and promote it through some of the above-mentioned outlets.

CANDY SUBSCRIPTION SERVICE

This novel idea involves selling a subscription service whereby a child will receive a small, decorative box of candy on each of seven holidays throughout the year.

Each gift the child receives will be symbolic of that particular holiday. For instance, at Christmas the child receives candy in a colorful Santa Claus-shaped container, Thanksgiving brings a turkey-shaped package, and so on.

Charge twenty dollars or so per year for your service. Aside from advertising through normal channels, you should find this an excellent mail-order product.

THE CANDY APPLE CAVALCADE

As a "candy apple king" (or queen), your most expensive equipment outlay will be for a commercial mixer. This is needed for stirring the syrup into which the apples are dipped. A dependable used model can usually be found for under $100.

Find a food broker through the Yellow Pages. Since he'll be selling you the apples and possibly distributing the finished product for you, he'll be more than happy to tell you where to buy equipment and how to set up your plant.

After getting into production, sell your product to supermarkets and convenience stores.

DOUGHNUT FACTORY

For some reason, most doughnuts bought in conventional restaurants taste flat, doughy—something, in fact, just this side of chewy straw.

You can do something about this deplorable situation by starting out small, in your home, and experimenting with several different varieties until you come up with the perfect product. Then take some samples around to restaurants, cafeterias, and food markets, and offer to supply them with your product on a regular basis.

BIRTHDAY CAKES FOR COLLEGE KIDS

At birthday time, it's not very easy for mom to bake, package, and ship a cake to the son or daughter away at school. Furthermore, the odds are against a mailed cake arriving in any condition other than a mangled pile of crumbs and icing.

Your solution to this problem is to contact out-of-town parents of local college students, offering to deliver a fresh, decorated cake in time for their children's birthday. You can either buy the cakes at a local bakery, or bake and decorate them yourself.

For further information:

Your Book of Cake Making and Decorating, Patsy Kumm. Levittown, New York, Transatlantic Arts, 1974.

Pillsbury Bake-Offs: Cake and Frosting Cook Books. New York, Simon & Schuster, 1969.

MAPLE SYRUP

If you have access to a grove of maple trees, you could pick up a nice piece of change by utilizing the syrup.

Simply tap the sap and boil it down to a sugary consistency. Maple sugar has a decidedly strong, sweet taste and can be used for making sugar cakes, maple butter, and a variety of candies.

You can sell the syrup to restaurants, the sugar to candy manufacturers, or the candy to any of a number of food outlets.

For further information:

Amateur Sugar Maker, Noel Perrin. Hanover, New Hampshire, University Press of New England, 1972.

Maple-Sugaring: The Way We Do It, Myrtie Fellows and Floyd Fellows. Brattleboro, Vermont, Stephen Greene, 1972.

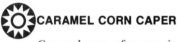

CARAMEL CORN CAPER

Caramel corn, of course, is that yummy-tasting popcorn coated with caramel. Starting with a recipe from any good cookbook, work up your own special recipe.

There are actually two ways to make money here. You could produce the product in your home (if regulations permit), packaging it and selling it wholesale to supermarkets and convenience stores. Or, you might open up your own shop in a high-volume area such as downtown or in a suburban shopping center. Either way, this enterprise should mean some sweet profits for you.

To get started, you'll need a commercial-sized popcorn machine, which you should be able to secure, used, from a popcorn or restaurant supply company for under $200.

DON'T BE A SUCKER—MAKE THEM!

Lollipops can be made in the shape of cats, bats, cars, stars, goats, boats, bucks, ducks, planes, or trains. They can be red, yellow, green, blue, chartreuse, or polka-dotted. They can be quarter-size or quarter-

horse-size. They can be sold to restaurants, variety stores, gift shops, and drugstores, and through mail order.

Climb aboard the good ship *Lollipop* and sail for "Greenland."

DESSERT CATERER

If your forte is creating exotic sweets, why not put your talents to work for yourself?

Your crème brulée, rum chocolate mousse, and soufflé Grand Marnier are sure to be a hit at wedding receptions, afternoon teas, bar mitzvahs, and just about anywhere else that good food is required.

If you're not already proficient at serving up these tasties, consult the books listed below or other good gourmet cookbooks. Experiment at home till you're proficient. Then spread the word through social groups, brides-to-be, gourmet restaurants, and specialty food shops.

For further information:

Maida Heatter's Book of Great Desserts, Maida Heatter. New York, Knopf, 1974.

The Dessert Lovers' Cookbook, Margaret Storm. New York, Bantam, 1973.

HOLIDAY GOODIES

Even though this enterprise involves creating desserts only for holidays, it's possible, through wide distribution, to earn enough to carry you through the entire year.

Your plum pudding, fruitcake, lepküchen, decorated cookies, mincemeat and pumpkin pies, as well as your own specialties, can be sold to bakeries, gourmet food shops, and restaurants—as well as through mail order—at Christmas, Thanksgiving, Easter, Valentine's Day, and on any other festive occasion.

MAKE WEDDING CAKES

As a baker and decorator of fine wedding cakes, you can get anywhere from $20 to

$500 and up for your creations, depending, of course, on their size and elaborateness.

If you're not a veteran cake baker already, study the books listed below, experimenting at home. When you're ready, spread the word through bridal salons, churches, and synagogues.

For further information:

The Wilton Book of Wedding Cakes, Norman Wilton. New York, Exposition, 1971.

Cake Icing and Decorating for All Occasions, Beryl Guertner. New York, Taplinger Publishing Company, 1967.

COUGH DROPS

We never heard anyone say that if you can manufacture a better cough drop, the world would beat a path to your door. But because these little medicinal candies are a multimillion-dollar-a-year business, *somebody's* door has a path beaten in front of it!

Most cough drops contain a combination of menthol, eucalyptus, and corn syrup in varying amounts, plus additional "medication" or flavoring. Try to come up with some unique flavors of your own. Mint, caviar, and Scotch are all flavors that might be winners for you.

6

An Avalanche of Art

Whether your interest lies in creating masterpieces in oil or in operating an art poster shop, the art field offers an excellent opportunity for high profits.

Let us again stress the value of promoting your product aggressively in order to obtain the best possible returns for your efforts. Art can be fun, as in the case of producing and selling caricatures. Or it can take on a more somber tone, as in reproducing in oil the likeness of a widow's deceased husband. Obviously, your promotional methods must harmonize with the nature of your service in order to be effective.

You may be unfamiliar with some of the materials and techniques used in the enterprises outlined in this chapter. Most art supply stores can provide you with needed materials and, in addition, will give you valuable free advice on technique.

Where and through what channels can you market your work? Two excellent sources providing valuable information on commercial markets are: *Artist's Market* and *Fine Arts Market Place*. These can be found at your local library or ordered through bookstores.

If you're attempting to sell your goods to, or through, retail outlets, have some samples of your better work to show the buyer or store owner. Naturally, you'll try to collect your money upon delivery. If the store owner balks at this arrangement, you might try leaving your products on consignment. That is, the store pays you for what is sold, after it is sold, with any unsold merchandise returned to you. Of course, you'll want to get a signed receipt for any goods left without payment.

The list below will give you some ideas on possible markets of a general nature. Stretch your thinking a bit and see if you can come up with others that might relate better to the enterprise you have in mind.

Display your work in, and sell it to or through:

- Arts and crafts shows
- Art galleries
- Museums or museum art shops
- Artist supply stores

- Gift shops
- Children's shops
- Toy stores
- Variety stores
- Drugstores
- Supermarkets
- Tourist centers
- Door to door
- Mail order
- Novelty shops, suppliers, manufacturers
- Restaurants, banks, department stores, and other high-traffic retail outlets

If your art involves "on-the-spot" work, set up a booth at a:

- College campus
- Shopping center
- Department store
- Flea market
- Fair, carnival, amusement park
- Public beach
- Boardwalk
- Public park

In addition, review the advertising and promotional ideas outlined in Chapter 1, and see if you can apply any of them to your particular enterprise.

Likenesses of People—Pets— Palaces—Personal Belongings

If you're an artist, you're undoubtedly aware that creating oil portraits or sketches of individuals can be a lucrative outlet for your creative talents.

Some of the more promising enterprises, such as sketching in public or creating oil portraits of business executives, are outlined in this section. But let's stretch things a bit further and see if we can't provide you with some subjects for oils and sketches that you may not have thought of. Here is a partial list. Can you come up with more?

- Business executives
- College and high school administrative officials
- Law enforcement officers
- Officers of civic and fraternal organizations
- Entertainment personalities
- Sports personalities
- Children
- Pets
- Race horses
- Stores and shops
- Houses
- Automobiles
- Racing cars
- Motorcycles
- National and local political figures, including your mayor and members of your city council

Other possibilities include:

- Creating portraits from other types of photos.
- Being commissioned by your city to paint your city hall in oil.
- Selling portraits or sketches of unique buildings to the architect or builder.

PORTRAIT SKETCHES

If you have the ability to sketch portraits quickly and accurately, you are indeed fortunate. You can set up your easel at fairs, carnivals, beaches, parks, shopping centers, department stores, flea markets—anywhere people congregate—anywhere in the world!

You can sketch adults, children, infants, and pets. You can work in pencil, charcoal, pastels, or watercolor, charging more, naturally, for the more colorful renditions.

For further information:

Drawing Portraits, Douglas Graves. Cincinnati, Watson-Guptill, 1974.

Portrait Painting in Watercolor, Charles Reid. Cincinnati, Watson-Guptill, 1973.

How to Paint Portraits in Pastel, Joe Singer. Cincinnati, Watson-Guptill, 1972.

SILHOUETTES

Silhouettes had their heyday around the turn of the last century as a precursor to modern photographic portraiture. Recently this art form has begun to enjoy an upsurge in popularity. Actually, in creating these pieces artistic ability is not as important as attention to detail.

Practice at home on the kids, your spouse—anyone who's convenient. When you feel confident enough, contact a shopping center or department store in your locality and ask them to rent you a small area where you can set up a booth. Or, instead of paying rent, perhaps you could just give them a percentage of the take. After all, aren't you doing them a favor by attracting potential customers to their store?

Each silhouette takes only a few minutes and a reasonable price is three dollars each or five dollars for a pair.

Two good instruction books on the subject are:

Beauty in Black and White: An Artist with Scissors, Nellie Quimby. Richmond, Virginia, Dietz Press, 1953.

Cut Paper, Silhouettes, and Stencils, Christian Rubi. New York, Van Nostrand, 1972.

BUSINESS EXECUTIVES IN OIL

It may take some time and careful planning, but if you merchandise your talents well you can profit greatly by specializing in "quality" oil portraits for business executives.

Your service would involve calling on these busy individuals several times weekly for sittings, with your paints, easel, and unfinished oil, working in their offices until the job is completed.

To start, you might call directly on prospects at their offices. Or, you could work through civic and fraternal organizations, perhaps giving others a commission for leads.

For further information:

Complete Guide to Portrait Painting, Furman Fenck. Cincinnati, Watson-Guptill, 1970.

Technique of Portrait Painting, Helen Van Wyk. Cincinnati, Watson-Guptill, 1970.

A BARRAGE OF BUSTS

If I were an artist capable of accurately reproducing human facial features, I would specialize in making busts for the wealthy, getting my customers through such sources as yacht and country clubs and the better art galleries and residential neighborhoods. I would work in marble, charging liberally for my time and talent.

Then again, you may prefer to work with the less expensive medium of terra-cotta, thus broadening the base of your potential customers. You might want to do busts of children or even of animals, working through schools and pet shops respectively.

For further information:

Modelled Portrait Heads, T. B. Huxley-Jones. Levittown, New York, Transatlantic Arts, 1968.

Modeled Portrait Sculpture, Louis Marrits. Cranbury, New Jersey, A. S. Barnes, 1970.

CURRENCY FROM CARICATURES

Most people get a kick out of seeing good caricatures of themselves and their friends. If you're talented in this line, set yourself up at a flea market, fair, carnival, or in a touristy section of town. Offer to work live or from photographs.

You can work either in charcoal or pastels, charging more for the latter. For extra profits, offer to enclose your sketches in folders or to frame them with colored matboard.

For further information:

Cartooning the Head and Figure, Jack Hamm. New York, Grosset & Dunlap, 1967.

A HOUSE SKETCHER

Pick out some of the better-cared-for homes in your area and sketch them on good paper. Then approach the lady of the house (they're easier to sell than the men), and offer to sell her your sketch for ten dollars. If she balks, drop down to five. As a last resort, offer to sell her your "masterpiece" for a dollar or two.

These sketches can either be framed and hung, or they can be taken to a printer's and printed onto stationery.

If you can sketch (and talk) fast, it's not impossible to bring in $75–$100 per day at this.

STATUES FROM PHOTOS

This novel enterprise involves creating ceramic statuettes of children from photographs. Practice copying, in clay, photos found in old magazines. When you can make a perfect replica, spread the word through your neighborhood, children's apparel shops, your local PTA, and advertise on school and supermarket bulletin boards.

You might also get permission to set up a stand in a department store or shopping center, working in open view of the public.

For further information:

Sculpture in Ceramic, Fred Meyer. Cincinnati, Watson-Guptill, 1971.

Ceramic Sculpture, John Kenny. Radnor, Pennsylvania, Chilton, 1953.

SKETCH-A-STORE

Most owners of small retail stores are proud of their businesses and might be willing to buy well-executed sketches of their store's exterior.

Test this idea out by sketching a few of the better-looking storefronts around town. Then present each to the owner framed in an inexpensive colored mat. Ask ten dollars for each sketch, and then drop your price if the owner balks.

If your work is good, you should be able to sell eight or ten pieces a day.

OIL PORTRAITS FROM PHOTOS

If you've got a perfect eye for detail, and a hand that will follow your eye, you can make a lot of money by creating oil portraits from photographs.

Make up some sample portraits of movie stars painted from their photographs and show them at local art shows. Or set yourself up in a booth at a department store, shopping center, or art gallery.

This enterprise is also being very successfully operated through mail order. With good promotion techniques, you could market much of your work in this manner.

For further information:

Character Studies in Oil, Joseph Dawley. Cincinnati, Watson-Guptill, 1972.

Complete Guide to Portrait Painting, Furman Finck. Cincinnati, Watson-Guptill, 1970.

SKETCH OLD HOUSES

In cities across the country, stately old houses are being torn down to make way for freeways, new housing developments, and other tokens of "progress."

You can help preserve some of these historical landmarks—and line your coffers at the same time—by making pen-and-ink sketches of these structures, matting and framing them, and selling them to art and gift shops.

After you've accumulated a number of them you might even want to publish a picture book of your town's old homes, giving historical information on each one.

A PET ARTIST

Americans pamper their pets to the tune of millions of dollars every year. Consequently, you can profit by sketching—or even painting in oils—dogs, cats, rabbits, hamsters, birds, and goldfish.

A good way to start is to sketch at dog and cat shows, selling your work on the spot. Also spread the word through breeders, grooming salons, pet shops, and veterinarians.

For further information:

Drawing All Animals, Arthur Zaidenberg. New York, Funk & Wagnalls, 1974.

Animal Drawing and Painting, W. J. Wilwerding. New York, Dover Publications, 1966.

On Paper and Canvas

BROKE? SMOKE

An almost unknown form of art involves cutting out a stencil, then holding it between a piece of paper and a candle flame. Smoke from the candle filters through the stencil to the paper and creates unique, fantastic designs.

Create an interesting array of smoke pictures, then have your local newspaper come get the scoop on this novel art technique. Be sure and have the paper mention that you will hold a one-man (or woman) show in the park next week, at which you will demonstrate your method.

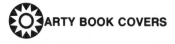 ARTY BOOK COVERS

Custom-made book covers would be a welcome item on any college or high school campus. Make your covers from some fairly stiff material such as burlap or canvas. Then you can paint, sew, or embroider them with portraits of movie or rock stars, sports personalities, politicians. You might also make up some covers adorned with abstract designs or clever sayings.

Create some samples to fit the various standard-sized textbooks, and sell them to bookstores around campus.

 POSTER PARADE

Hand-painted posters can be sold to churches, civic organizations, social clubs, colleges, and retail stores. An attractive, eye-catching poster can bring you anything from a few to a few hundred dollars, depending on the degree of detail involved.

Also, if you can come up with witty, sexy, or especially unique creations, they can be sold to poster distribution companies either for a flat fee or on a royalty basis.

To get started make up some samples and take them around to some of the above-mentioned organizations, asking for orders.

For further information:

Postercraft, Leo Rackon. New York, Sterling, 1971.

Poster Ideas and Bulletin Board Techniques, Kate Coplan, Dobbs Ferry, New York, Oceana, 1962.

 A COMIC STRIP ARTIST

Occasionally, while reading the Sunday funnies, you've probably thought that you could make up better comic strips yourself. Why not try by submitting some sample strips to newspaper editors? Their names and addresses can be found in the *Editor and Publisher Yearbook.*

Or you might submit them to comic book publishers or to a syndicate, some of which accept new comic strip material. Names of these can be found in the *Writer's Market.* Your public library should have both publications.

 HAND-PAINTED STATIONERY

With a little imagination you could come up with all sorts of interesting designs for personalized stationery: flowers, animals, colorful dots, swirls, lines—and, of course, hand-printed names and initials.

Make up some samples and take them around to stationery and department stores, gift shops, art galleries, and museums. If your work is well done you'll receive orders for more, and you'll be on your way.

CARICATURE MAPS

You could make a nice profit by creating, copying, and distributing maps of the area featuring cartoonlike sketches of local tourist attractions. These can be successfully sold through gift and souvenir shops.

In addition, local merchants could be sold ads to be placed around the borders of your maps.

DESIGN HANDBILLS

Handbills, or fliers, represent a low-cost, effective form of advertising for small businesses. Before being printed or distributed, however, the handbill must be "laid out," or designed, and this is where you come in.

Design a few sample handbills and take them around to small merchants in your town. Offer to custom-design some for them for a fee.

You might also consider providing an expanded service, including layout, printing, and distribution of the fliers. Of course, your fee will then be proportionately greater.

ANTIQUE CAR PORTRAITS

You can find pictures of old cars in encyclopedias, material published by auto manufacturers, and in the various motor magazines.

Make some large color pastel sketches or watercolor portraits of those fine old vehicles. Frame them and sell them to antique car collectors, auto supply stores, service stations, garages, art galleries, and gift shops.

For further information:

Vintage and Veteran Cars, P. G. Hendry. New York, Arco, 1974.

Great Collectors' Cars, Gianni Rogliatti. New York, Grosset & Dunlap, 1973.

MONTHLY ILLUSTRATION SERVICE

Many merchants would like to be more creative in their newspaper display ads but aren't able to draw eye-catching illustrations.

After selling them on your creative ability and getting an idea of what they need, begin to supply them with three or four new illustrations a month, charging them ten dollars monthly.

Fifty or more of these accounts will bring you a nice return every month.

For further information:

Book of Promotional and Program Artwork, Lauren Reinertsen. Plainfield, New Jersey, Galloway, 1974.

Commercial Artists Handbook, John Snyder. Cincinnati, Watson-Guptill, 1973.

HAND-PRINTED WEDDING INVITATIONS

If your penmanship is distinctive and flawless, you might turn this talent into cash by printing wedding invitations by hand.

Here's how: First make a master copy. Since the paper invitations are relatively thin, each one can be placed over the master and then copied by hand.

To get started make up some samples and take them around to bridal salons, asking them to display the invitations on their counter. Offer the proprietors a small commission for each customer they refer to you. Also, some small ads placed in the wedding section of your local newspaper should be a great help.

PERSONALIZED GREETING CARDS

Get started in this enterprise by making up some sample greeting cards covering unusual situations, such as congratulating a friend on that twenty-eight-pound bass he caught last week, or hailing that boy who just became an Eagle Scout.

Take them around to card and gift shops, offering them for sale. Be sure to include your name and phone number on the back of each card. Soon you'll be getting requests for your personalized greeting cards from all over town.

For further information:

How to Make Your Own Greeting Cards, John Carlis. Cincinnati, Watson-Guptill, 1968.

A CAREER IN CARTOONING

There are many outlets for fine cartoonists although, as in any creative field, the competition is keen.

If your forte is political cartooning, try submitting some of your work to newspaper editors. For their names and addresses, consult the *Editor and Publisher Year Book* or the *Ayer Book of Publications* at your library.

You might try submitting your gag cartoons to periodicals such as *True* or *Playboy.* Find out who's interested in receiving cartoons by checking *Artist's Market.*

For further information:

Cartoonist's and Gag Writer's Handbook, Jack Markow. Cincinnati, *Writer's Digest,* 1967.

How to Draw and Sell Cartoons, Dave Breger. New York, Putnam's, 1966.

CUSTOM-DESIGNED WALLPAPER

Another way of putting your creative talents to use is to produce custom-designed wallpaper.

The paper can either be hand-painted or created by the silk-screen method.

To get started advertise in new housing tracts, as well as in the older, more affluent sections of town. If you're good, you can work through interior designers, wallpaper firms, or building contractors.

For further information:

Wallpaper and Fabric Designs, Fiona Clark, New York, St. Martin's, 1973.

PAINT PAINT-BY-NUMBER SETS

We've always believed that people would buy just about anything, but this belief was recently reinforced when we discovered that it's possible to make a living by buying paint-by-number sets, then painting and selling them.

Obviously, no artistic talent is needed. They are best sold through restaurants, taverns, gift shops, and other retail stores. Ask permission to display your work on the walls of these businesses. Attach your name and address to the corner of each picture and every time you sell one give the store owner a small commission.

DESIGN PLAYING CARDS

Get names of playing card manufacturers from the *Thomas Register of American Manufacturers* at your library. Write them asking if they'd be interested in seeing your designs. If you get the go-ahead, mail off your work.

Be sure not to send the same design to more than one manufacturer at the same time. Designs must measure, or be in direct proportion to, 2½ by 3½ inches.

SPRAY GUN ART

Many unique abstract art designs can be made by using spray guns filled with various colors of paint. By varying the spray and the distance from the gun to the canvas a multitude of different effects can be achieved.

Start by buying a half-dozen or so inexpensive spray guns, some paint, and some cheap canvasboard. Practice until you can come up with some professional work, then peddle your masterpieces to, or through, the outlets listed at the beginning of this chapter.

HUMOROUS PLACE MATS

This idea involves supplying, at no charge, paper place mats on which gag cartoons have been printed, to cafés and restaurants. Either you'll think up the gags yourself, or you'll consult a cartoon joke book for ideas. If necessary, work with an artist who will draw the cartoons.

You'll be responsible for having the mats printed up as well as for distributing them to the restaurants. Where's the profit here? From local merchants who agree to take small ads appearing around the edges of the mats.

For further information:

The Art of Cartooning, Syd Hoff. New York, Stravon, 1973.

Cartoonist's and Gag Writer's Handbook, Jack Markow. Cincinnati, *Writer's Digest,* 1967.

SHOWCARD ARTISTRY

Department stores and other large retail outlets are in constant need of fancily lettered and illustrated showcards for window displays.

Make up some samples of your better work and take them around to these establishments, offering to design their showcards on a piecework basis. If you continue to do good work, you may even be commissioned for other work, such as illustrating newspaper ads and painting designs on delivery trucks.

For further information:

Lettering and Lettering Display, William Mann. New York, Van Nostrand, 1974.

Lettering for Advertising, Mortimer Leach. New York, Van Nostrand, 1956.

A TV CARTOONIST

If you're a truly imaginative cartoonist, or can develop this talent, the possibility exists for you to have your own TV show. Offhand, we can think of a half-dozen themes; there are probably dozens more.

Cartoon the weather, tell the news in cartoons, make caricatures of kids on camera, have a gag cartoon show, tell children's stories while drawing cartoons, tell adult stories while illustrating them with cartoons.

Take some samples and your ideas to program directors of local TV stations. You just might get that big break.

For further information:

Complete Course in Professional Cartooning, Stan Fraydas. Huntington, New York, Krieger, 1972.

The Art of Cartooning, Syd Hoff. New York, Stravon, 1973.

Other Art Forms . . .

TAPING YOUR ACT

Here's a nifty idea for cashing in on those hot, sultry days at the beach. Arrive at the beach early Saturday morning with rolls of easily removable masking tape in assorted widths and a big sign: *Natural Body Tattoos—Only $2!* Peddle your unique service from group to group. Use your tape to create any design—or perhaps a sweetheart's name—your customer wants on his skin.

After a weekend under the sun, he'll peel off the tape for a unique masterpiece in suntan skinpainting. Be prepared to attract crowds of curious spectators as you work on your customers.

DECORATIVE T-SHIRTS

Using the T-shirt for a canvas is not a new idea, but with a little imagination it can be mighty profitable for you.

You can harness your creative talents by custom-painting T-shirts in many different ways. A few of the endless number of possibilities are portraits of movie or rock stars, politicians, historical figures, or of the wearer or his/her boyfriend or girl friend. Colorful abstract designs and witty sayings will likewise sell.

For further information:

The Craft of Fabric Painting, Kathleen Monk. New York, Ballantine, 1972.

Textile Printing and Painting Made Easy, Ursula Kuehnemann. New York, Taplinger, 1967.

PISCATORIAL PAINTINGS

Another way to put your artistic talents to work is by painting colorful backgrounds on the outsides of goldfish bowls and aquariums. By creating representations of underwater caves and rocks, flora and fauna, you can not only make things more scenic for the unfortunate aquarium-confined fish, but you can turn a few fins at the same time.

For the round goldfish bowls, use opaque paint to decorate all around the outsides. For the rectangular bowls and the aquarium tanks, it would be best to merely paint the rear side as a background.

Start by buying a few plain glass goldfish bowls. Then decorate them attractively and take them around to variety stores and aquarium supply shops, asking for orders. With the first flush of success, begin buying your basic stock wholesale in large lots.

TIE ADS

Believe it or not, some people actually *like* to wear ties! Furthermore, many would wear ties advertising their product, if someone would provide them.

For prospective customers contact food chains, store merchants, insurance companies, travel agencies—just about anyone who offers a product or service. Offer to hand-paint ties for them, even in large quantities, with their company name or a picture of their product on them.

For further information:

The Craft of Fabric Painting, Kathleen Monk. New York, Ballantine, 1972.

Textile Printing and Painting Made Easy, Ursula Kuehnemann. New York, Taplinger, 1967.

TIE UP YOUR PROFITS

If you prefer not to adorn your ties with commercial advertising, here's another nifty necktie idea.

Endow your ties with abstract designs, portraits of body organs, likenesses of politicians, entertainers, sports figures, and historical figures such as Beethoven, Shakespeare, and Socrates—the possibilities are infinite. With an aggressive advertising campaign, you should be able to sell thousands of the things.

For further information:

The Craft of Fabric Painting, Kathleen Monk. New York, Ballantine, 1972.

Textile Printing and Painting Made Easy, Ursula Kuehnemann. New York, Taplinger, 1967.

BE A MURALIST

It may not be in the history books, but it's not inconceivable that Michaelangelo got his start by painting murals in Roman taverns and restaurants.

You may never get the chance to paint the Sistine Chapel, but you can certainly put your artistic talent to work by "muralizing" business offices, banks, hotels, children's nurseries, stores—even taverns and restaurants. Create each mural to match the surroundings.

To get started paint some unique designs on small canvases and take them around to prospective customers, offering to paint small or large murals on their walls.

For further information:

Technique of Fresco Painting, Gardner Hale. New York, Dover, 1966.

Art of Fresco Painting, Mary Merrifield. Levittown, New York, Transatlantic Arts.

Fresco Painting; Modern Methods and Techniques for Painting in Fresco and Secco, O. E. Nordmark. New York, American Artists Group, 1947.

INTERIOR BOTTLE PAINTER

Actually, the artist can perform this work indoors or out. The above title derives from the fact that the artist paints scenes on the interior of the bottles.

These very unique works might feature flowers, birds, seascapes, or pastoral scenes. They can be sold to gift and tourist shops, and to better department stores.

The secret of interior painting? Before painting, the bottle is cut in half lengthwise, along its original seam, with a glass cutter. The painting is done, then the two halves of the bottle are skillfully rejoined. Voila!

FIGURE YOUR PROFITS!

This enterprise involves wood carving, by hand, and selling to local merchants, anything from ants to anteaters, from baubles to bicycles. You might suggest that the local tobacconist order a wooden Indian for his storefront. A saddler might like the idea of a wooden horse in his window.

Make up some small samples of your work

to show various merchants around town—and don't forget your order book!

For further information:

> *Wood Carving for Fun and Profit,* Al Ball. Jericho, New York, Exposition, 1971.
>
> *Creative Light Wood Carving,* John Matthews. New York, St. Martin's, 1971.

FREE-LANCE WINDOW DRESSER

Ladies' and men's apparel shops, gift shops, jewelry stores, variety stores, shoe stores, toy stores, hardware stores—they all could sell more merchandise with clever, eye-catching window displays.

Get started in the business of hiring out your window-dressing talents by donating your services to a few such stores badly in need of a good window display. These stores will then serve as showcases for your talents and, if you're good, merchants will soon be beating a path to your door (or to your window).

For further information:

> *First Official Window Decorating Guide,* Marie Graber. New York, Essandess Specials (orders to Simon & Schuster), 1968.
>
> *Modern Display Techniques,* Emily Mauger. New York, Fairchild, 1964.

A COUNTERFEIT SCULPTOR

If you're good at imitating famous original works of art—*The Thinker, Venus de Milo,* or the *Pietà*—you may just find a market in small art galleries, museums, and gift shops.

Find pictures or reproductions of these famous sculptures at museums and art galleries, and practice until you can make a perfect reproduction. Then take some samples around to these places offering your reproductions for sale.

CUSTOM-PAINTED TABLE LINENS

The well-to-do can always be sold unnecessary items like hand-painted tablecloths, place mats, and linen napkins. A pastoral scene, a seascape, or the client's house are a few of many possible subjects. Special fabric paint must be used, which can be obtained at any art supply store.

To get started make up some samples, using various pastel shades as backgrounds. Then take orders from fine gift shops and department stores, and by calling on people at their homes.

For further information:

> *The Craft of Fabric Painting,* Kathleen Monk. New York, Ballantine, 1972.
>
> *Textile Printing and Painting Made Easy,* Ursula Kuehnemann. New York, Taplinger, 1967.

A CLOTHES PAINTER

Blouses, skirts, jackets, scarves, aprons, trousers—these are also possible items that can be colorfully decorated with special fabric paint.

If you have a flair with color and line, make up some samples and contact local department stores offering your services as a fabric painter. Propose to set up a small booth in the store. The store will then offer to its customers a free paint job on each blouse, shirt, or other item sold, and will pay you a dollar or two for each item you paint.

STORE WINDOW PAINTER

Try persuading merchants to commission you to paint, on their front windows, cartoon figures, pictures of the merchant's product, nature scenes—anything that would help the merchant sell his product. A saddlery might want a Western-style storefront portrayed, while a toy shop might like an animal scene.

Start by pounding the pavement—simply making the rounds of local merchants—and selling your service.

CHINA PAINTING

Sorry, but this enterprise doesn't mean an art trip to the Orient. Rather, it's a form of art which involves the painting, by means of a ceramic glaze, on china dinnerware. Possible subjects are pastoral scenes, seascapes, and the house of the owner.

As an artist, your fee would cover materials and labor, including the necessary firing of the material after painting, and the dinnerware itself, if the customer doesn't provide his own.

For materials and instruction, contact your local art supply store.

For further information:

Techniques of China Painting, Gunhild Jorgensen. New York, Van Nostrand, 1974.

China Painting, Step by Step, Doris Taylor and Anne Hart. New York, Van Nostrand, 1962.

SIGN PAINTER

No great investment is required to get started as a sign painter and, at least initially, you can work right out of your home. A few brushes, paints, and a ladder or two are all you need.

A good way to get work is to walk through the business district, keeping your eye peeled for needed signs and for signs that have deteriorated and ought to be repainted. Once found, simply approach the owners and ask for the job.

For further information:

Sign Painting Techniques: Beginner to Professional, Ralph Gregory. Cincinnati, Signs of the Times, 1973.

Practical Sign Shop Operations, Bob Fitzgerald. Cincinnati, Signs of the Times, 1965.

Shops and Services

ART LENDING LIBRARY

Contact some local artists through an art gallery or exhibition and tell them that you are starting an art lending library. If they will loan you some of their unsold work, you will split 50-50 with them on the proceeds of your library.

You can set up the library in a spare room of your home and charge your customers five dollars per month and up (depending on the quality of the art) for each piece borrowed. It need not be a painting. Collages, pottery, sculpture, mobiles, and bronze work can all be used as rentals.

To get started put an ad in the art or women's section of your local newspaper. Perhaps the local art museum will allow you to leave some leaflets in their shop or put up a notice on their bulletin board. Also offer your rentals to offices, banks, restaurants, and other business firms.

POSTER PALACE

As a poster palace proprietor you'll rent a store in a low-rent area, preferably around a college or university, and stock it with a large inventory of posters which you can buy wholesale from poster distributors. These are found in the Yellow Pages of any large city's phone directory.

Of course, you'll want to decorate your "palace" attractively inside and out, in order to appeal to the largest number of potential customers.

INTERIOR DESIGNER

Good interior designers are knowledgeable about furniture, fabrics, and finishes. They are able to plan color schemes, draw floor plans, and make sketches of proposed designs.

If you feel you're qualified, start by spreading the word through friends, relatives, and neighbors. Contact local builders, architects, and real estate brokers. Work through social and civic organizations. Initially, you might donate your services to a few small shops or offices, letting word spread through these satisfied clients.

For further information:

Your Future in Interior Design, Michael Greer. New York, Arco, 1970.

Your Career in Interior Design, Robert Doyle. New York, Julian Messner, 1969.

ART CONSULTANT

You can become an art consultant by simply making arrangements with a few of the better art galleries in town. Tell them you'd like to work as their agent, selling and renting art to offices, banks, hotels, motels, fine shops, and other such establishments. Better yet, eliminate one middleman by dealing directly with the artists themselves.

Commissions vary but you, as salesman, should get about 40 percent of the selling price for your efforts.

RUN A PRINT GALLERY

Here you'll open up a small shop in, preferably, a hip or mod area of town. The residents of these areas generally don't have a lot of cash, but they'll usually appreciate a good art print enough to spend ten or fifteen dollars for it.

An investment of less than five hundred dollars should be sufficient to allow you to open your gallery—a few hundred dollars for rent and an initial inventory of prints, plus a hundred dollars or so for paint and fixtures. Of course, you'll want to paint and decorate your gallery attractively, both inside and out.

MOBILE ART GALLERY

Find some "starving artists" in your area who would be willing to consign some of their better paintings. Then simply load up a station wagon or small truck with these goods and drive to a busy location such as a gas station or shopping center.

After getting the owner's permission, display your paintings all around your vehicle, perhaps even putting up a few streamers or balloons to attract attention. You may have to pay the lot owner a small fee or commission, but since you'll be in a high-traffic location, your sales should more than make up for this.

COMMUNITY ART EXCHANGE

Many people tire of looking at the same paintings or fine reproductions on their walls year after year and would gladly play you a small fee for the privilege of using your art exchange to trade these pieces for other, equally fine works of art.

To get started it will be necessary either to buy an initial inventory of paintings or reproductions, which could be quite costly, or to get friends and neighbors to "donate" their art until such time as you get something from another customer that they would like to have.

CUSTOM FRAME SHOP

As the owner of a custom frame shop, you'll get anywhere from a few dollars for a small job to a few hundred dollars for a large, ornate, six-inch gold leaf frame.

To start you'll need at least 100 sample moldings, which you can obtain from a molding manufacturer. Find the names of these in a copy of the *Thomas Register of American Manufacturers* at your local library.

Initially, you can obtain customers through local art galleries and by putting up notices at museums. Yellow Pages advertising should likewise be an effective medium for you.

For further information:

Professional Picture Framing for the Amateur, Barbara Wolf. Blue Ridge Summit, Pennsylvania, TAB, 1974.

Making Picture Frames, Manly Banister. New York, Sterling, 1973.

PROMOTE ART SHOWS

Although they are primarily thought of as cultural events, art shows are a mighty big business, too. The individual artists invariably do well and the promoters even better.

To start, arrange to rent space in pleasant outdoor surroundings on weekends, or arrange for warehouse space if the weather is inclement. Then contact local artists offering them space in your exhibit for a flat rental fee or for a percentage of their sales.

Your job, of course, will be to promote the event as a free cultural exhibition through the media, as aggressively as possible. In order to be sure of continually attracting new customers you'd be wise to hold your show in a different nearby town every week.

PACKAGE DESIGNER

There's an old saying in the merchandising game: "Sell the sizzle, not the steak." Unfortunately, many firms pay no heed to this old adage. They package their products in lackluster and unimaginative containers, and their slumping sales are a sad monument to their cobwebbed thinking. Here's what to do about it.

From the shelves of any retail store select several items whose packages, in your estimation, are poorly designed. Buy these products and take them home. Then put your artistic talents to work and see if you can't come up with a more attractively designed—a more alluring—product.

Next, send each product to its respective manufacturer *in its new package.* Include a cover letter explaining what you've done and

outlining any special qualifications you might have. Offer to design packages for their products on a regular basis.

For further information:

The Silent Salesman: How to Develop Packaging That Sells, James Pilditch. Boston, Cahners, 1973.

Color Sells Your Package, Jean-Paul Favre. New York, Hastings House, 1970.

ART ACADEMY

If you have a large, well-lighted loft, hall, or basement and would enjoy teaching others the fine points of art, your own art academy may be just what the doctor ordered.

In addition to oil painting, you'll offer classes in drawing, watercolor, clay and metal sculpture, and related arts. Not only will you charge each student for attending classes, but you'll profit from the sale of materials as well.

Initially, you might teach at the local Y or evening adult school in order to round up students. Also leave notices at art supply stores and galleries, and at art shows and exhibitions.

For further information:

Learning to Teach Art, Robert Paston. Lincoln, Nebraska, Professional Educators, 1973.

Teaching Art Basics, Roy Sparkes. Cincinnati, Watson-Guptill, 1973.

SET DESIGNER

In any large city there are usually a number of theater groups, TV studios, and TV commercial producers, and in Hollywood there are scads of motion picture studios. They all employ set designers.

If you've got confidence in your creative inventiveness, make up a small photo portfolio of your better work. Take it around to these concerns, offering your services as a set designer.

For further information:

Theatrical Set Design: The Basic Techniques,
David Welker. Boston, Allyn & Bacon,
1969.

**HOME ART GALLERY**

In any community there are many fine
artists who could sell much of their work if
they only had the opportunity to display it in
conducive surroundings.

If you have a large room in your home,
open it up as a gallery in which local artists
can display their work. For providing these
facilities you would charge each artist 25 percent of the selling price of each piece sold.
Naturally, you'll want to publicize your gallery extensively throughout your community.

After your enterprise gets off the ground
you can move to a more commercial location,
eventually taking on the work of foreign artists in addition to local ones.

7

A Career in Crafts

Even more than the art field, the world of crafts allows you to let your imagination soar, bound only by the limitations you yourself impose. For here not only is your subject matter unlimited, but materials can be drawn from any segment of the animal, vegetable, or mineral worlds.

This opens up an infinite source of supply of free materials. Products can be made from driftwood or seashells gathered from the seashore, pine cones from the mountains, leaves from the trees—even weeds from the fields!

Of course, the decision as to what items to produce is entirely up to you. However, if your interest in the craft field is mainly monetary, you'll probably be better off creating functional items rather than decorative ones. A gourd totem pole in the front yard makes an excellent conversation piece—but what can a person *do* with it? One exception here is jewelry, which can be said to serve a functional purpose in that it enhances the appearance of the wearer.

As in the art field, materials and much free advice can be obtained from retail outlets such as arts and crafts suppliers and hobby shops. Public libraries represent another excellent source of information. In addition, classes are frequently held at crafts centers, and in evening adult classes.

In exploiting your creations use every promotional method you can think of, plus those outlined in Chapter 1. Since the line between arts and crafts is many times indistinguishable, your products can be marketed through most of the outlets listed in the previous chapter on art, giving special consideration to arts and crafts shows and exhibitions as marketing outlets.

Although the competition is keen, tourist centers both here and abroad offer excellent opportunities for the craftsman to display and sell his work. San Francisco and Berkeley, California; Taos, New Mexico; Provincetown, Massachusetts; and Sugar Loaf, New York are just a few of many such places.

Many large cities have crafts cooperatives or guilds which will not only put you in touch with others possessing the same interests, but will serve as valuable marketing outlets.

In attempting to sell your crafts to retail stores or to buyers for department stores bring your best samples along. If your product is too large, bring along a model or a good-quality color photograph of it. And remember, when selling your products outright to retail outlets collect cash on delivery. If you're selling them your articles on consignment, get a signed receipt upon delivery.

The following list of books will help you get started:

Artist's Market, Cincinnati, *Writer's Digest.* Contains a listing of commercial markets for the craftsman.

Craft Shops/Galleries USA, American Crafts Council, 44 West 53rd Street, New York 10019. Directory of craft stores.

The Craftsman's Survival Manual: Making a Full or Part-Time Living from Your Crafts, George Wettlaufer and Nancy Wettlaufer, Englewood Cliffs, New Jersey, Prentice-Hall, Inc., 1974.

Selling Your Handicrafts, William Garrison. Radnor, Pennsylvania, Chilton, 1974.

How to Make Money with Your Crafts, Leta Clark. New York, Morrow, 1974.

Handcrafts Marketing. New York, Unipub, 1972.

Craft Horizons, 44 West 53rd Street, New York 10019 (bimonthly).

Creative Crafts, P.O. Box 700, Newton, New Jersey 17860 (published nine times a year).

Functional Items

☀OUT OF YOUR GOURD!

Did you know that in many primitive societies utensils such as drinking cups, dippers, and bowls are fashioned from dried gourds?

You can introduce this unique practice into our culture by growing and drying your own gourds, then fashioning and selling attractively painted gourd-shaped utensils to gift, variety, and department stores.

Better check first, however, on any regulations involving the manufacture and sale of utensils made of this plant. If regulations prohibit you from doing this, there's nothing to stop you from selling these products as decorative pieces for the home.

A WINDFALL FROM WEATHER VANES

Weather vanes have always had wide appeal and are the type of product that invariably sell well if exposed to potential buyers in gift shops or as a mail-order item in gift sections of national magazines.

Weather vanes can be made of just about any material—wood, plastic, metal—and are topped off with some unique figure such as a replica of a bird, hunting dog, or tiger. The main requirement, however, is that they be built sturdily enough to hold together and to remain firmly anchored to the roof even in severe windstorms.

For further information:

Weather Vanes: The History, Manufacture, and Design of an American Folk Art, Charles Klamkin. New York, Hawthorn, 1973.

A VERY BRIGHT IDEA

Lamps can be made from wine jugs, seashells, rocks, transparent plastic, etched metal—even silver and gold! Why not put your imagination to work and "electrify" local consumers?

You can either sell your creations directly from your home or they can be sold to department, gift, variety, and lighting stores.

PRODUCT EMBELLISHMENT

There's hardly any product around the house that couldn't be cleverly and aesthetically improved upon and sold for a profit.

Some examples are colorfully quilted facial tissue containers, a toilet tissue or paper towel dispenser featuring small wooden or plastic figures on each side, children's hangers resembling animals, and bookends featuring risqué adult figurines. Using your creative ability you should be able to come up with many, many more.

Make up some samples and take them around to gift and variety stores.

DOLLARS FROM DESKS

In secondhand stores and warehouses across the country there are thousands of old-fashioned children's school desks—the kind with seat and inkwell attached. Scout these out by making a "buying tour" or by placing ads in magazine classifieds.

These relics can then be refinished, painted in bright colors, decorated attractively, and sold through furniture and department stores and children's shops.

HORN SHAKERS

You won't find this item listed in the dictionary, for we've just given it the most descriptive name we can come up with.

These are salt and pepper shakers made from cow horns. The horns are purchased from packing houses, then hollowed out and drilled with tiny holes in the top, cleaned, sanded, and coated.

Sell your stylish shakers to gift shops, restaurants, department and variety stores, and supermarkets.

THE GAVEL GAME

Although one may exist, we have never heard of a company dealing exclusively in the manufacture of gavels.

If you're handy in woodworking you might consider starting to manufacture and distribute these handsome, stately-looking items.

To begin, take some samples around to local civic, fraternal, and business organizations, as well as to gift shops. In addition, you may want to advertise in national business publications or make up attractive brochures and send them, along with order blanks, to boards of directors of large corporations and to governmental bodies.

GOURD LAMPS

Here's another way of turning dried gourds into "green paper." If you've ever seen a lamp with a base of dried gourd you know how quaint, how almost surrealistic it looks.

Buy a number of dried gourds, or grow and dry them yourself. Then create some of these products, painting and glazing the gourds. Sell them through gift shops and variety and department stores. You might even set up a booth at a flea market, selling them direct to the customer.

MAKE WICKER BASKETS

Any well-crafted, decorative item will find a ready market, especially if it can be made to serve some functional purpose.

Such an item is the wicker basket. These can be painted different colors, lacquered, laced with ribbons, or decorated in a number of other unique ways. Make them in the form of clothes hampers, gift baskets, wastebaskets—even small Easter egg baskets for the children.

Sell your beautiful basketry to gift shops and variety and department stores, as well as through mail order.

For further information:

The Techniques of Basketry, Virginia Harvey. New York, Van Nostrand, 1974.

Basket Weaving. New York, McGraw-Hill.

Weaving with Cane and Reed, Grete Kroncke. New York, Van Nostrand, 1967.

ROCKING CHAIRS

In this day of split-level homes and modular furniture, rocking chairs continue to maintain their popularity.

If you've at all dabbled in furniture making you might try turning out some of the fancier versions of rocking chairs, selling them to better furniture and department stores.

QUALITY CHOPPING BLOCKS

Good chopping blocks—the kind that won't chip and splinter—command handsome prices.

Anyone can easily mass-produce these by stacking hardwoods one on top of the other, gluing them together with a nontoxic cement, then cutting, lengthwise, down through the stock with an electric saw. After sanding and finishing, the blocks can be sold to gift shops and to variety, hardware, and department stores.

CUSTOM WASTEBASKETS

If you stop and think about it, wastebaskets can be made in just about any shape or consist of just about any material, color, or decoration you can think of—as long as they have a hole in them!

They can be round, square, rectangular, triangular, octagonal, or hexagonal. Materials can include wood, leather, plastic, metal, ceramic, glass, or paper.

Put your creative talents to work, wastebasketwise, and see if you can't come up with a salable product.

OUTDOOR FURNITURE

Picnic tables and benches, coffee tables, card tables, sun chairs, chaise longues—these and other accoutrements of the outdoor life, if they are well made, are constantly in demand.

You can make and sell your products from your home if local regulations permit. Simply display your handiwork on your front lawn, or on a lot on a busy thoroughfare. Once your business gets off the ground you'll want to open a store in a suburban shopping center.

 **GOURD PLANTERS**

Planters represent still another avenue to profits in the wide world of gourds.

Hollow out some dried gourds, which you can buy or grow and dry yourself. After painting and glazing them attractively, plant ivy, fuchsia, or wandering Jew inside. The flat-bottomed specimens can serve as table planters, while the round-bottomed varieties can be suspended by ribbons, leather strips, or wire.

Sell your masterpieces to gift and variety stores, nurseries, and garden centers.

BUCKS FROM BULLETIN BOARDS

Bulletin boards are a popular item for home use, as well as for businesses, schools, and churches. They're easy to make, consisting of a large sheet of corkboard, tackboard, or flannel board with a frame around it. For your wealthy customers there is self-sealing plastic bulletin board facing.

Both the board and the frame can be colorfully painted so that a customer can select the color that best matches his/her decor.

Make up some small boards as samples and sell your product to children's stores, department and variety stores, and hardware stores.

WELCOME CASH FROM WELCOME MATS

Too many welcome mats nowadays are falling down on their primary responsibility of welcoming visitors to the household. Tat-tered, lackluster, and expressionless welcome mats across the country seem to be littering, rather than beautifying, their owners' doorsteps. By reversing this trend, not only can you help beautify America, but you can make some handsome profits as well.

Mats can be made from rubber, plastic, nylon, felt, straw, or any other soft or semihard material. Experiment with different shapes and colors. Imbue your mats with distinctive personalities. Then, take some attractive samples door-to-door. It'll be a simple matter to see who needs your product—and to sell it.

Personal Items

RAISE CANE!

If you have access to a wooded area you already have the raw materials you'll need for making walking canes. Cut only hardwoods that closely resemble the cane shape in its natural state. Then it's simply a matter of sawing a little here or shaving off a little there, sanding, varnishing, and presto! You have a cane that's worth eight to ten dollars.

Sell your finished products to hospital gift shops, sickroom supply companies, and department and variety stores.

A PLETHORA OF PIPES

Throughout history pipes have been fashioned from every conceivable material. Stone, wood, porcelain, meerschaum, corncobs, and bone represent just a few.

Try your hand in this field by making up some high-quality samples, taking them around to tobacconists, fine men's shops, gift shops, and department stores. Mail order might likewise represent a good market for some of your more unique creations.

 **THE BEAD GAME**

Beads can be made in all styles, fashioned from all materials, and sold through all types of outlets. There are Indian beads, hippie beads, mother-of-pearl beads, seashell beads, plastic beads, diamond beads, shark's-tooth beads—ad infinitum.

Whichever segment of the bead game turns you on, why not get a large, assorted batch and some nylon string from a wholesale supplier and see what unique creations you can come up with and successfully market?

TIE-DYEING

Tie-dyeing involves tying various lengths of fabric or finished garments into knots, then dipping the material into one or more colored dyes. When the material is untied and allowed to dry, colorful patterns are permanently dyed into the fabric.

There are many fine books on the subject. Study these, practicing at home, then market your creations through boutiques and department stores.

For further information:

Tie-Dye, Sara Nea. New York, Van Nostrand, 1972.

Tie-And-Dye as a Present Day Craft, Anne Maile. New York, Taplinger, 1963.

YOUR NAME IN LEATHER

Here's a unique impulse item that can be manufactured on the spot and peddled from a sidewalk booth or in a weekend flea market: Personalized leather snap-on bracelets. Precut the bracelets in various lengths and widths. Then press the names in on the spot, stain, and sell for a dollar or two apiece.

In addition to a supply of metal snaps and leather, you'll need a few simple woodworking tools and some dye. Make up some attractive samples and display them prominently.

For further information:

Leather Tooling, Charles Leland. New York, Sterling, 1975.

Leather Tooling and Carving, Chris Groneman. New York, Dover, 1974.

BE A LAPIDARY

As a lapidary you'll be concerned with cutting and polishing semiprecious stones. From them you'll create items such as rings, pendants, cuff links, tie clips, and earrings.

The craft of the lapidary is not difficult to learn, but as with others, practice makes perfect. Study books and attend classes. When you can start turning out marketable items, sell them at gem and mineral shows, craft exhibitions, jewelry stores, and through other retail outlets.

For further information:

Rock and Gem Polishing: A Complete Guide to Amateur Lapidary, Edward Fletcher. New York, International Publications, 1974.

Gems and Minerals, P. O. Box 687, Mentone, California 92359 (monthly).

Lapidary Journal, P. O. Box 80737, San Diego, California 92138 (monthly).

CUSTOM-MADE SANDALS

Tourists traditionally have money to burn on unique items and twenty-five to thirty-five dollars spent for a pair of custom-made sandals while on vacation is not unusual. The material will cost you less than five dollars.

Set up a stand or small shop in the most heavily traveled tourist section of town and display samples of various styles and colors for customers to choose from. With experience you can knock them out fast and either deliver the finished product the same day or agree to send them to the customer by mail.

If you don't know anything about leatherwork, enroll in a night course or offer to work free at a shoe repair shop in order to learn the fundamentals.

For further information:

Jonathan Ervin's Leather Notebook: Making Sandals, Belts, and Bags, Jonathan Ervin. Philadelphia, Running Press, 1973.

 **COSTUME JEWELRY**

This field is one that's truly as limited or as unlimited as your own imagination. Since time began, man has fashioned jewelry from every conceivable type of material. Rocks, seashells, tree bark, fruit pits, glass, plastic, metal, ceramic, rubber, teeth, hair—you name it and it's been used. The trick, however, lies not in thinking up a material that hasn't been used, but in applying fresh ideas to any usable material.

Get your findings from wholesale jewelry suppliers and sell your finished products to department, variety, drug, and jewelry stores; gift and specialty shops; and through various crafts guilds and organizations.

For further information:

Jewelry Making for Fun and Profit, Helen Clegg and Mary Larom. New York, McKay, 1951.

Inventive Jewelry-Making. Ramona Solberg. New York, Van Nostrand, 1972.

 **MONEY FROM MACRAME**

Macrame is the art of making garments or decorative articles by knotting threads or cords in a geometrical pattern. As the craftsman's material may include anything from a fine thread to a thick rope, a multitude of products and effects can be produced: Purses, belts, sandals, flowerpot holders, and wall hangings are just a few of the many possibilities.

Sell macrame products from your home, from a shop, or by mail order. You can also profit by holding classes or writing a book on the subject.

For further information:

Macrame Made Easy, Eunice Close. New York, Macmillan, 1973.

Macrame: Advanced Technique and Design, Norman Rack and Lilian Rack. Gloucester, Massachusetts, Peter Smith, 1972.

CELEBRITY DOLLS

Every child has her favorite TV personality, movie actor, or sports figure. With this in mind, make up doll models of such heroes and heroines as Cher, Robert Redford, and Joe Namath. Naturally, you'll want to match the clothes to the personality.

Market your dolls through toy and children's apparel shops and variety and department stores. If your products are truly unique, they should also sell quite well through mail order.

BATIK BOUTIQUE

Batik is a centuries-old Indonesian method of decorating fabrics. It's done by applying a design of melted wax to the surface of the cloth. The material is then dipped in cool vegetable dye, leaving a design on the portions protected by the wax.

You can profit from this ancient art by opening a "batik only" shop in which you specialize in batik wearing apparel. You could also teach classes or write a book on the subject.

For information:

Creating in Batik, Eleen Bystrom. New York, Van Nostrand, 1973.

Batik: Material, Techniques, Design, Sara Nea. New York, Van Nostrand, 1972.

Decorative Items

 **STAINED GLASS**

We've all seen stained glass in churches, but lately there has been a trend toward this type of decorative artwork in commercial establishments. Banks, restaurants, hotels, department stores, and office buildings are all excellent prospects for the stained-glass craftsman.

You can learn this craft through adult

evening classes. Then, make up some attractive sample panels and take them around to likely prospects in your area, asking for jobs.

An even better bet is to work with architects and builders, getting contracts for your work while the buildings are still in the planning stage.

For further information:

> *Making Stained Glass: A Handbook for the Amateur and Professional,* Robert Metcalf and Gertrude Metcalf. New York, McGraw-Hill, 1973.

> *Working with Stained Glass: Fundamental Techniques and Applications,* Jean-Jacques Duval. New York, Thomas Y. Crowell, 1972.

GOURD TOTEM POLES?

Why not? After buying some dried gourds, or growing and drying your own, make up a couple of outrageously tall specimens by gluing gourd on top of gourd and painting faces on the front of each. Stand these in your front yard by running a stake through the bottom two or three gourds and into the ground.

Then take some color photos of these and blow up the prints to 8 by 10. Leave the prints, with some order blanks, in gift and novelty shops, variety and department stores. Pay the proprietors a 20 percent commission on each order.

HORSESHOE HANDINESS

Horses aren't the only critters that can benefit from horseshoes. By buying or making a blacksmith's forge, you can turn old horseshoes, or even homemade new ones, into such items as decorative lawn displays, bookends, door knockers, lamp bases, water faucet handles, and decorations for the top of bars and coffee tables. You might also sell a horseshoe pitching game set combination, in which you'd not only supply the horseshoes, but install backyard horseshoe pitching pits as well.

Get your business through feed shops, riding stables, western apparel stores, variety and department stores, and mail order.

For further information:

> *Art of Blacksmithing,* Alex Bealer. Totowa, New Jersey, Funk and Wagnalls (orders to Thomas Y. Crowell Company), 1969.

> *Forging Materials and Practices,* A. M. Sabroff et al. New York, Van Nostrand Reinhold, 1968.

CASH FROM CANDLEMAKING

Many creative candlemakers have waxed ecstatic over the profits they've made from this enterprise!

Candles can be made in any conceivable shape. They can be scented, colored, stood on a table, hung on a wall, or suspended from a ceiling. What better medium for the creative craftsman?

Practice creating your wax wonders at home. When you feel you have some salable products, take them around to gift shops, department and variety stores, craft shops and shows. As a profitable sideline, sell candlemaking supplies.

For further information:

> *Creative Candlemaking: From the Simple Basic Candle to the Most Intricate Sculptural Form,* Thelma Newman. New York, Crown, 1972.

> *Candlemaking for Profit,* Eugenia Bourn. Cranbury, New Jersey, A. S. Barnes, 1973.

A WORLD OF DECOUPAGE

Using decoupage, ordinary items such as trays, wastebaskets, table tops, doors, and wooden walls can be turned into eye-catching—and salable—works of art.

To get started, simply cut out from old magazines, colorful designs, pictures of animals, flowers, toys, human faces, and reproductions of works of art. Paste these on the object you're working on, then simply apply varnish or lacquer over the surface.

For further information:

The Beginner's Book of Decoupage, Rebecca Hyman. New York, Bantam, 1974.

The Craft of Decoupage, Patricia Nimocks. New York, Scribner's, 1972.

CARVE WOODEN INDIANS

The once-familiar wooden Indian native to the fronts of cigar stores has all but vanished. (Come to think of it, cigar stores have also vanished!)

You can help bring back this friendly fellow—and make money doing it—by carving these life-sized figures out of logs, then painting and selling them to tobacconists, antique shops, hardware stores—even art galleries and museums.

For further information:

Artists in Wood: American Carvers of Cigar Store Indians, Show Figures, and Circus Wagons, Frederick Fried. New York, Clarkson N. Potter, 1970.

POTTED PLASTIC

If you despise plastic flowers as much as we do, better pass this idea up for something more "real." However, the plastic flower industry is growing by leaps and bounds, and it's possible for you to share in the wealth.

This enterprise involves buying batches of plastic flowers wholesale and arranging them attractively in vases, bottles, decorative flowerpots—even in old washtubs and commodes! As in any creative experience, the more you can put your imagination to work, the more successful you'll be.

Sell your products to anyone but florists!

PLASTIC GARDENS

If you want to get even more entrenched in making profits with plastic plants you can jump into the fray by designing whole gardens of these plastic wonders yourself.

There is a big demand for these products in apartment complexes, office buildings, factories, and industrial plants. They are used to decorate foyers, courtyards, and outdoor gardens. Large displays can sell for hundreds of dollars.

Start by reading up on the subject and practicing at home. Then arm yourself with color photographs of your work and call on officials of the above-mentioned types of establishments.

HAND-CARVED PICTURE FRAMES

This product won't be for the masses. Selling only in the better frame shops, galleries, and art supply stores, your ornate, hand-carved gilded frames will be made to order. Naturally, your prices will likewise reflect your exquisite craftsmanship.

Make up some samples, leaving them in the above establishments. Make your prices high enough so that you can make a nice profit, even after giving retailers a healthy discount.

For further information:

Woodcarving, Alan Durst. New York, Viking, 1969.

Handbook of Woodcarving and Whittling, Elsie Hanauer. Cranbury, New Jersey, A. S. Barnes, 1967.

DECORATIVE SCREENS

These are made of three framed panels, about five feet high, and hinged together. The panels can be made of plywood, plastic, fiber glass, or other solid material. They can be painted or wallpapered, decorated with plastic flowers or other colored material. The possibilities are endless.

Make up some samples and take them around to furniture and department stores and gift shops, taking orders as you go.

MONEY FROM MOBILES

Mobiles can be made from all kinds of materials—wood, plastic, paper, metal, glass.

One man in Oregon creates his mobiles from nuts and bolts.

You can get started in this field just by hanging things together, using your own imagination. You might also tour local art museums and galleries or refer to art books for ideas.

Market your work through museums, galleries, art shows, and art supply stores.

For further information:

> *Mobiles: A Practical Guide for Beginners,* Peter Mytton-Davies. New York, International Publications, 1971.

> *Making Mobiles,* Guy Williams. Buchanan, New York, Emerson, 1969.

MAKE MOSAICS

A mosaic is composed of many small varicolored pieces of such materials as glass, ceramic, and porcelain. Seeds, beans, or gravel may also be used. Viewed as a whole, these materials blend together to form striking works of art or to decorate such functional items as serving trays, table tops, and water pitchers.

Attend classes or read books on the subject and practice this craft. Then sell your creations at craft shows and through retail outlets.

For further information:

> *Making Mosaics,* Edmond Arvois. Totowa, New Jersey, Littlefield, Adams, 1974.

> *Making Mosaics,* Beatrice Lewis and Leslie McGuire. New York, Drake, 1973.

HOUSE SIGNS

Most people are proud of their names and find it hard to resist a personalized item such as a hand-carved name plaque for the front of the house. These can be attached to the house itself or stuck into the lawn on the end of a stick.

Create some samples by carving plaques out of wood, then chiseling in, or painting on, family names. For quick sales, take them door

to door, making sure to get a deposit with each order.

LAWN DECORATIONS

A whole world of possibilities exists when it comes to thinking up items for the lawn. Ceramic likenesses of children or animals, a pushcart flower bed, a bicycle or small car, birdbaths, likenesses of famous statues—any one of them will appeal to somebody.

The best way to start is simply to create a large batch of various items, and spread them out on your own front lawn or on a lot on a well-traveled street, along with a "For sale" sign. Soon people will be stopping to look over your unique products. Word will spread, and you'll be on your way.

For ideas:

> *Complete Book of Garden Ornaments, Complements, and Accessories,* Daniel Foley. New York, Crown, 1972.

SUN STENCILS

Catering to man's (and woman's) age-old penchant for skin decoration, this specialty—already being successfully offered in some areas—combines the appeal of the traditional tattoo with the advantage of a novel, painless method. It may range from the simple to the very elaborate design, merely consisting of a stencil to be applied to the body before an individual gets a suntan. When the stencil is removed, voilà! A "natural" tattoo.

You can offer one-tone stencils or multiple stencils, parts of which are removed after every few days of sun exposure. The result will be a tattoo in various shades ranging from flesh color to tan. Let your imagination run rampant!

Market your suntan stencils through beach shops, boutiques, and cosmetics departments of drug and department stores.

DECORATIVE SHUTTERS

Even if you live in an area that's not subject to hurricanes and tornadoes, you could probably do very well creating storm shutters—for decoration.

In this day of prefabricated and mass-produced houses, homeowners will welcome the touch of individuality that attractively styled and painted window shutters provide.

To get started, take some of your samples door to door and to building contractors. If you can sell a builder on the idea of installing a set of these on each of his future homes, your local banker will be very happy.

BUCKS FROM BOTTLED BOATS

You may *think* that you need spaghetti-thin fingers to assemble a ship inside a bottle but it's simply not true. What you will need, however, are a few simple tools and a lot of patience.

You can learn the secret of this ancient art, free for the asking, at any craft or hobby shop, or from the books listed below.

Sell your bottled boats, your jarred junks, and your glassed-in galleons through gift shops, marine hardware stores, hobby shops, and craft exhibitions.

For further information:

Ships in Bottles; A Step-by-Step Guide to a Venerable Nautical Craft, Don Hubbard. New York, McGraw-Hill, 1971.

Modelling Ships in Bottles, Jack Needham. New York, Macmillan, 1973.

INFANT PRINTS

How many mothers could resist buying a ceramic plaque of their newborn infant's footprint or handprint? Not many!

Check the "new births" column of your local newspaper, and call on new mothers within a few days after they get home from the hospital. Take the print, fire it in a small home kiln, then deliver it and collect your fee. Easy money? You bet!

SILVER FROM SUNDIALS

Sundials were first used in Egypt around 1500 B.C., yet they still retain their appeal as decorative pieces for lawns, patios, and gardens.

Get some picture books on sundials at your library. Using the illustrations as models, construct a few. Offer to put them on display in garden shops, nurseries, public parks, and museum courtyards. Naturally, you'll want to have a plaque affixed to each containing your name and phone number.

For further information:

Sundials, Their Theory and Construction, Albert Waugh. New York, Dover, 1973.

Choice of Sundials, Winthrop Dolan. Brattleboro, Vermont, Stephen Greene, 1974.

SKILLET SKILL

Many interesting and unique wall hangings can be created from various-sized kitchen skillets.

They can be painted or used as a base on which to paint clever sayings or affix amusing decals. A woman in Tennessee employs formed and painted paperboard within each pan to create three-dimensional likenesses of such dishes as bacon and eggs, steak and potatoes. She's sold these to gift shops, variety stores, and restaurants throughout her area.

Try your creative talents here and see if this business will pan out for you.

Services

RICHES FROM RIFLES

If your forte is working with guns, you can profit by designing and producing hand-carved, custom-made rifle stocks.

Once the serious hunter finds he can get a stock built exactly to his own physical requirements, he'll wonder how he ever got along without one.

Get customers through sporting goods stores and hunting clubs.

For further information:

Checkering and Carving of Gunstocks, Monty Kennedy. Harrisburg, Pennsylvania, Stackpole, 1952.

Shotgun Stock: Design, Construction and Embellishment, Robert Arthur. Cranbury, New Jersey, A. S. Barnes, 1970.

OPERATE A CRAFTS MARKETPLACE

In large cities everywhere there are literally thousands of talented leatherworkers, candlemakers, weavers, potters, doll makers, and other craftsmen who have no effective central outlet for their work.

As the owner and operator of a crafts marketplace you would lease a large warehouse or shed and rent floor space to local craftsmen where they could display their goods. Your responsibility would be to provide electricity and sanitary facilities, and to advertise and promote the enterprise.

Find interested craftsmen through crafts schools and centers, and craft suppliers.

CRAFTS CONSIGNMENT SHOP

A variation on the foregoing is the operation of a shop where, instead of each craftsman selling his own goods, you take all merchandise in on consignment, selling it yourself. In arrangements of this type the shop normally gets 15–25 percent of the selling price of each item. Of course, any unsold merchandise will be returned to the person who brought it in.

As in the previous enterprise, since there is no investment in inventory, your financial risk is limited to rent, store fixtures, and advertising.

For further information:

Starting and Managing a Swap Shop or Consignment Sale Shop, Small Business Administration. Washington, D. C., Superintendent of Documents, U. S. Government Printing Office.

CRAFTS CENTER

As a crafts instructor versatility is your most important asset. If you can work with facility in leathercraft, pottery, jewelry, mosaic, and candlemaking—as well as other crafts—you have an excellent foundation for success.

One way to get initial students is to teach at your local Y or evening adult school. If you're well liked, they'll come for more lessons after the semester is over. Also, advertise in craft and hobby shops, in the newspaper, and in the Yellow Pages.

For further information:

Craft Manual. Arts and Crafts Section, Department of Recreation and Parks, 3191 West Fourth Street, Los Angeles, California, 90005.

CHAIR CANING

There are at least two ways to make money caning chairs. One is to do it for customers who bring their chairs in for repairs; you can get these customers through furniture stores and by advertising in the newspaper and Yellow Pages.

Another avenue lies in seeking out damaged chairs at flea markets, garage sales, and secondhand stores. Recane these and sell them through the same outlets at a profit.

For further information:

How to Repair and Reupholster Furniture—Caning Simplified, Donald Brann. Briarcliff Manor, New York, Directions Simplified, 1974.

Seat Weaving, C. Perry. Peoria, Illinois, Bennett Company, 1917.

Also, a twenty-five-cent pamphlet on chair caning is available from the North Carolina Agricultural Extension Service, North Carolina State University, Raleigh, North Carolina 27607.

 MAKE MODELS!

If you've got an eye for detail you may be able to profit greatly by working with architects, making detailed models of their proposed projects. Government agencies, industrial firms, owners of office buildings, and private homeowners are other potential buyers.

Start out by making a replica of a well-known local landmark as a sample. Then contact the above-mentioned parties, making them aware of your extraordinary talents and offering your services.

For further information:

> *Minature Building Construction,* John Ahern. New York, International Publications.
>
> *Getting Started in Model-Building,* Herbert Lozier.'New York, Hawthorn, 1971.
>
> *Model Building for Architects and Engineers,* J. R. Taylor. New York, McGraw-Hill, 1971.

☀ TEACH FLOWER ARRANGING

People make money by arranging music, marriages, and motorcycle races. Why not by arranging flowers? To teach effectively, however, you must be proficient in all the various styles.

Get started by notifying florists and garden clubs in your area of your services. Teaching classes at the YWCA and in evening adult schools are other possible outlets for your multifarious multifloral money-making machinations.

For further information:

> *Basic Guide to Flower Arranging,* Florence Hillier. New York, McGraw-Hill, 1974.
>
> *The Complete Flower Arranger,* Amalie Ascher. New York, Simon & Schuster, 1974.

Novelties

☀ PERSONALIZED JIGSAW PUZZLES

Customers will supply you with a photo of themselves, their sweetheart, their house, or other subject. Copy the picture, blow it up

to 8 by 10 or larger, and glue it firmly onto a thin slab or wood or fiberboard. After the glue dries, cut the slab into jigsaw-like pieces with an electric jigsaw.

Sell your products through camera shops, novelty stores, and by mail through national publications.

☀ THINK SMALL!

You probably are aware that the antique business is a multimillion-dollar industry. But how about *miniature* antiques?

If your bag is working with minuscule objects, try creating tiny, precisely detailed replicas of antiques out of wood or ivory. If your work is good you should be able to successfully market these miniature wonders —at fairly high prices—to fine gift shops, antique shops, and department stores, as well as to individual collectors.

☀ GIANT INSECTS

A foot-long ant . . . . a giant butterfly . . . a ladybug as big as your head: These and other replicas of small insects and animals, made out of stuffed fabric, wood, or welded wire and painted convincingly, would sell especially well in toy and variety stores, pet shops, department stores—even to school science classes!

Try your hand at this unique enterprise, getting started by consulting some well-detailed animal picture books at your library. Practice until your imitations look exactly like the real thing, and then start showing 'em off.

☀ GOURD CREATURES

Dried gourds, because of their unique colors and shapes, can be put to good use as bodies for various animals. Plastic eyes, felt ears, button noses, and cloth feet will endow them with the necessary "equipment."

Plant gourd seeds, which you can obtain from a local supplier, in the spring. After the gourds mature, cut them and allow them to dry in the house or in an arid shed for a few months.

Potential outlets for these products are toy and children's shops, and variety and department stores.

☼ SILVER FROM SEASHELLS

Ashtrays, lamp bases, bookends, cuff links, tie clasps, money clips, pendants, earrings—these are just a few of the multitudes of unique products that can be handcrafted by using seashells.

Large quantities of various types of shells can be obtained from suppliers, usually found in large coastal cities both here and abroad.

Sell your products to gift shops and jewelry and department stores, as well as to other retail outlets.

For further information:

Shell Crafts, Elizabeth Logan. New York, Scribner's, 1974.

Shellcraft, Cleo Stephens. Radnor, Pennsylvania, Chilton, 1974.

 DECANTER PEOPLE

A unique artistic enterprise involves the designing of small caricatures of people in your community, using clay. The figures are then attached to corks or stoppers of decorative decanters. You may even use plain wine bottles as a base and decorate the body of the bottle with miniature clothes.

Make up some samples, using people you know as models. Show them to some of the people's relatives and suggest that these caricatured decanters would make nice gifts.

If people like your work, you'll have all the business you can handle come Christmas or birthday time.

 SLINGSHOT SALESMAN

We've all heard of the hotshot salesman who can sell anything under the sun and usually does. A slingshot salesman, is different,

however. Here, you'll specialize exclusively in carving and selling fancy, even ornate, children's slingshots to toy and gift shops, department and variety stores.

In fashioning these minor weapons use a hardwood such as oak or maple. If you can find slingshot-shaped pieces in their natural forms, these, after a little sanding or shaping, should make especially attractive products.

☼ MAKE FACE MASKS

A face mask is a likeness in plaster of paris of an individual's face. First a liquid wax-rosin mold of the face is made. Then plaster of paris is poured into the mold, where it hardens into a cast.

First get some books on molding and casting. Then practice on children or friends until you can get a perfect likeness every time.

The quickest way to get business is to take some samples door to door in child-populated neighborhoods. Offer mothers face masks of their children for five dollars each.

For further information:

Molding and Casting: Its Technique and Application, Carl Clarke. Butler, Maryland, Standard Arts, 1972.

☼ WOODEN GREETING CARDS

You can capitalize on this unique idea by carving greeting cards out of such materials as plywood, birch bark, oak, mahogany, or hickory veneer.

Practice until you can make attractive cards. Then make up some samples, taking them around to gift and novelty shops, variety stores and drugstores.

For further information:

Creative Light Wood Carving, John Matthews. New York, St. Martin's, 1971.

Wood Carving for Fun and Profit, Al Ball. Jericho, New York, Exposition, 1969.

☼ BOOTY FROM BUTTONS

Even an item as unglorified as the common button can be made into an object of distinction and admiration.

Using plastic as a base, you can embed all sorts of objects in your buttons: Flowers, leaves, insects, foreign coins and postage stamps, charms, teeth, and locks of hair are just a few of the endless possibilities.

Sell your products to sewing and yardage shops, gift shops, and variety stores, as well as to suppliers of these stores.

ANTLER ART

If you live in a big-game area such as Montana or Wyoming, you can obtain antlers of elk, moose, and deer by the hundreds from firms that specialize in dressing hunters' game.

These can be formed and fashioned into a multitude of unique items such as belt buckles, tie clips, cuff links, ashtrays—even toothbrushes and flutes!

Sell your creations through gift and variety stores. Give serious consideration, here, to mail order.

DOLL PALACES

Ordinary dollhouses are sold in just about every toy store in the country. What you'll specialize in, however, are quality "doll palaces" with all the trimmings. Miniature pieces of fine furniture and kitchen appliances, attractive drapes, elegant chandeliers, and colorful wallpaper will all add distinction to your unique creations.

Of course, you'll somehow have to get one of your palaces displayed in a home show, the local country club, an uptown gift shop—but if your work is as good as your prices are high, word should spread soon and you'll be on your way.

For further information:

Furnishing Dolls' Houses, Audrey Johnson. Newton Center, Massachusetts, Branford, 1972.

How to Make Dolls' Houses, Audrey Johnson. Newton Center, Massachusetts, Branford, 1957.

GOURDS FOR THE BIRDS!

Any product that is decorative, functional, *and* inexpensive invariably sells well. Such is the case with birdhouses made of dried gourds. You can either buy the gourds or grow and dry them yourself.

First weatherproof the gourd by giving it a coat of lacquer or bright paint. For carving out the "front entrance," you'll need a saber saw or a keyhole saw. Directly beneath this opening, drill a small hole and insert a short peg, which will serve as a "doorstep." In the top of the gourd, insert a screw eye for hanging, and drill a few holes in the bottom for drainage. This last operation is extremely important. It will prevent the house from filling up with water, which might result in a tragedy.

Sell your creations to gift and pet shops, variety and department stores. And don't neglect the mail order market!

DRIFTWOOD DOLLARS

If you live near the coast, chances are you have access to unlimited quantities of a material that you can get free, just for the pickin'—driftwood.

Put your creativity to work and you'll come up with many unique and salable items to make: lamps, bookends, statuettes, abstract forms, walking canes, chessmen, ad infinitum.

Sell your creations to gift shops, variety and department stores, art galleries, and other retail outlets.

For further information:

Driftwood: Techniques and Projects, La Dora Erdmann. New York, Drake, 1974.

Creating with Driftwood and Weathered Wood, Elyse Sommer and Mike Sommer. New York, Crown, 1974.

MANUFACTURERS' MODELS

Manufacturers of large equipment such as trucks, farm tractors, and construction cranes are always eager to promote their products and to keep them in the public eye.

If you can come up with some clever ideas for authentic-looking toy models of this equipment, you can get valuable help from the companies concerned. They can supply you with blueprints of their products, and may even help finance their production or assist in marketing them to toy stores and hobby shops.

Names and addresses of heavy-equipment manufacturers can be found in the *Thomas Register of American Manufacturers,* at your local library. Write them a letter proposing your idea.

WITTICISMS ON WOOD

If you have a ready wit—or access to a good one-line joke book—you might be able to pick up some nice change by painting or silk-screening some clever short sayings onto small decorative wooden plaques.

This product lends itself especially well to sale by mail order and direct sale to novelty supply firms.

KNICKKNACK POSTCARDS

These are regular color postcards, but stapled onto the end of the card is a small plastic bag containing a seashell, a dried flower, a leaf, a few pebbles or grains of sand—anything that could be considered a "souvenir" of the area.

Get your postcards from a local distributor, then simply attach any suitable knickknack to each. Sell them through gift shops, variety, and drugstores—anywhere regular postcards are sold.

MAP MAGIC

State and city maps are often yours for the asking at service stations, state highway departments, and city halls. Affixed to a piece of plywood or plastic, and shellacked, these maps can be made into framed posters, serving trays, souvenir plaques, or other tourist items.

Sell your creations to gift, souvenir, and variety stores.

WEIRD WIND CHIMES

We've all seen wind chimes made of short lengths of bamboo and small pieces of metal. Use your imagination and come up with wind chimes utilizing some really unique materials. Possibilities are bones, seashells, old silverware, frying pan covers—even a giant model made of manhole covers! This last one could be donated to the town plaza as a promotional stunt.

And how about an electronic model with varicolored lights, flashing on and off at the will of the prevailing breezes?

RICHES FROM RESIN

Some extremely decorative and functional items can be made by the art of resin casting. Molded articles such as paperweights, ashtrays, trivets, soap dishes, and light-switch cover plates can be made in a variety of colors and designs. Such things as seashells, coins, flowers, and colored rocks can be embedded in items made of clear resin.

Your products should find a ready market at gift shops, variety, and department stores.

8

Home Is Where the Heart Is— and the Money!

The U. S. Department of Commerce estimates that there are ten million businesses in the United States. How many of these are operated out of the home is anybody's guess. How can one accurately count the many "businessmen" with a few dozen laying hens in their backyards, or the multitudes of little old ladies taking in mending or ironing? Nevertheless, you can bet these "mom and pop" industries account for a sizable percentage of the total number of businesses.

What are the advantages of running a business in, or from, your home? One is the personal service that you can offer. Another is that, as opposed to your competitors in the business district or the suburban shopping centers, your overhead will be lower, so you'll be able to pass most or all of these savings on to your customers in the form of lower prices.

Now for the big question: How are people going to find out that you exist and that your prices are, indeed, lower? You'll normally not have the advantage of heavy foot traffic or be allowed to erect outdoor signs, as is the case with merchants in the business district. Therefore, you'll have to depend heavily on a combination of word-of-mouth and media advertising, clever promotional campaigns and, in general, your own imagination and ingenuity. To help you along, we suggest you reread the advertising and promotional ideas outlined in Chapter 1.

An especially effective way to get business is to concentrate your sales and promotional efforts on such organizations as women's and church groups, scouting troups, PTA's, Little Leagues, and civic, business, and fraternal organizations. Members of these groups are in constant communication with one another. If you please one or two members, word will spread throughout the organization. In the same vein, if your work is unsatisfactory you can expect to swiftly establish a reputation —of another sort.

Again, we urge that before you start you check thoroughly all local, state, and federal regulations which might bear upon your activities, as well as any applicable deed restrictions on your property.

All set? Now let's journey through the vast array of home-based money-making activities and see if we can find something to your liking.

Personal Services

CUSTOM CLOTHING

Design and make everything from baby booties to wedding trousseaus.

If you have confidence in your creative abilities, an excellent way to start would be with some unique, perhaps controversial, outfits and give a fashion show in one of the better hotels.

Advertise in advance, being sure to invite the press.

For further information:

Basic Tailoring. New York, Time-Life Books (orders to Little, Brown, & Co.), 1974.

Modern Pattern Design, Harriet Pepin. New York, Funk & Wagnalls, 1970.

A FORTUNE IN FINDERS' FEES

What is a finder's fee? A "finder" is an individual who brings two parties together for the purpose of making a transaction. When the transaction is consummated, the finder receives a commission—his "fee."

These transactions can include anything from locating an apartment for a bachelor to arranging a merger between two manufacturing concerns. Millions of dollars are made by finders every year.

There are several good books on the subject, and studying these can help you avoid many pitfalls when starting out.

For further information:

How to Make a Fortune in Finders' Fees, Jack Payne. New York, Frederick Fell, 1973.

Finders' Fee Guide. Business Opportunities Digest, 301 North Orchard Avenue, Farmington, New Mexico 87401.

DATING SERVICE

Contrary to expensive—and sometimes unscrupulous—"computer dating" schemes, this service operates in a very straightforward manner.

Each male client is charged ten to twenty dollars, for which he receives five names and phone numbers of females who have registered with you. The females are listed free of charge. If she's interested when he calls, they can arrange to meet. If not, he'll just call the next one.

Advertise your service at singles bars, in the cafeterias of large office buildings, and in the entertainment section of your local newspaper. This venture may or may not make you a millionaire, but one thing is certain: You'll never have to spend your Saturday nights alone!

VISITATION SERVICE

Many elderly or convalescing individuals who live alone, and their relatives, would welcome a service in which they are visited a few times each day. Visits would serve two purposes: Should such persons become ill or have an accident, you would be there to call a doctor for them; also, at each house, you'd "socialize" for a few minutes, thus helping to ease the loneliness that some of these people face.

Get clients through doctors, hospitals, convalescent homes, and senior citizens' groups. Charge each client ten to twenty dollars per month.

HOME HAIR STYLING

If you've never held comb and scissors to another person's head before, get some training from library books, a correspondence course, or by attending a school of cosmetology.

When you're ready to hang out your shingle spread word to your friends and neighbors, and distribute leaflets throughout your area.

Before starting, however, check local and state licensing requirements.

For further information:

Hairdressing in Theory and Practice, T. W. Masters. New York, William S. Heinman, 1971.

Hair Design and Fashion: Principles and Relationships, Miriam Cardwell and Marion Rudoy. New York, Crown, 1970.

HOME GYM

How to compete with commercial exercise gyms? Well, for one thing, your prices will be a lot lower. Second, and more important, you'll be giving *personalized* attention to men and women who need help with weight problems.

Start with a few mats on the floor and some light equipment such as stretch cables and exercycles. As your business grows you can add more equipment.

Get your initial customers by teaching classes at the Y or at an evening adult school. Also, print and distribute leaflets in health food stores as well as supermarkets.

For further information:

Keep Moving: Easy Workouts for Figure Control, Olga Ley. New York, Dial, 1974.

Slimnastics, Pamela Nottidge and Diana Lamplugh. New York, St. Martin's, 1972.

RUN A REST HOME

If you have a fairly large house and enjoy helping others, you may be suited to operating a rest home.

Unlike the inhabitants of nursing homes, your clients won't need nursing care. They'll mainly be folks who are advanced in years and prefer not to live alone, or persons needing an extended rest period following a surgical operation. In any event, you must conform to community health and safety regulations before opening your doors.

To get started, notify physicians, hospitals,

and nursing homes; contact senior citizens' centers; and advertise in the newspaper and the Yellow Pages.

LIVE-IN COMPANION

Many elderly individuals who live alone would like the security and companionship that another person or family could provide. These people will often take others into their homes—even buy their food and give them a small allowance—in return merely for their reassuring presence. Although you may occasionally be called upon to perform small favors such as taking your companion for a ride in the car, you'll not be expected to be a nursemaid or to prepare any more than your share of the meals.

To find someone who desires a live-in companion, check the newspaper classifieds and advertise there yourself if necessary. Be prepared to give personal references.

A COMFORTABLE LIVING

Here's a real soft way to make some money. Get permission from stadiums and gymnasiums in your town to rent out cushions to the spectators at sports events.

You'll probably have to give the owners a percentage, but there should still be a handsome profit in it for you.

A HAIRY BUSINESS

Hair removal by the electrolysis method is safe and permanent. The most frequent customers for this service are women desiring removal of unwanted facial or leg hair. However, the method is occasionally used by men who are tired of shaving or don't like their hairy chests.

For information on training in this field, write Kree Institute of Electrolysis, Inc., 152 West Forty-second Street, New York 10036.

For further information:

How to Be a Successful Electrologist,

Maryland Manger and Robley Stevens. Boston, Branden Press,

Electrolysis, Thermolysis and Blend: The Principles and Practice of Permanent Hair Removal, Arthur Hinkel and Richard Lind. Los Angeles, Arroway, 1968.

BE A GENEALOGIST

Tracing one's ancestry back through the ages has fascinated people since mankind began. It's possible to learn this practice through books—and to earn a living from it.

Since it carries with it a certain snob appeal, you'll want to advertise your genealogical services in country and yacht clubs, libraries and art museums, the programs of classical performances, and magazines catering to the intelligentsia.

For further information:

Genealogy as Pastime and Profession, Donald Jacobus. Baltimore, Genealogical Publishing, 1971.

How Book for Genealogists, George Everton, ed. Salt Lake City, Deseret, 1964.

LAUNDRY FOR LOVERS

Bachelors and bachelorettes alike have more important things to do than their laundry! Give them time by taking in their laundry at rates comparable to what they would pay at a laundromat.

If you live in an area containing singles apartment buildings it'll be easy for you to round up customers. Simply distribute handbills in these buildings. As a sideline, you might also offer to do mending and alterations.

For further information:

Simple Laundrywork and Fabric Care, Marion Mennie. Plainfield, New Jersey, Textile Book Service.

Let's Talk Laundry, Frederick Dearmond. Springfield, Missouri, Mycroft Press, 1957.

More Services . . .

 TRY TRAILERS!

Many individuals and families have need for a trailer at moving time, or perhaps just for picking up a newly purchased piano or refrigerator.

You can get into the business of renting out trailers by buying or making some in various sizes. If you're handy and can build them yourself, you should be able to produce a half-dozen for under $1,000.

Then make arrangements with a local service station to rent them out for you, letting the proprietors keep 25 percent of the rental fee. Naturally, you'll want to keep an eye on expanding your "fleet," perhaps to eventually include one-way rentals between cities.

A FORTUNE IN FLOCKING

Flocking is a fuzzy, velvetlike material used for coating such things as wallpaper, greeting cards, lamp shades, Christmas ornaments, car interiors, and—in some extreme cases—car exteriors.

Flocking is applied by means of a spray-type gun called a flock gun, used in combination with a small compressor. Both of these can be purchased for under fifty dollars. A large supplier of flock guns and flocking material is Advance-Chicago, 400 North Noble Street, Chicago, Illinois 60622.

Potential customers are everywhere: used car dealers, hotels, restaurants, secondhand furniture dealers, and interior decorators, to name a few. Or you can turn out your own unique flocked products, selling them through retail outlets.

FLOWER PARADE

Here customers contract, either for themselves or as a gift, to have a fresh bouquet of flowers delivered to homes, businesses, or sickbeds every week.

In addition to thoughtful husbands and boyfriends, other customers might include restaurants, banks, beauty salons, doctors' and dentists' offices, hospitals and nursing homes.

Get started by giving away some free sample bouquets to these places, along with some descriptive literature about your service.

For further information:

Success in Selling Flowers, Stanley Coleman. New Rochelle, New York, Sportshelf and Soccer Associates.

The Retail Florist Business, Peter Pfahl. Danville, Illinois, Interstate Printers and Publishers, 1973.

 GET IT ON TAPE!

If you've got some good-quality tape recording equipment there's money to be made by tape recording such events as weddings, convention and political speeches, church choirs, and the like.

You can record the proceedings directly onto a tape cassette, selling the cassette to your customer. Or you can use more sophisticated equipment and then have a local recording company dub the tape onto an LP disc. This would, of course, enable your customers to replay the record on their home record player.

HOME MAINTENANCE AGENCY

As the owner of a home maintenance agency you'll hire high school and college students, retired persons, and casual laborers to perform tasks such as rug and wall cleaning, attic and garage cleaning, floor waxing, painting, and minor repairing.

Get your clients through telephone or door-to-door canvasing, or through leaflet distribution. Find employees by contacting your state department of employment. Or advertise for both in the newspaper classifieds.

For further information:

Home Cleaning Guide, Barbara Molle and Irv Charles. Phoenix, Arizona, Sincere Press, 1972.

PLANT-SITTER

You've heard of baby-sitters, house-sitters, and pet-sitters—why not be a plant-sitter?

A family going away on vacation can always get a neighbor to water the lawn, but how about caring for the potted plants, hanging baskets, delicate rose bushes, and thirsty petunias? Your job will be to call at customers' homes several days a week to water and generally care for their growing things.

Get business through nurseries, travel bureaus, and your local garden club. Promote your enterprise heavily during the summer months.

For further information:

Home Owners' Complete Garden Handbook, John Melady. New York, Grosset & Dunlap, 1960.

Making Things Grow, Thalassa Cruso. New York, Alfred A. Knopf, 1968.

PACK IN THE PROFITS

In addition to transporting household goods, most moving companies will provide, for an extra fee, a service whereby they'll pack the goods prior to moving. However, their rates are exorbitant.

You could perform this service for a fraction of the cost—and still profit nicely. (In addition to the physical work involved, you'll supply the containers necessary for packing the goods.)

Homeowners who have their homes up for sale will make excellent prospects. Find these by watching for lawn signs and by contacting real estate brokers. In addition, newspaper and Yellow Pages advertising should bring you a brisk business.

CARPET AND DRAPERY CLEANING

Private homes, apartment buildings, hotels, office buildings, and department stores are a few of your potential customers.

To clean carpets you'll need a commercial vacuum machine and a carpet-cleaning machine. Together these units should cost around $500. Clean the drapes in a self-service dry-cleaning machine or farm this work out to a professional cleaner.

BE A HOUSE-SITTER

Many vacationers would more fully enjoy themselves if they knew someone was holding down the fort while they were away.

As a house-sitter your job may consist of actually living in the house, or the owners may just want you to drop by once or twice daily, watering the plants, feeding the pets, picking up the mail, and so on.

Advertise your service heavily just prior to the summer months. Distributing leaflets and advertising in the newspaper classifieds are both good bets.

FLOOR-POLISHING SERVICE

As a "floor-polishing expert" contact homeowners, industrial plants, and everyone in between, contracting with them to wax their linoleum floors periodically.

Hardware stores and supermarkets often rent out floor polishers as well as providing waxing material. As you expand, however, you'll want to own your own equipment and buy your materials wholesale.

GOLF CLUB RENEWAL SERVICE

For the golfer who likes to keep his equipment in good condition—and most golfers do—a battered, rusty club is a disgraceful club. That's why golf club refinishing and replating services are big business at pro shops. However, their prices are high and they're swamped with business.

You can start your own golf club renewal service in one of several ways. Either open your own shop or take out a concession in an established shop or subcontract for the jobs from an established shop, doing the work in your garage. Get information on club care from the various golf club manufacturers.

HOME MAINTENANCE EQUIPMENT RENTALS

Most apartment dwellers, and many homeowners, don't like the idea of investing in such seldom-used equipment as rug shampooers and floor polishers. Rather, when the need arises they prefer to rent these units.

Buy a number of these machines and install them in supermarkets and hardware stores as rentals.

Let each store owner keep 25 per cent of the amount he takes in on the rentals. The rest is yours.

TUNE PIANOS

This has always seemed to us to be one of the more pleasant ways in which an individual can earn his daily bread. Piano tuning is not difficult to learn, and although there are several schools around the country teaching this subject, it can also be learned through correspondence courses.

Get information on the necessary training by calling a few piano dealers. When you're proficient at the trade you might be calling them again, this time to offer them your piano-tuning talents.

Three firms offering home study courses in piano tuning and repair are:

- Niles Bryant School, 3631 Stockton Boulevard, Sacramento, California, 95820.

- American School of Piano Tuning, P. O. Box 707, Gilroy, California, 95020.

- Capital Piano Tuning School, 3160 S.W. Sixteenth Court, Fort Lauderdale, Florida, 33312.

For further information:

Complete Course in Professional Piano Tuning, Repair, and Rebuilding, Floyd Stevens. Chicago, Nelson-Hall, 1972.

A FORTUNE IN FORMICA

Because of Formica's durability most modern homes use it for counter tops in kitchens and bathrooms, and sometimes on cabinets and walls.

With a little practice you can learn, and specialize in, the installation of this material. Then work with home-improvement companies and builders on a subcontract basis —as well as going after your customers directly.

As sidelines you could also do tilework, flooring, cabinetry, and general remodeling.

TV RENTAL

If you can repair television sets, or can find a partner with this ability, it's possible to accumulate and have on rental hundreds of TV sets—each bringing you twenty to twenty-five dollars every month.

Buy old TV sets from dealers who have taken them in as trade-ins, at flea-markets and garage sales, and through the newspaper classifieds. Aside from renting them out to individuals, you can rent sets en masse to hospitals, nursing and convalescent homes, hotels, and motels.

Food and Entertainment

NEWS FOR THE ELDERLY

Failing eyesight and hearing, limited means, and lack of entertainment among the elderly all add up to a simple way for you to make money and help these senior citizens at the same time.

Arrange to appear at senior citizens' centers and convalescent homes at a specified time each day or several days each week. For a quarter apiece, interested oldsters will hear your half-hour earful of local and national news, together with select short fiction and humor from magazines such as *Reader's Digest*. Or, you might try getting your fee from the organization itself.

START A THEATER GROUP

Although we can't guarantee you'll go from Medicine Lodge, Kansas, to the Broadway stage overnight, it's possible, with talent and hard work, to profit by forming a local theater group.

After getting your acting troupe together, generate community interest by giving free performances in parks and school auditoriums. You can also solicit funds from local merchants, the city or state art commission, and wealthy patrons of the arts.

For further information:

> *The Art of Play Production*, John Dolman and Richard Knaub. New York, Harper & Row, 1973.
>
> *Amateur Theatre: A Guide for Actor and Director*, Van Cartmell. New York, Funk & Wagnalls, 1968.

MELODRAMA MADNESS

Perhaps you're interested in a more frolicsome, less formal, type of theater than the conventional type. If so, consider the melodrama.

In eighteenth-century England the melodrama was a serious theater form characterized by romance, violence and, invariably, the triumph of virtue over evil.

Today some acting groups still perform a comical, exaggerated type of melodrama in which the villain (who is roundly hissed and booed by the audience) attempts to win the pretty naïve young thing (with whom the audience empathizes). But in the end the hero

(whom the audience enthusiastically applauds) subdues the villain and finally wins the girl.

At these performances popcorn is served, which is more often thrown at the villain than it is eaten. In general, a good time is had by all.

Why not start a melodrama theater in your community?

COUNTRY COOKIN'

If you live a little ways out of town and can come up with some good country cooking, you've got the ingredients for a lucrative restaurant business.

Of course, you'll specialize in some popular dish like fried chicken, ham, or steak. But just as important, a good country restaurant is known for its trimmings: fresh-baked cornbread or biscuits and honey; fresh vegetables and fruits; homemade pies or ice cream. And, of course, generous helpings and a congenial atmosphere.

For further information:

> *Mary Meade's Country Cookbook*, Ruth Church. Chicago, Rand McNally, 1974.
>
> *The Farmhouse Cookbook*, Yvonne Tarr. New York, Quadrangle, 1974.

WEDDING PLANNER

Another name for this enterprise might be "wedding wizard," as you'll be required to plan every phase of the affair from the first engagement announcement to the honeymoon trip.

Fees, on an average, are based on 10 percent of the wedding budget, so a few elaborate shindigs, along with a good number of normal-sized affairs, should add up to a healthy annual income.

To learn more, study the books below. Then spread the word through friends and neighbors, wedding salons, and ads in the wedding section of your local newspaper.

For further information:

Planning a Beautiful Wedding, Mary Wilkinson, ed. New Rochelle, New York, Sportshelf and Soccer Associates, 1969.

The Wedding Planner, Diana Bright. Los Angeles, Nash, 1970.

PARTY PLANNER

Like the wedding planner, the party planner takes over all the details of the affair. These include printing and sending out invitations, and arranging for food, alcohol, flowers, decorations, and entertainment.

Find your clients through social organizations, social contacts, catering services, and newspaper and Yellow Pages advertising.

Fees, as in the preceding entry, are usually set at about 10 percent of the cost of the affair.

For further information:

Party Planning and Entertainment, Jan Adair. Cranbury, New Jersey, A. S. Barnes, 1972.

The Party Planner, Bernice Hogan. Old Tappan, New Jersey, Fleming H. Revell, 1967.

BE AN IMPRESARIO

If you know of a good rock group, comedian, singer, trained dog act, or other talents in your area, why not organize four or five of these acts into a show? Then rent an auditorium, hall, or abandoned theater and sell tickets for performances.

Promote your show well in advance by distributing leaflets, putting up large posters, and advertising in the local newspaper.

PROMOTE ANTIQUE SHOWS

There are probably a number of antique dealers in your area who can profit greatly by participating in an antique show or exhibition. Your job will be to organize these shows, which will be free to the public. Rent a lot or a

large hall or warehouse for a week or a weekend, and then vigorously promote the show throughout the community. Naturally, you will collect rental fees from each exhibitor in exchange for floor space at the show.

In order to continually find "new blood," keep your show on the move by holding it in a different town each week.

FOREIGN LANGUAGE RADIO SHOWS

If you are the outgoing type and can speak one or more foreign languages, you may be able to have your own foreign language radio show. There are several possible types of programs you could do. Ethnic news or music, personality features, and quiz shows are a few possibilities.

To get the ball rolling, contact program directors of various radio stations in your area and propose your idea.

HOME COOKING FOR STUDENTS

Many college students living away from home haven't had a good, home-cooked meal in months. If you live near a college or university you can capitalize on this unfortunate state of affairs by cooking for students in your home.

You could provide them with more appetizing meals, and probably at less expense, than similar fare served in local restaurants.

Start by advertising in the school paper and on school bulletin boards.

A RECORD INCOME

If you have a large collection of various types of records and are the disc jockey type, combine these two assets and offer your services as a DJ for social functions and discotheques in your town.

The best way to start would be to check the Yellow Pages for listings of fraternal organizations, social organizations, and nightclubs, and then call offering your services.

HOME THEATER

You can rent, at a reasonable rate, old movies from any one of a number of film libraries found in just about any metropolitan area in the country. Find the names and addresses of these firms in any big city Yellow Pages under "Motion picture film libraries." Write and ask them to send you their catalogues.

Next, buy a projector, screen, and any necessary furniture. Used goods will do.

Advertise your "grand opening" a week or so in advance by distributing leaflets, advertising in the entertainment section of your local newspaper, and putting up notices on school and supermarket bulletin boards. For the first few nights offer a price reduction, free popcorn, dancing girls—anything to get 'em into your theater.

SCHOOL LUNCHROOM

If you live near a school, and have a spacious home, you might consider turning part of your home into a lunchroom for local students, which many schools do not have.

First check the schools near you and find out what lunch facilities are already available for the students. Next, you'll want to check existing licensing and zoning regulations.

Assuming you've decided to go ahead with the venture, spread word throughout the schools and leave notices on their bulletin boards.

For further information:

A Menu Planning Guide for Type A School Lunches (PA-719), U. S. Department of Agriculture Consumer and Marketing Service. Washington, D. C., Superintendent of Documents, U. S. Government Printing Office, 1966.

Buying—Selling—Investing

A FORTUNE IN FURNITURE

Profits galore reside in secondhand furniture. The trick is to seek out bargain-priced items such as dressers, coffee tables, desks, chairs, sofas—anything that can be resold.

Find these pieces in secondhand stores, thrift shops, at garage sales—even on the curb at rubbish collection time. Then make minor repairs: covering scratches, refinishing, perhaps mending a bit of upholstery or repairing a loose leg.

Resell the furniture to, or through, the same outlets, through newspaper ads, or even through an auctioneering firm.

For further information:

Complete Book of Furniture Repair and Refinishing, Ralph Kinney. New York, Scribner's, 1971.

How to Sell Furniture, Stanley Slom. New York, Fairchild, 1970.

RARE BOOKS

Any needed item that is in short supply invariably carries a high price tag. Such is the case with rare books.

Naturally, if you're not already familiar with the market the first thing you'll have to do is to make a study of the field. But once you've learned the basics, there's no limit to your earnings.

You can buy, sell, and trade your books, or you can rent them out. Your business can be transacted from your home, in a shop, or through the mail.

For further information:

The Book Collector's Handbook of Values, 1972–1973, Van Allen Bradley. New York, Putnam's, 1972.

Bookman's Price Index: A Guide to the Values of Rare and Other Out-of-Print Books (10 vols.), D. F. McGrath. Detroit, Gale Research, 1964–73.

INVEST IN INVENTIONS

The automobile, the airplane, even the lowly paper clip at one time represented an opportunity for the alert investor.

If you possess risk capital—that is, money that you can lose without depriving yourself or your family of food or shelter—you might consider advertising for new inventions. If you find a potential money-maker, either buy the rights to the invention outright or enter into a profit-sharing agreement with the inventor.

Plenty of clever inventions never get off the ground for lack of someone like you—the Great American Promoter!

For further information:

> *How to Make a Fortune from Your Invention,* Norman Carlisle. New York, Warner Paperback Library, 1972.
>
> *How to Be a Successful Inventor: Patenting, Protecting, Marketing, and Selling Your Invention,* Clarence Taylor. Jericho, New York, Exposition, 1972.

ANTIQUES—AND ALL THAT JUNQUE

If you live in a community or along a well-traveled highway where there is a dearth of antique outlets, and you are a sharp trader, to boot, you've got the ingredients for a successful antique operation. You'll also want to deal in assorted "junque." Junque, naturally, is high-class—or high-priced—junk. Old Pepsi-Cola bottles, gumball machines, traffic signals, dresses from the twenties. Even an old streetcar falls into this category and, if placed in your front yard, can attract a lot of attention to your operation.

Start your shop by scouring garage sales, flea markets, used-furniture stores, attics, and by reading the newspaper classifieds. Promote your enterprise heavily throughout the area.

For further information:

> *Antiques: How to Identify, Buy, Sell, Refinish, and Care for Them,* Ann Cole. New York, Macmillan, 1962.
>
> *Official Guide to Antiques and Curios,* Hal Cohen. New York, House of Collectibles, 1974.
>
> *The Antique Dealer,* Ebel Doctorow Publishers, 101 Springfield Avenue, Summit, New Jersey 07901 (a monthly publication).

 **BE A BIG WIG!**

The wig business is big business. You can successfully run a "wig boutique" from your home by giving *personalized* service that large department stores and commercial wig outlets can't provide.

You'll need at least a few hundred dollars' worth of inventory to begin with, and enough space for display. To find out what's selling in your area, visit wig and department stores and talk to beauty shop operators. To become more knowledgeable about wigs, get some books on the subject and also study wig manufacturers' catalogues.

For further information:

> *Wigs: A Complete Guide for the Profession,* Sally Cooney and Charlotte Harper. Englewood Cliffs, New Jersey, Prentice-Hall, 1973.
>
> *Complete Guide to Synthetic Hairpieces and Wigs,* Rebecca Hyman. New York, Grosset & Dunlap, 1971.

BUY AND SELL AMERICANA

Relics of bygone days such as old wagon wheels, buggies, horse collars, flatirons, commodes, and bean pots can usually be bought for a song and sold for a pretty penny. Finding these items is the trick, however.

Start your search by getting out into the country. Many farmers have items like these just lying in the fields and, in many cases, aren't aware of their true value.

Sell the items through newspaper ads or just by displaying them on your front lawn. Word-of-mouth advertising should make your business snowball into a lucrative enterprise.

BOAT BOOTY

A small fortune can be made every year by buying small boats in the off-season and reselling them during the summer months at a premium. Your best bet, initially, would be to concentrate on small fishing craft such as duck boats, bass boats, rowboats, and canoes.

As your business prospers, you can branch out into big-ticket items such as cruisers and yachts.

You'll need a large garage or shed for storage over the winter. In addition, a good comprehensive insurance policy is advisable.

Find your boats through newspaper ads and sell them through the same medium. If you live on a busy throughfare, you might also display them on your front lawn.

BOOK BARGAINS

Most large cities have at least several used book stores, but many small and medium-sized towns do not. If your town's population is over 100,000 and it has no used book store, you're in virgin territory.

It's possible to start your enterprise right in your own home. Advertise the fact that you buy and sell used books in the newspaper classifieds. You may have to make occasional buying trips to the big city, but this will be well worth your while.

For further information:

Beginning in Bookselling, Irene Babbidge. New York, Academic Press, 1971.

BOTTLE BOOTY

We once met a man in California who claimed that he put his two kids through college by buying and selling old bottles. Since he seemed to be the reliable type, we'll have to take him at his word and say that if he can profit from bottles, you can, too.

Find your bottles on the curb at rubbish collection time, in city and county dumps, and by paying janitors to collect them for you. The most valuable specimens, however, are the old relics which are found by digging in the earth around ghost towns, in farmers' backyards, and in historical communities.

Check your Yellow Pages for dealers and get names of collectors through them.

For further information:

Twelve Hundred Bottles Priced: A Price

Guide and Classification System (2 vols.), John Tibbits and Dan Smith. Sacramento, Little Glass Shack, 1970–73.

Bottle Collector's Handbook and Pricing Guide, John Yount. San Angelo, Texas, Educator Books, 1970.

The Old Bottle Magazine, Box 243, Bend, Oregon 97701 (a monthly publication).

For the Handyperson

JEWELRY REJUVENATOR

You've probably seen ads in the newspaper "Cash paid for old jewelry" and wondered what the purchasers did with the stuff. With a little soldering, buffing, polishing, and improving, junk jewelry can be transformed into beautiful—and salable—articles.

Find old jewelry by inserting ads in the newspaper classifieds and by canvassing jewelry dealers, pawn shops, secondhand stores, garage sales, flea markets, and swap meets. Then, by reading up on the subject and perhaps signing up for an evening course on it, you too can learn the secrets of turning junk into jewelry.

For further information:

Jewelry Repair Manual, Allen Hardy and John Bowman. Cincinnati, Van Nostrand, 1967.

BARBECUE BUCKS

Ever since that caveman accidentally dropped that chicken into the fire, barbecues have been popular.

As a burgeoning builder of better barbecues you'll build and install everything from small, built-in kitchen barbecues to giant outdoor models.

Start by contacting home improvement firms, offering to work for them as a subcontractor. If your work is of high quality, word will get around and you'll soon have plenty of customers on your own. In the meantime don't be afraid to solicit business by knocking on doors.

For further information:

> *Sunset Ideas for Building Barbeques,* Editors, *Sunset* magazine. Menlo Park, California, Lane, 1971.

BE A SHARPIE

At this moment, countless millions of knives, scissors, chisels, scythes, and lawn mowers are languishing in shameful disuse. Or worse, performing substandard service, because of a malady that could just as easily have been prevented: dullness.

You can give new life to these unfortunate instruments—and reap some handsome rewards from their owners—by starting your own sharpening business.

Find manufacturers of sharpening equipment in the *Thomas Register of American Manufacturers,* at your library. They'll provide you with information on their products and give you hints on how to get started in this rewarding field.

For further information:

> *Home and Workshop Guide to Sharpening,* Harry Walton. New York, Harper & Row, 1967.

A FORTUNE IN FIREPLACES

In cold-weather areas the good old-fashioned fireplace will always be a hot sales item for the home, especially at remodeling time. Combined with the creating and selling of fancy fireplace accessories, a fireplace-installation service should bring in some heavy cash.

The best way to start is to work on contract for such outfits as Sears, Montgomery Ward, or even for several smaller firms. Naturally, you'll also want to try drumming up some of your own business by going door to door and by advertising in the newspaper.

For further information:

> *How to Plan and Build Fireplaces,* Editors,

Sunset magazine. Menlo Park, California, Lane, 1973.

> *How to Install a Fireplace,* Donald Bram. Briarcliff Manor, New York, Directions Simplified, 1974.

PAPER PROFITS

The average homeowner *might* paint the interior of his own home if needed, but not many would attempt hanging their own wallpaper. Doing a good, wrinkle-free job is more difficult than it looks, and this is where you come in.

To get started, call on homeowners, announcing your wallpaper-hanging talents and showing alluring color photographs of your past work. Building contractors and interior decorators are likewise good prospects.

For further information:

> *How to Do Your Own Painting and Wallpapering,* Jackson Hand. New York, Barnes & Noble (orders to Harper & Row), 1968.

> *Painting and Wallpapering,* Morton Schultz. New York, Arco, 1969.

UNLOCK YOUR DOOR TO SUCCESS

Locksmithing is not difficult to learn, yet the field is specialized and technical enough to justify fairly high fees for services performed.

To learn the basics, study up on your own, attend night classes, or enroll in a correspondence course. When you're ready to unlock your doors, leave notices at hardware stores, distribute leaflets to houses, and advertise in the Yellow Pages.

For further information:

> *Complete Course in Professional Locksmithing,* Robert Robinson, Chicago, Nelson-Hall, 1973.

> *All About Locks and Locksmithing,* Max Alth. New York, Hawthorn, 1972.

 **PUBLIC WOODWORKING SHOP**

If you have a fairly large area and some heavy woodworking equipment, why not pay for some of your equipment by opening your facilities to the public?

Advertise your shop in the newspaper classifieds. Another good bet would be to contact teachers of woodworking classes in your area, asking them to send their students to you.

Charge by the hour. In addition, you could make some extra profits by holding classes and by selling needed materials. But make sure you have adequate insurance to cover any unforeseen accidents.

 **ASSEMBLY SERVICE**

More and more products ordered from catalogues, as well as many items purchased at discount stores, come to the customer unassembled. A service based on assembling these products should prove to be a source of easy money. After all, assembling a bicycle or baby carriage according to instructions is a relatively simple task.

Assemble customers for yourself by spreading the word to catalogue stores such as Sears and Montgomery Ward, and to other large discount houses. These sources, along with newspaper ads, should get you all the business you can handle.

BUILT-IN FURNITURE

As with the creation of any custom-made product, the craftsman of built-in furniture can command handsome prices for his work.

Many homeowners would like to have such additions to their homes as built-in breakfast nooks, window seats, desks, shelves, and storage space. Get the ball rolling yourself by printing up some colorful brochures and taking them around personally to some of the higher-class homes in your area. If your work is good, your reputation will be your best salesman.

For further information:

How to Make Built-in Furniture, Mario Dal Fabbro. New York, McGraw-Hill, 1974.

Built-Ins for Home Improvement, James Waters. New York, Drake, 1970.

WEATHER STRIPPING

Installing weather stripping—strips of material laid around doors and windows to keep out rain and cold air—can be turned into a profitable enterprise if you're willing to get out and beat the bushes.

The best way to start would be simply to call on older homes in your area, offering your services. Also place classified ads in your newspaper and advertise in the Yellow Pages.

Buy your stripping from a wholesaler, whose name you can find in the Yellow Pages.

A FLOORING CONTRACTOR

The biggest market for this service is in an area enjoying widespread new construction.

As a flooring contractor you would hire out your carpet-, linoleum-, and tile-laying services to building contractors and owners of apartment houses, office buildings, and individual homes.

Either you or your customers would supply the material, or you might work on a commission basis with a local supplier.

KITCHEN REMODELING

If you're crazy about carpentry, a wonder with walls, and a crackerjack on cabinetry, you could make a lot of housewives happy by putting these talents to work remodeling their kitchens.

Get customers by going door to door or by doing work on contract for Sears, Montgomery Ward, or small home improvement outfits.

For further information:

Planning and Remodeling Kitchens.

Editors, *Sunset* magazine. Menlo Park, California, Lane, 1974.

Remodeling Your Kitchen or Bathroom, Walter Salm. New York, Arco, 1967.

FURNITURE REFINISHER

In this business you'll be called upon to do everything from removing a few scratches from a dining room table to completely restoring a valuable antique. Of course, the latter requires specialized knowledge that can only be gained with experience.

If you need some training enroll in a night course or refer to the books below. When you feel you've got it, hang out your shingle.

To get customers, make friends and neighbors aware of your services, and promote your enterprise as you would any other home business.

For further information:

How to Refinish Furniture, H. W. Kuhn. New York, International Publications, 1974.

Furniture Repair and Refinishing, Donald Meyers and Richard Demsky. Reston, Virginia, Reston (Orders to Prentice-Hall, Inc., Englewood Cliffs, New Jersey), 1974.

STEREO CABINETS

With today's preponderance of high fidelity and stereo equipment an excellent market exists for creating made-to-order cabinets for speakers, amplifiers, and other components.

The best way to get business is by arranging for local hi-fi dealers to refer interested customers to you. You'll have to compensate the dealers in some measure, but if you do good work you can easily pass this expense on to your customers.

TOOL STORAGE SHEDS

A Florida man has built up quite a successful business by manufacturing and selling small metal sheds for tool storage. Because of their ease of assembly and disassembly these sheds have found a ready market among owners of mobile homes. They're also sold through hardware and building supply firms.

Try creating and marketing similar products in your area. For variety, style your sheds after barns and outhouses.

BUILD SECRET COMPARTMENTS

Homeowners lose millions of dollars worth of valuables every year in burglaries. Why don't you help outfox these thieves?

If you can perform basic carpentry you can profitably specialize in creating secret compartments in the home for the storage of valuables. Inside a wall, inside a false bottom for a drawer, or inside a false fireplace log are just a few possible hiding places. The following book will give you many more:

How to Hide Almost Anything, David Kratz. New York, Morrow, 1975.

Instruction and Consultation

INFANT INSTRUCTION

If you've got one or more children past the diaper stage, you already know more than enough about infant care to teach it to others. To the uninitiated, diapering, feeding, even proper ways of holding the new baby can be a source of great mystery.

Offer to solve these perplexities by holding regular classes in infant care for expectant first-time mothers and fathers. Use a large doll for your demonstrations. You can also teach related subjects such as buying baby furniture, clothing and toys, and infant psychology.

Find your students through maternity shops and baby supply stores, and by advertising in the newspaper classifieds.

For further information:

Baby and Child Care, Benjamin Spock. New York, Pocket Books, 1968.

The Know-how of Infant Care, Sylvia Close. Baltimore, Maryland, Williams and Wilkins, 1972.

☀ FOR THE BRIDE-TO-BE

If you're a seasoned homemaker, chances are you're well-versed in such subjects as home economics, interior design, minor home repairs and maintenance, effective cleaning methods, and cooking. Why not put your domestic talents to additional good use and teach new brides and brides-to-be the secrets of your success?

You could hold classes right in your home one or two days each week. Get your students through bridal consultants and registries, and through classified ads in your local newspaper.

For further information:

Introductory Homemaking (text and teacher's manual), Aleene Cross. Philadelphia, J. B. Lippincott, 1970.

Home Management and House Care, E. E. Carpenter. New York, International Publications, 1968.

☀ HOUSE CONSULTANT

When faced with the task of buying a home many individuals, especially young people, do not know how to determine properly the condition of a house.

If you are knowledgeable about such things as electrical wiring, plumbing, insulation, roofing, and furnaces, as well as general construction, you might be able to merchandise this knowledge by advising prospective homeowners on the condition of the home they're thinking of buying.

To get started, place classified ads in the "Homes for sale" section of your local newspaper.

For further information:

How to Judge a House, A. M. Watkins. New York, Hawthorn, 1972.

☀ HISTORICAL HIGHLIGHTS

Secluded in dusty tomes in the history section of your local library lie interesting and colorful facts and legends surrounding the birth and growth of your town. With a little research you can come up with a show and tell course in local history that will be the talk of the town.

Advertise in the library and in local clubs. Let the town newspaper know what you're up to. Take your nostalgic listeners on walking tours of famous and infamous landmarks, and intersperse your facts and dates with colorful anecdotes on how things used to be in the old days.

You needn't limit your history homilies to your town. The procedure can be repeated endlessly in communities all around your area.

☀ BE A HEAT REDUCTION CONSULTANT

In the summertime many homeowners could avoid having excess heat in their homes by utilizing such simple measures as proper shading and ventilation, glass tinting, and improved insulation. Instead, many people suffer needlessly or invest in large, expensive air conditioners which in many cases still don't do an adequate job.

You can help these people by first studying up on the nature of heat and how best to reduce it, and then offering your services on a consultation basis, or working with suppliers of awnings, insulation, glass-tinting products, and air conditioners on a commission basis.

For further information:

How to Cool Your House, Editors, *Sunset* magazine. Menlo Park, California, Lane, 1961.

JOB-FOR-A-DAY

Many people have a hankering to try on someone else's shoes for a change. They may simply be curious, or they may be interested, from a more practical point of view, in entering a new occupation. That's where you—the career advance-glance arranger—come in.

You can give anyone the chance to be anything, including king or queen, for a day. Work out a deal with someone already so occupied to let your client tag along on a typical day as a one-day apprentice. Split the fee for this chance of a lifetime with the person who'll coach your client.

For business, contact the graduating classes of local high schools and colleges. A first hand advance-glance arranged by you can save these graduates miserable years of misplaced labor.

LANGUAGE LESSONS

If you speak a second tongue fluently why not turn this ability into dollars by setting up language classes—or even a small language school?

Feature a "crash," six-week course for those getting ready to travel, as well as normal-length classes. You might also tutor high school and college students who need additional help in learning a foreign language.

Check the possibility of teaching at Ys as well as holding classes in evening adult schools. Notify travel agencies, and otherwise promote your classes aggressively.

For further information:

> *How to Teach Foreign Languages Effectively,* Theodore Huebener. New York, New York University Press, 1965.

> *On Teaching Foreign Languages to Adults,* A. M. Lowe and J. Lowe. Elmsford, New York, Pergamon, 1965.

BRIDGE SCHOOL

No, this is not an educational institution located over a river! Naturally, we're talking about your holding instructional classes in the popular card game of bridge.

Start attracting students through bridge clubs and newspaper advertising. Teach classes at the local Y or at adult education classes. If you're proficient and well-liked, when these classes end you'll find students wanting to come to your home for lessons. Soon you'll be able to call yourself a "school."

For further information:

> *Master Bridge Teachers Manual,* Charles Michaels, Port Chester, New York, Barclay Bridge Supplies, 1974.

> *4-3-2-1 Bridge Student Text,* Charles Michaels and Ruth Cohen. Port Chester, New York, Barclay Bridge Supplies, 1969.

HOME MAINTENANCE SCHOOL

Many homeowners, especially young people, know next to nothing about repairing such simple things as clogged drains and broken wall switches. Since most homeowners aren't really in a position to support plumbers and electricians, many would rather learn to fix these things themselves.

If you're knowledgeable about fixing furnaces and repairing roofs, patching plaster and doctoring door hinges, servicing screens and mending mowers, you can teach these unhandy homeowners a thing or two!

Start by holding classes in your home, at the Y, or at an evening adult school. Garner students by distributing handbills throughout new suburban housing developments.

For further information:

> *Home Repair and Improvement,* Alfred DeCicco. New York, Drake, 1973.

> *Family Handyman Magazine's Home Emergencies and Repairs,* Editors, *Family Handyman* magazine, New York, Harper & Row, 1971.

> *How to Fix Almost Everything,* Stanley Schuler. New York, M. Evans, 1963.

TEACH SEWING

You won't become a millionairess by holding sewing classes, but by combining this with selling sewing books and patterns you can earn a comfortable income.

In order to avoid buying your own machines (each of your pupils will need one for class), see if you can make an arrangement with a local sewing machine shop whereby you'd hold your classes on their premises, using their equipment. They'll cooperate because in promoting your classes you will be providing them with valuable advertising and bringing potential customers into their shop.

For further information:

The Complete Book of Sewing, Constance Talbot and Isabelle Stevenson. New York, Crown, 1972.

Modern Sewing Techniques, Frances Mauck. New York, Macmillan, 1962.

USED CORRESPONDENCE COURSES

Thousands upon thousands of correspondence courses are sold in this country every year. Many of these valuable courses eventually end up collecting dust on somebody's shelf or in a used book store.

Make it your business to purchase as many of these courses as you can find, at a low price, by scouring used book stores and garage sales. When you've collected a large inventory advertise in national publications the fact that you buy and sell them.

9

A Fortune in Photography

A famous photographer once said that if you took him up in an airplane and dropped him over any city in the world—with only a parachute on his back and a camera over his shoulder—he'd be grinding out dollars for himself in no time.

Of all the ways for a person to earn his daily bread, the field of photography is perhaps the most flexible and varied.

But where to start in this vast wilderness of lenses and lights, filters and film? The best way may be to ask yourself what type of subject you'd like to work with: infants, adults, animals, plant life, scenery, commercial products, industrial plants. . . . Make this decision and you've won half the battle.

What about equipment? The equipment you use will depend on what phase of the business you've decided to enter. Most photographers feel that the 35 mm single-lens reflex camera is the most versatile. However, more critical work, such as shooting magazine covers or high-quality portraits, demands a large-format camera, such as a 4 by 5 or 8 by 10.

In "fast-buck" photography, such as taking snapshots at the beach or creating "instant postcards," a Polaroid camera may be the best choice. The customer's realization that he will receive immediate delivery of his print is an attractive incentive to buy. Here, however, your finished print costs will be double or triple the amount they would have been had you used a conventional camera. So when using a Polaroid, you'll have to either work on extremely high volume or pass these higher costs on to your customers.

There are many fine books explaining the pros and cons not only of various cameras but of related equipment as well. If you're in doubt, we suggest you consult these sources.

Before buying new equipment you'll probably want to consider purchasing some good used equipment. Shop for bargains in the newspaper classifieds, on bulletin boards of college media arts departments, and in pawnshops and photo supply stores. When it comes to more expensive gear, such as movie cameras, don't overlook the possibility of renting your equipment.

Color or Black and White? Again, this depends on your subject and purpose. You wouldn't attempt to sell a black and white photograph of a beautiful sunset as a magazine cover, nor would you offer to print up thousands of color postcards if you were trying to sell a small local merchant on the idea of an inexpensive postcard promotion.

Figure your costs for both and judge beforehand whether the market will bear the relatively higher costs of using color.

Processing and Printing—You or a Lab? If you'd rather spend all your working time shooting, and can still make a nice profit after paying a lab to process and print your work, by all means send your work out. Otherwise, set up your own darkroom.

Speculation or Prior Commitment? Many photographers will shoot pictures on speculation, or "spec," hoping that the finished product will be so attractive that the customer will want to buy it. Almost all photos sold to publications by free-lancers are sold on spec. In addition, in some cases shooting on spec may be the only way to work, as when a hot news item presents itself.

Generally, however, you should require a firm commitment before shooting anything that may involve a large expenditure of money or time. In such cases, get a deposit—50 percent of the selling price—or, better yet, ask for the total amount in advance. If a customer wants the pictures enough, he won't refuse.

Selling Your Work. Many entries in this chapter involve selling your work directly to the customer. Here, good salesmanship often takes precedence over photographic ability. Why, we once saw a photographer sell a woman a "portrait" of the top of her baby's head! The baby had been lying down facing the camera, and the photographer happened to snap the picture just as the toddler put his head down.

In selling photo-related items to or through retail outlets collect your money upon delivery, leaving your goods on consignment only as a last resort.

In quoting prices—like any artist—you'll ask what the market will bear.

Delivery. You can save yourself a lot of time on delivery of presold material by sending it out C.O.D., if there is a balance due. In such cases the customer usually pays both postage and C.O.D. charges. If the material has already been paid for in full, it should be sent postage prepaid.

Releases. A signed release must be obtained from the subject if the photo in which he or she appears is to be used for advertising or public relations, or if it is going to appear in a house organ or other sponsored publication. Parents must sign if the model is a minor.

Insurance, Licenses, Etc. Once you purchase valuable equipment protect yourself from loss with a good theft insurance policy. Also, if you deal directly with the public, you'd be wise to obtain liability insurance. If your home studio generates any significant customer traffic you'll be required to conform to existing zoning laws and to be licensed like any other commercial enterprise.

Further Reading. Artist's Market and *Writer's Market,* which can be found in libraries and bookstores, contain valuable information on such subjects as captioning and mailing, model releases and, most important, where to market your work.

The Eastman Kodak Company puts out an extensive array of publications for both amateurs and professionals. To get a list of their material, write them at Rochester, New York 14650, and ask for Index L-5.

You can pick up a lot of tips on photography, as well as discover new products and sources of supply, in any of the monthly professional or amateur photography magazines.

Two publications catering to the professional trade are: *The Professional Photographer,* 1090 Executive Way, Des Plaines, Illinois 60018, and *The Rangefinder,* 3511 Centinella Avenue, Los Angeles, California 90066.

At the newsstand you'll find copies of such publications as *Popular Photography* and *Modern Photography,* which will likewise give you valuable tips.

The following references will provide further information on the subject:

Visual Impact in Print, Gerald Hurley and Angus McGougall. Chicago, American Publishers Press, 1971. Contains visual examples of what editors require.

Audiovisual Market Place. New York, R. R. Bowker, (Published every two years). Lists producers and distributors of slides, filmstrips, kinescopes, motion pictures, phonograph records, cassettes, and videotapes.

Photographic Principles and Practices, Harry Asher. Englewood Cliffs, New Jersey, Prentice-Hall, 1974.

Professional Photography, Philip Gotlop. New York, Van Nostrand, 1974.

Photography: Materials and Methods, John Hedgecoe and Michael Langford. New York, Oxford University Press, 1971.

L. P. Clerc's Photography: Theory and Practice (6 vols.), D. A. Spencer, ed. New York, American Photographic Book Publishing, 1970.

Shoot People!

☀ EXECUTIVE PORTRAITS

Busy executives usually won't take time out to go to a studio for a portrait of themselves but will sit still for the few minutes it takes you to shoot them in their office.

Either call on these individuals directly or approach them through civic or fraternal organizations. Or you could pay others a commission to drum up business for you.

For further information:

Professional Portrait Techniques (0-4). Rochester, New York, Eastman Kodak, 1973.

Candid Photographic Portraiture, Kevin Aston. New York, American Photographic Book Publishing, 1965.

SLOW-MOTION SPORTS FLICKS

Many athletes could improve their performance by watching themselves in action by means of motion pictures in slow motion. Make arrangements in advance to get paid for filming the action.

Arm yourself with a super-8 movie camera and offer your services to coaches of such sports as baseball, football, basketball, track, and field. Other possibilities are golfers, bowlers, tennis players, and equestrians.

For further information:

The Complete Book of 8 mm (Super-8, Single-8, Standard-8) Movie Making, Jerry Yulsman. New York, Coward, McCann, 1972.

Independent Filmmaking, Lenny Lipton. San Francisco, Straight Arrow, 1972.

COSTUME PHOTOGRAPHER

Have available a number of costumes for your subjects to don. You might have a superman outfit for the men, a nineteenth-century gingham dress and bonnet for the ladies, pirate outfits for the kids.

Make arrangements to set up your studio in a large department store. Customers, upon purchasing a shirt or blouse, will get a free 8 by 10 of themselves in whatever costume they desire.

You'll get a few dollars from the department store for each picture taken. On a busy day you can shoot 50–100 pictures or more.

FOTO FUND RAISING

Contact organizations interested in fund raising, such as scout troups, civic and fraternal groups, and charities. Offer to help them put on a drive whereby people will come into their meeting place on a specified day for portraits at bargain prices in a small "studio" you'll have rigged up with camera, lights, and backdrop.

The customers will get a good deal on por-

traits, and the sponsoring organization will get all the cash taken in, except 10–25 percent, which goes into your pocket for your efforts.

For further information:

Practical Portrait Photography for Home and Studio, Charles Abel and Edwin Falk. New York, American Photographic Book Publishing, 1967.

Croy's The Photographic Portrait, O. R. Croy. New York, American Photographic Book Publishing, 1968.

COMPOSITES

These consist of four 4 by 5 pictures, in different poses, on an 8 by 10 sheet. Models and aspiring actors and actresses need them by the score for distribution to modeling, theatrical, and casting agencies.

Get your customers through the above agencies as well as through modeling and acting schools, local theater groups, and by advertising in trade magazines.

COMPANY YEARBOOK

Contact large corporations and sell them on the idea of buying several thousand "yearbooks" to give to their employees at Christmas.

It would be your responsibility to appear at the plant several times during the year, taking shots of employees at work, eating lunch, punching out. You'll also be on hand to shoot company picnics, softball games, and bowling leagues.

When you've got all your photos do the layout, arrange for printing, deliver the final product to the company, and collect your fee.

LEGAL PHOTOGRAPHER

Attorneys are called upon to handle a wide variety of cases, some of which—such as divorce and fraud cases—might necessitate obtaining photographic evidence.

Make your photographic services known to them through direct introduction, through mutual acquaintances, or through form letters.

Keep in mind, however, that once you're in business, many of your assignments will involve obtaining photos without the permission of the subjects, catching them in various compromising situations. If your moral code doesn't conflict with this type of activity, go to it!

PASSPORT AND I.D. PHOTOS

The big money in this enterprise lies in opening up your own small, quick-service, high-volume photo shop, preferably in a large city or town. It's best to be located near the federal office that issues the passports.

Of course, many such shops are well entrenched in these areas already. But, as in any business, if you can think up a new slant or gimmick to draw the customers in, you can get the lion's share of the business.

POST EXCHANGE PHOTOGRAPHER

Get permission from the officer in charge of the PX at a nearby military installation to set up a small photo studio in or near the PX.

Take pictures of the men and women of the military and have a mailing service to send the pictures to their friends or relatives anywhere in the world.

For further information:

Basic Principles of Business Management for the Small Photographic Studio. Rochester, New York, Eastman Kodak, 1971.

Portrait Manual, Edward Bomback. Dobbs Ferry, New York, Morgan and Morgan, 1967.

NIGHTCLUB PHOTOGRAPHER

Make an arrangement with a nightclub owner to station a beautiful female photog-

rapher in his club in the evenings, taking pictures of the patrons at their tables. Have her collect for the pictures at the time they're ordered.

The trick is to have rapid processing and printing facilities, either in the club's basement or in a trailer outside. Mount the prints in an inexpensive folder and have them back to the customers within an hour.

The owner will most likely demand a percentage of your gross, but if you can get into a good club, you can clean up.

BEACH PHOTOS

Go to a beach and offer to take Polaroid snapshots of the vacationers for a few dollars each. Better yet, bring a donkey (if the authorities don't stop you) and shoot your subjects while they're sitting on the beast.

If you don't make a lot of money you'll at least draw a crowd and have some fun in the bargain.

For further information:

How to Make Better Polaroid Instant Pictures: Complete Guide to Successful Use of the Polaroid Land Camera, Paul Giambarba. Garden City, New York, Doubleday, 1970.

Polaroid Photography, Kalton Lahue. Los Angeles, Petersen, 1974.

COMMUNITY YEARBOOK

During the year have your camera with you constantly, shooting people at their jobs, painting their houses, at parties—everywhere. You'll also shoot events such as parades, graduations, and the swearing-in of city officials. Toward the end of the year take all your material to a printer and have "community yearbooks" printed up.

Where's the profit? From the sale of full-page ads to local merchants as well as from the sale of the book itself throughout the community.

Special Events

☀ COMMENCEMENT DAZE

What picture is more salable to parents than that of their child receiving his or her diploma or degree at commencement exercises?

Station yourself in the center of the audience, toward the front. Using a long lens, take a close-up shot of each graduate as he receives his parchment. Usually the graduates appear in alphabetical order, as listed on the program, so your shooting sequence will match the program.

Get the addresses of the parents from school records, sending each a tiny print of their son or daughter as a sample. Offer packages of 8 by 10s for a certain price, with discounts for larger quantities.

For further information:

Tips for Good Pictures of Commencement Day (AC-34). Rochester, New York, Eastman Kodak, 1971.

☀ SHOOT WEDDINGS

Because of the sentimental value of wedding pictures, just about every wedding of any size has a photographer in attendance. Shoot everything from the bride's readying herself in her home to the joyful couple making their getaway.

It's a demanding job but a top photographer can consistently sell several hundred dollars' worth of prints from every wedding.

Get your leads through wedding chapels, bridal shops, caterers, jewelers, and anyone else who might possibly be connected with the wedding ceremony.

For further information:

Successful Wedding Photography, M. K. Arin. New York, American Photographic Book Publishing, 1967.

Candid Wedding Photography, Kenneth

Tydings. New York, American Photographic Book Publishing, 1959.

☀ SHOOT PARTIES

There are several ways to make contacts in this business. You can get your tips through the society pages, dropping by the host's home when a big affair is announced, introducing yourself, and asking for the job. Or you can work through friends, country clubs, civic, social, or fraternal organizations.

As a special attraction, offer your clients a certain number of prints in a handsome album.

For further information:

Wedding and Party Photography, Barney Stein and Les Kaplan. New York, American Photographic Book Publishing, 1968.

☀ SHOOT SHOWS

Take pictures of young performers and their groups at such events as plays, dance and music recitals, beauty contests, and high school baseball and football games.

Station yourself, with a long zoom lens, in the audience. Make sure to get flattering poses of both individual performers and the groups involved.

Print up your work and sell it to the parents of the children who participated.

☀ GRAND OPENINGS

To celebrate their start in business many new stores will stage a "grand opening," complete with clowns, giveaways, and musical entertainment. Be on hand with your camera to shoot the goings-on. After processing and printing, call on the owner and offer him color prints of the affair at a reasonable price.

Of course, if you can find out about grand openings in advance make your arrangements with the owners beforehand, thus assuring yourself a sale.

WEDDING MOVIES

Here's a new twist to the old wedding photography game. Set yourself up in business as a movie producer—of weddings! You'll need a super-8 movie camera, which you can either rent, or buy for under $200 used. You may also need lights, depending on the lighting conditions where you'll be shooting.

Get your business through bridal salons and caterers. Also advertise and check wedding announcements in your local paper.

You might offer sound movies for an extra fee. You can at some point expand your business to include Bar Mitzvahs, First Communions, christenings, and private parties.

For further information:

The Complete Book of 8 mm (Super-8, Single-8, Standard-8) Movie Making, Jerry Yulsman. New York, Coward, McCann, 1972.

How to Plan Your Super 8 mm Movies, C. V. Wilson. New York, American Photographic Book Publishing, 1973.

How to Make Good Sound Movies (AD-2). Rochester, New York, Eastman Kodak, 1973.

THE TRADE SHOW CIRCUIT

In any big city there are bound to be several big trade shows going on every month. The exhibitors go to great lengths to design their booths and display their equipment distinctively. If they had photos of these exhibits they could be put to good use for advertising and publicity purposes. So here you have a captive audience.

During the first day of each show visit all the booths, taking orders for pictures. Shoot them on the spot, then process and print them up, delivering the final prints before the show is over.

COVER FASHION SHOWS

There is a good market for quality photos taken at fashion shows. They can be sold to the manufacturers or designers, the sponsor of the show, fashion magazines, or local newspapers.

Query these organizations by letter on upcoming shows, proposing your project and stating your qualifications.

For further information:

Fashion Photography Techniques. A Belson. New York, Hastings House, 1970.

BARBER AND BEAUTY SCHOOL GRADUATES

The graduates of these schools are usually required by their state to supply one or more identification photos prior to receiving a license to practice.

Make arrangements with the owners of these schools to take pictures every time a class graduates. You will be performing a service for the school, the students and, of course, yourself.

Price your photos competitively with studios in your area.

PROM PHOTOS

A photographer who can beat the competition and get permission from high schools to shoot their proms has indeed found his El Dorado.

One of the authors once shot a prom for another photographer who had suddenly taken ill. Out of 370 couples in attendance, 340 of them posed for and purchased pictures—over 90 percent of them!

THE BANQUET CIRCUIT

Have the owners of restaurants with banquet facilities provide you with the names of people arranging upcoming banquets.

Then contact these individuals offering your services as photographer for the event.

Explain that there is no charge for the service—only for prints purchased. At the banquet take both group and individual shots, getting orders as you go. After printing, mail your orders out C.O.D.

You may have to cut the restaurant owner in for a percentage, but if you do your job well you should come out way ahead in the long run.

More Shooting

 PECULIAR PIX

Keep your eye peeled constantly for unusual, clever, weird, humorous, ironic, or other visual anomalies. Last Christmas, in a small town near us the exterior of the one-room police station was painted a bright red, with a painted yellow ribbon around it, making the small building resemble a giant Christmas package. A friend snapped it and sold the print to a law enforcement magazine for twenty-five dollars. One of the classics, however, has got to be the night shot of the neon sign of the Hotel Essex, whose four middle letters went out during a thunderstorm.

Sell your peculiar pix to magazines, newspapers, or newspaper syndicates. For markets, consult *Artist's Market, Writer's Market,* or *Editor and Publisher Syndicate Directory,* at your library or bookstore.

A DOCUMENTARY FILMMAKER

This enterprise isn't as difficult as it may sound. You can get by with a super-8 movie camera, which you should be able to pick up, used, for under $200.

You may talk local environmental groups into a conservation film. An elementary school may buy a film on safe bicycling. The possibilities are endless.

For information on potential markets for your films consult *Audiovisual Market Place,* available at your library or bookstore.

For further information:

Technique of Documentary Film Production, W. Hugh Baddeley. New York, Hastings House, 1973.

MAKE MONEY BY GIVING AWAY YOUR WORK

That's right! Offer to do a specific amount of free work, such as publicity photos and promotional shots, for local theater groups, orchestras, civic and fraternal organizations, conservation groups, and other community organizations. Your payoff will come when individual members of these groups start buying prints of themselves that you've so thoughtfully provided.

For best sales results these shots should show the members "in action," engaging in a particular activity.

For further information:

Kodak Job Sheet No. 2—Publicity Portraits (P-100-2). Rochester, New York, Eastman Kodak, 1971.

THE COVER GAME

It's doubtful you could earn a full-time living from selling cover photos to magazine editors, since the field is extremely competitive and editors are exceedingly selective. However, this sort of work pays handsomely, so it might be worth a try.

Two main requirements are that you match the cover with the image of the publication, and that you use a large-format film, preferably 4 by 5 or larger.

For potential consumer and trade publication markets consult *Writer's Market.* For information on the house-organ market refer to the *Gebbie House Magazine Directory.*

For further information:

Photography with Large-Format Cameras (0-18). Rochester, New York, Eastman Kodak, 1973.

ROVING INDUSTRIAL PHOTOGRAPHER

Most large industrial plants have their own photo department, complete with photographers and darkroom. Many medium and small-sized plants do not, yet they, too, have a continuing need for photographs.

Get started as a roving industrial photographer simply by contacting industrial plants and offering your services. To pave the way, perhaps you could take a picture of their front entrance and send it to them, along with an announcement that you'll be calling on them soon with your proposal.

For further information:

Industry in Focus, Michael Cahner. Boston, Cahners, 1974.

Commercial & Industrial Photography, D. Charles. New York, Halsted, 1958.

MERCHANT'S PHOTO QUIZ

Make a deal with a local merchant whereby you'll supply the local newspaper with a daily black and white print of some hard-to-recognize object around town, such as the hand of the statue in the city park or the ornate doorknob of the local art museum.

These pictures will run in the newspaper as a promotion for the merchant, along with an explanation that the first reader to show up at the merchant's store and properly identify the article in the picture will win five dollars' worth of merchandise.

Of course, the merchant will pay for the ad, as well as compensating you for each picture published.

PUBLICITY PHOTOG

Public relations firms are in constant need of photos to publicize their clients.

Compile a portfolio of your best work, taking it around to various firms. You may have to make several visits to each firm, but if your work is top-notch, your persistence should soon pay off in the form of some lucrative assignments.

For further information:

Kodak Job Sheet No. 2—Publicity Portraits (P100-2). Rochester, New York, Eastman Kodak, 1971.

PRODUCE PHOTO ESSAYS

Trade journals and newspapers, as well as general-interest magazines, are interested in photographic essays on timely topics.

Whether you photograph art shows for art magazines or zebras for zoo publications, you're sure to find a market if your work is good.

Query by letter first, however, tracking down potential markets in *Artist's Market* or *Writer's Market,* both of which may be found in your library or bookstore.

For further information:

Free Lance Magazine Photography, Lou Jacobs, Jr. New York, Hastings House, 1970.

The Photo Essay: How to Share Action and Ideas through Pictures, Paul Fusco and Will McBride. New York, Crowell, 1974.

A PRODUCT PHOTOGRAPHER

Contact shops specializing in such things as gift items, jewelry, furs, luggage, and antiques. Persuade the owners that pictures of their unique items in newspaper and magazine advertisements will have a sales impact they never thought possible. Take some pictures for them to try out in their advertising. Charge them a minimal amount.

If you can help stores move their merchandise in this manner, your photographic talents will soon be much in demand.

For further information:

Photographing Your Product for Advertising and Promotion: A Handbook for Designers and Craftsmen, Norbert Nelson. New York, Van Nostrand, 1971.

 PRODUCE BROCHURES

If you can combine photographic ability with a good sales pitch you should be able to do very well selling business firms, hotels, motels, chambers of commerce, and government agencies on the idea of having colorfully illustrated brochures made up as promotional items.

After getting the go-ahead from a firm take color shots of whatever your customer wants to appear in the brochure. You'll also have to help the customer write the copy. Then bring your transparencies and copy to a printer who specializes in brochures.

Of course, the price you quote your customer will cover the complete package. You'll make your money on the printing, which you'll get wholesale.

RARE COLLECTIONS AND VALUABLE POSSESSIONS

Look for individuals who have valuable collections of such items as coins, stamps, seashells, fine china, weapons, gems and jewelry, and antique furniture.

Offer to photograph these collections for their owners, thus providing an attractive and useful photographic record. Other prospects might be owners of racing cars, yachts, and airplanes.

In addition, photos of these unique items find a steady market in trade or consumer magazines.

INTERIOR DECORATOR'S PHOTOGRAPHER

Before and after pictures are a great sales tool for the interior decorator, who can use these in newspaper advertising, as well as show them to prospective customers.

Offer to work with the decorators on a per-picture or per-job basis. Of course, the pictures must be in color in order to fully bring out the decorator's abilities.

 HOT NEWS PHOTOS

If you and your camera happen to be on the scene when the first flying saucer lands on the White House lawn, or when a blizzard hits Miami Beach in July, you'll have a valuable commodity to sell to a national news syndicate.

Of course, happenings needn't be this spectacular for you to sell your news photos. Even a picture of a farmer with a head-sized grapefruit or a shot of a kitten on a large dog's back may be sold to your local paper.

You'll find a list of news syndicates in *Writer's Market* or the *Editor and Publisher Syndicate Directory.*

DISPLAY SUBSCRIPTION SERVICE

Contact department stores, as well as one-man shops, offering to photograph their in-store merchandise displays. Offer the larger stores a service whereby they'll receive ten or twelve photos of various displays every month for a set fee. The smaller stores, of course, will have fewer displays, so charge them less.

After a time, a sizable collection of these display photos becomes very valuable to the store owner. In addition to having a complete in-store photographic record for his own files, he can use these shots in his advertising and publicity.

DENTAL PHOTOGRAPHER

Many dentists and oral surgeons like to have photographic records of their more difficult and unique operations. The photos are used for later discussions with other specialists, as well as for self-instruction.

Start your dental photography service by contacting local dentists and oral surgeons directly, or by sending them informative printed matter on your service.

For further information:

Dental Photography, Philip Adams. Baltimore, Williams & Wilkins, 1968.

THE GREAT PICTURE GIVEAWAY

Offer a merchant in a suburban area a "package" consisting of 500 black and white 4 by 5s of individual houses in the area and 500 black and white picture postcards of the merchant's business. You'll shoot these pictures yourself. The printing can be done in your darkroom or by a professional lab.

On the reverse side of the postcard, which is sent to the homeowner, the merchant offers a free picture of the homeowner's house for just coming into the store. It's good advertising for the store owner and good money for you.

FAN PHOTOS

If you're clever, and live anywhere near a star-studded town like Hollywood, you can get needed photos of stars by wangling your way into parties, premieres, motion picture sets—even into their homes.

Movie and TV fan magazines buy these photos by the hundreds and will pay $25 and up for a black-and-white print. A color cover shot can bring up to $1,000. Check *Writer's Market* for outlets for your work.

A TV NEWS FREE-LANCER

This enterprise has big money-making potential for the alert motion picture cameraman. Like the newspaper "stringer" who writes up news stories and features for the local newspaper, you'll take 16 mm motion pictures of local news events and produce featurettes for local TV stations.

Naturally, before buying equipment or shooting any film you'll want to check with TV stations in your area. Find out if, indeed, they'll accept material from free-lancers and, if so, what subjects they'd be interested in.

For further information:

> *Television Newsfilm Techniques,* Vernon Stone and Bruce Hinson. New York, Hastings House, 1974.
>
> *Television News: Writing, Filming, Editing,*

> *Broadcasting,* Irving Fang. New York, Hastings House, 1972.

Novelties

CHRISTMAS CARDS

A few months before Christmas, print up and distribute a few thousand handbills advertising personalized Christmas cards. Offer to come to the home to take either a family portrait or a picture of the outside of the house itself. Both make excellent subjects for Christmas cards.

After getting a few estimates, have the cards printed up by a local printer. Then simply mount the photos on the cards and send them out to your customers.

For further information:

> *Ideas for Photo Greeting Cards (AC-18).* Rochester, New York, Eastman Kodak, 1972.

MUGS ON MUGS

Through the use of photo sensitizers you can print photographs on just about any item, coffee and beer mugs included.

Make up some samples of these mug mugs and leave them at coffee shops, beer joints, gift and photo shops, and department and variety stores. Either take the pictures yourself, or have the customers provide their own.

You might set up a stand in a tourist area, where you can use your own camera and mail the finished product to the customer. Or another possibility is that old standby, mail order.

Photo sensitizers can be purchased at photo supply stores, or ordered through: Rockland Colloid Corp., 599 River Road, Piermont, New York 10968.

PHOTO T-SHIRTS

Here we put photo sensitizers to work in applying photos to T-shirts. Through your own custom photo T-shirt business individuals can obtain T-shirts illustrated with likenesses of their favorite people—or enemies.

Open a small shop, preferably in a tourist area, or sell your services through photo stores, department stores, clothing stores, or at fairs, carnivals, and other celebrations.

☼ PHOTO DOLLS

Here is another possibility in the field of photo-application.

Buy yourself some inexpensive rag dolls with blank faces. These can be ordered, wholesale, from most large doll manufacturers. Then, through the use of a photo sensitizer, imprint on the face of the doll a photograph of a child's—or any other—face.

Make up some samples and display them at toy and children's shops, photo stores, department stores, and your local voodoo center.

For further information:

Photographic Sensitizer for Paper and Cloth (AJ-5). Rochester, New York, Eastman Kodak, 1972.

☼ CASH FROM CALENDARS

You've probably wondered, from time to time, where calendar printers get those pretty pictures for their calendars. The answer? From photographers who are willing to seek out and shoot exceptional outdoor scenes.

You'll need a large-format camera, 4 by 5 or larger. Submit your work directly to lithographic printers. Some of the larger ones are: Brown & Bigelow, 1286 University Avenue, St. Paul, Minnesota 55101. Kaeser & Blair, Inc., 593 Martin Place, Cincinnati, Ohio 54202. National Calendar Co., Inc., 617 Summer Avenue, West Lynn, Massachusetts 01905. Von Hoffman Press, Inc., 1002 Camera Avenue, St. Louis, Missouri 63126.

For further information:

Photography with Large-Format Cameras (0-18). Rochester, New York, Eastman Kodak, 1973.

☼ PHOTO STAMPS

Photo stamps are just what they sound like. Postage stamp-sized photos, complete with perforations on the sides and gum on the back.

Start a fad in your town by taking some samples around to junior high and high schools. Kids love 'em and, you should be swamped with orders. Also display your samples at photo supply stores. This item is also an excellent candidate for mail order.

You can print up the photo stamps yourself or they can be ordered through: Photo Stamp Co., 173 North Ninth Street, Brooklyn, New York 11211.

☼ PRODUCE COLOR POSTCARDS

Merchants, suppliers, and manufacturers can greatly benefit from postcard mail-out advertising. Hotels, motels, and resorts will want their picture featured so they can sell or give away the cards to their guests. Naturally, tourist and gift shops, variety and drugstores are always in the market for scenic postcards.

As photographer you'll take the shots yourself. Then either you can do the printing up of the negatives on postcard stock or you can have a postcard manufacturer do it. Some companies are listed below.

Kolor View Press, 11854 W. Olympic Boulevard, Los Angeles, California 90064.

Lithochrome Press, 5364 Venice Boulevard, Los Angeles, California 90019.

Tichnor Bros., 185 Amory Street, Jamaica Plains, Massachusetts 02130.

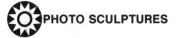

PHOTO SCULPTURES

This enterprise involves taking pictures of children and blowing them up to a foot high or more. The print is then glued onto a piece of plywood, which is cut along the outline of the figure in the photograph, using a coping saw or jigsaw. A brace is attached to the rear, and presto! You have a standing replica of a child.

Display these items in department stores, children's apparel shops, toy shops, and photo stores.

For further information:

Photo-Posterization (E-93). Rochester, New York, Eastman Kodak, 1973.

CHEESECAKE CALENDARS

Take some alluring color shots of nude or seminude models and commission a lithographer to imprint them on poster-sized calendar stock.

You can make up batches for individual companies on order, arranging with the lithographer to imprint the firm's name on the calendar, in addition to the photograph. These companies will then distribute the calendars as gifts to their clients for advertising purposes.

Or you can simply sell the photo calendars to individual service stations, garages, machine shops, trucking companies, and so on.

For further information:

Nude Photography, Karin Malin. Cranbury, New Jersey, A. S. Barnes, 1972.

How I Photograph Nudes, Bunny Yeager. New York, American Photographic Book Publishing, 1963.

PHOTO BUTTONS

Photo buttons, or badges, consist of a photograph pressed onto a disc which has a pin in the back for attaching to clothing. Thus the wearer can proudly display a photo of grandchildren, boyfriend, or girl friend.

They are successfully sold as novelty items at fairs and carnivals, and are in demand at conventions and in manufacturing plants as employee identification badges.

You'll need a Polaroid camera and a small button press. You'll find advertisements for these presses in the back of photography magazines.

Two large manufacturers are N. G. Slater Corporation, 220 West Nineteenth Street, New York 10011, and Badge-a-Minit, Box 618, LaSalle, Illinois 61301.

For further information:

How to Make Better Polaroid Instant Pictures: Complete Guide to Successful Use of the Polaroid Land Camera, Paul Giambarba. Garden City, New, York, Doubleday, 1970.

Polaroid Photography, Kalton Lahue. Los Angeles, Petersen, 1974.

PHOTO BOOKENDS

Create bookends, each set adorned with any photographic subject your customers desire.

Fashion your bookends distinctively in wood, plastic, ceramic, metal, or any other suitable material. Take the photos yourself and simply glue them neatly onto the finished bookends.

Attract customers by displaying samples of your work in gift shops, bookstores, libraries, children's shops, photo shops, and department and variety stores.

CUSTOM CALENDARS

Offer your customers calendars mounted with a photo of any subject they choose.

Order a large quantity of blank (without advertising) calendars from a printer or calendar manufacturer. Then make samples of your work and display them in gift and photo shops, stationery and variety stores.

You can either have the customers supply their own photos, or shoot them yourself.

PHOTO PLAQUES

These are photographs mounted on a plaque of plywood, oak, maple, or other wood. The plaque is then trimmed into an attractive shape with a jigsaw or coping saw, coated with varnish or lacquer, and used as a wall ornament.

Prospects for these decorative items are everywhere. Make up some samples and get your orders through photo stores and art shops.

You can either cut and carve the bare plaques yourself, or order them from: Creative Plaques, Box 131, Issaquah, Washington 98027.

PHOTO MATCHBOOKS

Matchbooks personalized with a photograph are useful to provide at parties and to give as gifts.

Make up some attractive samples and leave them with gift shops, photo stores, and department stores. When you get an order either take the picture yourself or copy an existing one onto the matchbooks.

Order your matchbooks from match manufacturers listed in the Yellow Pages.

INSTANT POSTCARDS

Stationing yourself near a well-known landmark anywhere in the world, advertise personal picture postcards for your customers to send to the folks back home.

After snapping your Polaroid shots, simply affix the print to blank postcard stock by means of fast-drying glue. Buy your postcard stock wholesale from a large paper supply house.

For further information:

How to Make Better Polaroid Instant Pictures: Complete Guide to Successful Use of the

Polaroid Land Camera, Paul Giambarba. Garden City, New York, Doubleday, 1970.

Polaroid Photography, Kalton Lahue. Los Angeles, Petersen, 1974.

PHOTO STATIONERY

What family wouldn't enjoy writing letters (especially to the grandparents) on stationery imprinted with a portrait of the family on top?

Solicit business by leaving samples with gift shops, stationery, and department stores. When you get an order, go out and photograph the family. Then make arrangements with a lithographer to do the printing. Naturally, you'll have to pay the store a commission, but can you think of an easier way to get business?

Services 'N' Such

BLOW THEM UP!

People are always fascinated by poster-sized photographs of themselves and their friends. Offer this service in tourist areas, at fairs, carnivals, shopping centers, or in downtown business districts. Blow up, on the spot, either the customer's own photo or one you've taken yourself.

You'll need some fairly expensive enlarging equipment. If you're lucky, you'll be able to pick it up from someone who's going out of the business. Be sure to find a good location and promote your service heavily.

Poster-sized photos also sell well through mail order.

For further information:

Photo-Posterization (E-93). Rochester, New York, Eastman Kodak, 1973.

PHOTO DUPLICATION SERVICE

Many people have photographs of sentimental value which they would like to get copied in order to send them to relatives, or just to have for safekeeping.

It's relatively easy to "take pictures of pictures." The item to be copied is secured to a stand, the camera is placed on a tripod, and the lights are positioned correctly. Special copy film must be used, and there are a few additional technical points that can be picked up by referring to any good book on the subject.

Advertise your service in the newspaper, Yellow Pages, and in photo supply stores.

For further information:

Copying (M-1). Rochester, New York, Eastman Kodak, 1971.

Restoration and Photographic Copying, Alexander Shafran. New York, American Photographic Book Publishing, 1967.

SLIDE DUPLICATION SERVICE

You can provide this service simply by using a slide copier, which can be purchased for about $25, from any camera store. The copier will fit on the front of any 35 mm camera.

Advertise in the local newspaper, in photography magazines, and in photo supply stores.

For further information:

Making Slide Duplicates, Titles, and Filmstrips, Norman Rothschild. New York, American Photographic Book Publishing, 1973.

The Fourth Here's How (AE-85). Rochester, New York, Eastman Kodak, 1973, pp. 26–36.

BE A PHOTOMURALIST

Photographic murals can be sold just about anywhere, including private homes, businesses, hospitals, museums, libraries and government buildings.

The murals are usually composed of several sections on panels which are printed up,

then mounted on a wall or large piece of plywood so that each section joins to form the overall picture.

For further information:

Making and Mounting Big Black-and-White Enlargements and Photomurals (G-12). Rochester, New York, Eastman Kodak, 1973.

CAMERA EXCHANGE

Here you'll be buying, selling, and trading everything in used cameras from twenty-dollar Instamatics to fancy motor-driven reflex jobs worth thousands.

Watch the want ads and shop at photo stores and pawnships for bargains. When you've built up a small collection run classified ads in the local paper, advertising the fact that you'll buy high and sell low. Take a commission when you arrange for two customers to trade equipment with each other.

START A PHOTO CENTER

Some of our larger cities, through their parks and recreation departments, provide complete darkroom facilities—including enlargers—for their photographically inclined citizens.

Unfortunately, most cities and towns have no such program. Why not start a photo center in your town? Have several small rooms fitted out with enlarger, running water, trays. Charge an hourly fee, with each user supplying his own chemicals and paper, which you can have for sale.

For further information:

How to Start a Photo Center (AT-104). Rochester, New York, Eastman Kodak, 1971.

Photolab Design (K-13). Rochester, New York, Eastman Kodak, 1968.

OPERATE A RETOUCHING SERVICE

Many times a portrait negative will show perfect framing, composition, and posing, only to have a stray hair sticking out from the subject's head, or an objectionable mole or unflattering wrinkle on the subject's face. It's the retoucher's job to remove these imperfections by using retouching fluids, dyes, and assorted small tools.

Consult any of the books listed below and offer local photographers and photo studios your services.

For further information:

Modern Retouching Manual, Kitty West. New York, American Photographic Book Publishing, 1973.

Guide to Retouching Negatives & Prints, Kitty West. New York, American Photographic Book Publishing, 1972.

PHOTOS INTO BOOKS

This enterprise involves searching for rare old photos of such subjects as the Civil War, old-time movie stars and political figures, early American culture, and other hard-to-find treasures. These can be found in secondhand stores, junk shops, attics, through newspaper ads or at garage sales and flea markets.

A good-sized collection is sure to be of interest to a publisher dealing in such subjects. If you can't find enough photos for a book, individual prints can be sold to private collectors, photo agencies, or museums.

FILMSTRIPS

A filmstrip may be thought of as a series of connected transparencies, arranged in sequence so as to tell a story or demonstrate a process. These can be either silent or with sound.

The filmstrip market is only as limited as your imagination. A strip on upholstering may be sold to a school and shown to a group of students interested in the subject. An insurance agency might want to purchase a strip which would present the facts about their company to prospective salesmen.

Study the books below and then make up a short sample strip. Potential markets can be found in *Audiovisual Market Place*, available at your library or bookstore.

For further information:

Making Slide Duplicates, Titles, and Filmstrips, Norman Rothschild. New York, American Photographic Book Publishing, 1973.

The Filmstrip Collection: Complete Instructions on How to Process and Organize, Dale Shaffer. Salem, Ohio, Dale E. Shaffer, 1972.

Producing Slides and Filmstrips (S-8). Rochester, New York, Eastman Kodak, 1970.

SELL TO PHOTO AGENCIES

Photo agencies sell hundreds of thousands of prints to publishers, manufacturers, and advertising agencies every year. Therefore, these firms constantly need to replenish their stock.

You can profit by supplying photos to these firms. A comprehensive list of them can be found in *Artist's Market*.

OPEN A PHOTO AGENCY

If you have a substantial number of black and white photos or color transparencies start your own photo agency.

First decide what subjects you want to specialize in, then send out form letters to consumer magazines, trade journals, house organs, advertising agencies, and manufacturers who might be interested.

Find names of publications in *Artist's Market* and *Writer's Market*. Names of advertising agencies can be found in the *Standard Advertising Register*. The *Thomas Register of American Manufacturers* will provide you with names of manufacturers. You'll find these publications in any well-stocked library.

A VERY NEGATIVE SERVICE

Many amateur as well as professional photographers like to work with good negatives, printing them up in their own way and in any quantity they desire. If you have acquired a collection of high-quality negatives, duplicate them and sell copies to photo agencies, as well as by mail to private individuals.

Query photo agencies, a list of which can be found in *Artist's Market*. Also place ads in any of the popular photography magazines.

For further information:

Now Make Duplicate Negatives as Readily as You Make Prints (P3-590). Rochester, New York, Eastman Kodak, 1972.

REPAIR CAMERAS

If a camera needs repair in our town of 100,000 persons the camera owner is in trouble, as there isn't a camera repairman within 100 miles. No doubt there are many towns like this across the country that would be virgin territory for a competent camera repairman.

Get yourself some ' night school or correspondence-course training, then notify local camera shops of your service. Put a few ads in the newspaper classifieds, too. That way you'll have direct customers as well.

MAKE OFFSET NEGATIVES AND PLATES

Before a form is printed on an offset printing press, a "master" is made up which must first be photographed, and a negative obtained. This negative is then exposed to a sensitized metal plate which is inserted in the press. Thousands of copies can then be printed by coming in contact with this plate.

With thousands of offset presses in operation throughout the country, then, millions of these negatives and plates are required for the printing process.

Get into this active field by referring to the books listed below. Then offer your service to industrial firms, schools, stores, state and local government offices, banks—any organization that does its own offset printing.

For further information:

Basic Photography for the Graphic Arts (Q-1). Rochester, New York, Eastman Kodak, 1972.

Graphic Arts Procedures: Offset Processes —Strike on & Film Composition. Chicago, American Technical Society, 1967.

Guidelines for Better Platemaking (Q-213). Rochester, New York, Eastman Kodak, 1973.

A MICROFILMING SERVICE

This highly lucrative, largely overlooked field involves microfilming records for governmental agencies, libraries, banks, insurance companies, or any other large organization where record-keeping is a major task.

You'll need a special camera for this—a microfilm camera—which can be ordered through any large photo supply house or directly from Regiscope Corporation of America, 7 East Forty-third Street, New York 10017.

For further information:

Microfilm Techniques (P-4-3). Rochester, New York, Eastman Kodak, 1973.

RESTORE OLD PHOTOS

Many people have old spotted, stained and partly torn pictures of great-grandmother or great-grandfather that they would love to see in good condition again. These damaged prints can often be restored to almost perfect condition.

Study up by consulting any good book on the subject, one of which is listed below. Then contact photo stores and photographers and place ads in the paper and Yellow Pages. Photo restoration has also done well in mail order.

For further information:

Restoration and Photographic Copying, Alexander Shafran. New York, American Photographic Book Publishing, 1967.

 **CUSTOM PHOTO LAB**

A large market may exist in your area for a high-quality custom processing and printing lab. If you're a novice in the field, practice in your darkroom till you get perfect results.

To get business contact local photographers directly and spread the word through camera stores and photo supply houses.

For further information:

Photographic Lab Handbook, John Carroll, ed. Englewood Cliffs, New Jersey, Prentice-Hall, 1974.

The Home Darkroom, Mark Fineman. New York, American Photographic Book Publishing, 1973.

 **TITLING SERVICE**

Thousands of individuals and organizations put on slide presentations every year on subjects covering everything from ants to the zodiac. Although furnishing the slides is up to them, creating slide titles requires a more specialized talent.

You can provide professional-quality titled slides by using a titling device. Ads for these can be found in any filmmaking magazine.

Promote your titling service through ads in national photography magazines.

For further information:

Making Slide Duplicates, Titles, and Filmstrips, Norman Rothschild, New York, American Photographic Book Publishing, 1973.

Easy Ways to Make Still and Movie Titles (AC-60). Rochester, New York, Eastman Kodak, 1972.

 **TEACH PHOTOGRAPHY**

If you're a cyclone on cameras, a fireball on films, and dynamite in the darkroom, you just might set your sights on teaching the trade as a career.

A good way to start is to give a photo course several nights a week at your local Y or evening adult school. Invariably, trade schools have courses in the subject, for which they must hire full-time instructors.

If you're ambitious you'll eventually want to start your own school, hiring your own instructors and charging fancy tuitions.

For further information:

Designing a Photo Course (AT-56). Rochester, New York, Eastman Kodak, 1971.

Outline for Teaching a Course in Basic Photography (AT-105). Rochester, New York, Eastman Kodak, 1973.

Outline for Teaching a Course in Basic Darkroom Technique (AT-107). Rochester, New York, Eastman Kodak, 1973.

Outline for Teaching a Course in Advanced Photography (AT-108). Rochester, New York, Eastman Kodak, 1973.

CAMERA RENTAL

Buy yourself a number of inexpensive used cameras and some film and station yourself outside an amusement park or similar operation to rent out the cameras and sell the film, which you can buy wholesale.

For security, be sure to get identification and a small deposit from each customer.

GOLD FROM SILVER

An important operation in the photographic process is the use of the fixing bath—a solution which removes excess silver salts from the negative or print. The silver can be recovered from these solutions and sold to smelters and refiners.

Make arrangements with photography studios, commercial photo labs, graphic arts firms, and x-ray labs for them to let you haul away their used photographic materials on a periodic basis.

For further information:

Recovering Silver from Photographic Materials, J-10. Rochester, New York, Eastman Kodak, 1972.

PHOTO OILS

For about forty dollars you can have a studio create a 16 by 20 portrait in oil from any existing photograph or negative. If the work is of high quality the final product is almost indistinguishable from an actual oil painting.

Work either from photos you take yourself or from those given to you by your customers, and sell your photo oils for a minimum of $150 each.

Get business by leaving samples with photo stores and studios, art galleries, and department stores, giving them a commission on each customer they send you.

The following firms make oils from photos. They'll sell you samples, send you price lists, and give you help in getting started. Portrait Arts, 1807 West Magnolia Boulevard, Burbank, California 91506, and Carlan Photo Service, 35 Mill Road, Irvington, New Jersey 07111.

10

Travel- and Get Paid for It!

Ahh, travel! If your heart beats a little faster when you hear the whistle of a train or when you see the billowing sails of a seagoing yacht as its hull slices resolutely through the briny blue, then come along with us through this chapter and learn some of the ways in which you can earn a living by traveling.

The following entries are only a few of the thousands of ways in which people make their living while on the move or in a land foreign to them. Why don't you hear much about these activities? Because the people doing them are having too much fun to sit down and write a book about them!

If you're young at heart, and won't regret it later, it might just be a good idea for you to take a stroll down to the yacht marina, check the local train schedules, or call an airline for reservations.

Sailboats and Popcorn Wagons

SAIL AROUND THE WORLD—FOR A SALARY!

Impossible, you say? Not at all. Thousands of private yacht owners around the world are continually in need of crew to perform shipboard duties in exchange for a berth, meals and, in many cases, a steady paycheck.

There are several ways to get started here regardless of your sex, and even if you've had no experience. (Anyone can swab a deck or man a helm.) The most direct way would be to get yourself into an area where charter yachts abound: the West Indian islands of Antigua and Grenada in the winter; Nice in the Mediterranean during the summer months; Honolulu, the Virgin Islands, and Panama are other possibilities.

Check, and take out, classified ads in yachting publications such as *Yachting* and *Rudder Magazine,* both found on newsstands.

Another way would be to go to work for a yacht delivery service. Find these in the Yel-low Pages of large coastal cities. Also contact the Sail Crew Clearing House, P. O. Box 1976, Orlando, Florida 33102. Their business is putting available crewmen in touch with yacht owners, and vice versa. Happy sailing!

TRAVELING POPCORN WAGON

Find an old panel truck or minibus. Paint it in bright colors, fix it up to accommodate a popcorn machine and small serving window, and you're in business.

Travel to festivals, fairs, carnivals, rodeos, and the like. For profitable sidelines add peanuts, soda pop, candy, souvenirs, and whatever else sells.

TRAVELING WRITER OR WRITING TRAVELER?

It really makes no difference—except to the Internal Revenue Service, which will allow you to deduct all, or a portion, of your traveling expenses if you can show that writing is indeed your business.

Publications like *Holiday* and *Travel* are excellent markets for your contributions from afar. The more unique your subject, of course, the better chance your article has of getting accepted. Naturally, some good photos or color transparencies will likewise make your material more salable. Query first.

MARINE ELECTRONICS

Would you like to travel to the South Pacific, the Riviera, or the Costa del Sol and be able to work at your leisure, sunning and swimming on your many off hours?

In yacht harbors around the world, competent technicians are in constant demand by yacht owners needing repair work on marine radios, navigation equipment, and ships' wiring. If you're already skilled in electronics, why not add shipboard electronics to your bag of technical tricks? Then simply take off for any foreign port.

For further information:

Modern Marine Electricity and Electronics, P. D. Smith. Cambridge, Maryland, Cornell Maritime Press, 1966.

START AN ART COLONY

Famous art colonies like San Miguel de Allende in Mexico, Torremolinos in Spain, and Positano in Italy were once ordinary, run-of-the-mill peasant villages. Through word of mouth, as well as through some promotional activity, of course, these villages achieved the recognition they now possess.

If you're an artist and desire to get away from it all, convince your artist friends to join you in starting your own colony. Find a picturesque spot in a foreign country. Word will spread, tourists will appear with money, and your colony will soon be self-supporting.

TRAVELING PAINTER

Thousands of hotels, motels, and resort cabins across the United States could attract hordes of additional ocucpants if their exteriors were brightened by distinctive painting. Painted flowers, animals, polka dots, strips, geometric shapes—anything that complements the architecture and owner's desires.

You could work your way around the country—or around the world—doing this, and probably even have some nice change in your pocket when you get back home!

TOURIST HOUSES

If you have some capital, this is one way you can live in a foreign country and make money without working.

Because of low wage scales, the cost of building a new home or buying an older one in a foreign country is usually a fraction of the amount it would cost in this country. Find a tourist area in a country such as Mexico or Portugal and build or buy some houses there, renting them out to tourists—at U. S. prices.

The secret is to find an area that is just starting to attract tourists, thus allowing you to get in on the ground floor.

MOBILE GIFT SHOP

Want to escape from smog, traffic jams, and the soaring crime rate? Load up a small van with attractive gift items and head for the hills!

Plan your itinerary in advance, making up a small poster for each town. On it mention the date you'll be in town and list a few of the more catchy things you'll be selling. Mail the poster care of the general store in that town, with a request that the proprietor tack it up for the locals to see.

Residents of these out-of-the-way places haven't the shopping facilities normally found in larger communities. Therefore, if your selection is good and your prices right, you should be able to make a comfortable living and escape from the cares of the city at the same time.

MARINE ENGINE REPAIRMAN

If you're competent in the repair and maintenance of diesel and gasoline engines, why not sign on board a cruising yacht?

You can advertise your services in, and perhaps find work through "Help wanted" ads in any of the yachting magazines. Or you can just take off for a distant yacht harbor looking for work.

Four especially good centers of yachting activity are Antigua and Grenada in the West Indies, the Riviera, and Honolulu.

For further information:

Marine Engines and Boating Mechanics, Dermot Wright. North Pomfret, Vermont, David & Charles, 1974.

TEACH ENGLISH

With more of the world turning to English as a second language, it's not surprising that there is a heavy demand for English teachers in many foreign countries.

Anybody can teach English to foreigners, even without knowing their language. In fact, many experts claim that students learn faster if the teacher is not versed in the native tongue of the students.

Of course, no one can guarantee in advance that you'll find a job. The best thing is just to go. You won't make a fortune, but you will be able to get by on what you're paid.

For further information:

Teaching English as a (Second) Language, Robert Politzer and Freida Politzer. Lexington, Massachusetts, Xerox College Publishing, 1972.

Teaching English to Foreigners, Guy Wilson. New York, International Publications, 1971.

 IMPORT/EXPORT

There are literally thousands of items regularly being sold in other countries which, because of their uniqueness, could be successfully marketed in the United States. Likewise, many domestic products would sell well abroad.

Before starting your search for potentially profitable items, become thoroughly familiar with markets and sources of supply, as well as with the customs regulations of the various countries you'll be dealing with.

 TRAVEL COLUMN

If you're conversant with such subjects as tooling around Tokyo or busing through Belgium, put your expertise to use by writing a daily travel column for newspapers. Either write the entire column yourself or have readers ask questions for which you would provide answers.

Write up some sample columns and send copies to newspaper editors in your area—or across the country. Find their names in the *Editor & Publisher Yearbook,* at your library.

 A SIGN OF SUCCESS

There are thousands of small communities across the United States without any sort of sign welcoming travelers to their town. Visit the chambers of commerce of these towns offering to build roadside signs at each end of town, with "Welcome to . . ." painted on each one.

Offer to do the work for the cost of materials plus ten or twenty dollars per sign for labor. As a sample of your work show photos of signs you've done in other towns.

For further information:

Sign Painting Course, A Complete Self-Instruction Course For Home Study. E. C. Matthews. Chicago, Nelson-Hall, 1960.

Sign Painting: The New Way, Steve Prohaska. Cincinnati, Signs of the Times, 1964.

FREE TRAVEL

Many travel agencies will provide free passage for you if you can sign up a certain amount of people for a particular tour. Sometimes you may be required to actually lead the tour, sometimes not.

Better yet, work independently, chartering a plane or making your own deal with a steamship company for a "package rate." Put your own tour together, not only including yourself in on your trips but making a profit at it!

YACHT CHARTER

If you have, or can buy, a large sailing yacht or motor cruiser, you can make money with it in many areas of the world.

Staying aboard as captain, you can charter out your craft to business organizations, providing executives with company-sponsored vacations. Or you can take on crews of vacationers who will pay you for the privilege of working or relaxing aboard your boat.

To get business, work with charter associations that exist in such areas as the South Pacific, the West Indies, or the Riviera. Also advertise in national magazines.

MAP MONEY

Travel from town to town making money by drawing and printing up rough street maps of each town. Finance your printing costs—and your profit—by selling advertising around the edges of the maps to merchants, each of whom will receive a generous supply of the maps to give out to their customers.

A FAIR INCOME

By running a game booth at carnivals and fairs it's possible to make a year's income in six months—and travel at the same time! All you need do is devise some new, unique, and entertaining game with which to lure customers. Keep it simple and make your prizes attractive.

Get names and addresses of carnival and state and county fair headquarters from the chambers of commerce of states in which you're interested. Then write them for information.

BE A TRAVEL AGENT

Unfortunately, you can't become a travel agent overnight. You'll need two years' experience in the field before airlines will consider appointing you as an agent. Experience can consist of working for an authorized agent or as a ticket clerk for one of the airlines.

In addition to on-the-job training, you can take a correspondence course through the American Society of Travel Agents, 360 Lexington Avenue, New York 10017. Also, you'll want to consult trade publications such as *ASTA Travel News,* 488 Madison Avenue, New York 10022 and *The Travel Agent,* 2 West Forty-sixth Street, New York 10036.

Your Camera as Your Passport

For tips on equipment, film, selling your work, and related reading matter refer back to the introduction to Chapter 9, "A Fortune in Photography."

? ? ?

We don't quite know what to call this one, so you can place your own label on it.

Here's the way it works.

Station yourself in any foreign country in the world. Aside from your camera and film, be sure to take along a copy of *Editor & Publisher Yearbook,* (get it by writing 850 Third Avenue, New York 10022), which lists the names and addresses of all the newspapers in the United States.

From hotels obtain the names of tourists and their hometowns. Call these people and tell them you'd like to take a picture of them for their hometown newspaper—at no charge.

Meet them in front of a famous landmark, snap their picture, and get a little information on their itinerary. After you collect a number of these, process your film and send the negatives, along with a small caption with each, to the respective hometown newspapers, asking them to forward their standard payment for such photos.

Most newspapers will send a check for the negative they receive, considering the subject "newsworthy." Oh, yes . . . Why will hotels release the names of their guests? You'll promise to mention the hotel's name in each caption, thus giving them valuable publicity.

TRAVELING CAMERA

Believe it or not, it's possible for a photographer to travel anywhere in the world and get paid for it!

First decide where you want to go. Let's assume you'd like to travel to the Arctic. Contact manufacturers of whatever you'll need for your trip: winter clothing, including a parka and woolen underwear; perhaps a tent, snowshoes, sleeping bag, provisions, a portable stove—and, of course, a good camera.

Offer to supply the manufacturers with pictures of their products surviving the Arctic winter, which they can use in their advertising. If you convince them you're a professional you stand a good chance not only of obtaining this valuable merchandise but of having your trip expenses paid to boot!

 ROLLING PORTRAIT STUDIO

Build a complete photo studio in a trailer or mobile home. Aside from a camera, you'll need lights, props, backgrounds and a darkroom.

Get permission to take pictures at shopping centers, fairs, carnivals—anywhere people, especially children, congregate. Advertise a package deal in the local newspaper a day or so in advance, maybe giving an 8 by 10, two 5 by 7s, and six wallet sizes for $9.95.

Process and print your work in the trailer and let your customers pick up the finished prints a few days later.

For further information:

Studio, Time-Life Books Editors. Dobbs Ferry, New York, Morgan & Morgan, 1971.

Photolab Design (K-13). Rochester, New York, Eastman Kodak, 1968.

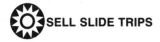 SELL SLIDE TRIPS

If you do a bit of traveling and can accumulate a series of slides of interesting places, you might have the basis for a slide-production business.

Package your slides in series of twenty-five or so. You can charge eight to ten dollars per package. Your catalogue might include such subjects as interesting cities, Disneyland, flowers of North America, Indians, famous racehorses—you name it.

These are best sold by mail to individuals through ads in whatever publication relates to the subject of your series, or to commercial slide-supply houses. Commercial markets can be found in *Artist's Market* and *Audiovisual Market Place,* available at your library or bookstore.

TOURIST PHOTOGRAPHER

This idea works best if you live in the vicinity of a famous landmark such as the cable cars of San Francisco or the leaning tower of Pisa.

Using a Polaroid enables you to give immediate delivery on your work. Otherwise, you'll have to mail the photos later.

Make up a simple sign saying "Souvenir San Francisco photo of yourself . . . only $1.50," or some other such message. Be aggressive: stopping people, flailing your arms, and generally making yourself obnoxious are all part of this tourist photo business.

For further information:

How to Make Better Polaroid Instant Pictures: Complete Guide to Successful Use of the Polaroid Land Camera, Paul Giambarba. Garden City, New York, Doubleday, 1970.

Color Photography Outdoors (E-75). Rochester, New York, Eastman Kodak, 1968.

Polaroid Photography, Kalton Lahue. Los Angeles, Petersen, 1974.

RESORT PHOTO ROUTE

Through various resorts offer a personalized vacation photo package to their clients. Your service will consist of following each of your subjects around for an hour or so, photographing him or her in the dining room, on the lake, playing tennis.

Charge twenty-five dollars or so for a

"quality" package. Supply each resort with your publicity material before you arrive there and arrange for customers to sign up in advance.

SUMMER CAMP PHOTOG

This idea is a variation of the preceding. Make the rounds of children's summer camps, shooting the kids as you go. Then send a set of proofs to the parents, along with a price list and order blank.

Get permission from the camp director beforehand, presenting your service as good advertising for his business.

Shoot the kids on horseback, in the swimming pool, playing baseball, shooting marbles, eating dinner, and in any other way that might evoke a favorable response from Mom and Dad.

For further information:

> *Petersen's Photographic Guide to Photographing Children.* Los Angeles, Petersen.

FOREIGN FASHION FOTOG

Textile manufacturers and fashion designers are always on the lookout for new fashion ideas. Of course, many of these ideas originate in foreign countries.

If you travel widely, and can accumulate a portfolio of the unique fashions of other countries, you may be able to sell your work to these firms.

Find the names of textile manufacturers and fashion designers in the *Thomas Register of American Manufacturers,* and write to them proposing your idea.

For further information:

Fashion Photography Techniques, A Belson. New York, Hastings House, 1970.

SCENIC PRINTS

Just about every tourist center in our country has outstanding points of interest that could be captured on color film, enlarged and matted, and then sold in tourist and gift shops, hotels, motels, art shops, and photo stores.

Whether you're in San Francisco, on the Arizona plains, or in the Rocky mountains, if you have a camera and film why not shoot what's around you and sell your finished products to the above outlets?

SLIDE-SHOW LECTURER

If you can gather a large collection of quality slides on different subjects and geographic locations, you can make good money as a traveling lecturer. Your audiences may consist of high schoolers, college students, nature lovers, or just ordinary folks.

Of course, the more unusual your subjects, the better. The wildlife of Africa, Tahitian culture, headhunters of Borneo, or life in an Eskimo village are suitably exotic examples.

Lecture bureaus are found in most large cities and, for a percentage, will get you your bookings.

For further information:

> *Effective Lecture Slides (S-22).* Rochester, New York, Eastman Kodak, 1973.

> *Planning a Slide Talk (P-100-4).* Rochester, New York, Eastman Kodak, 1973.

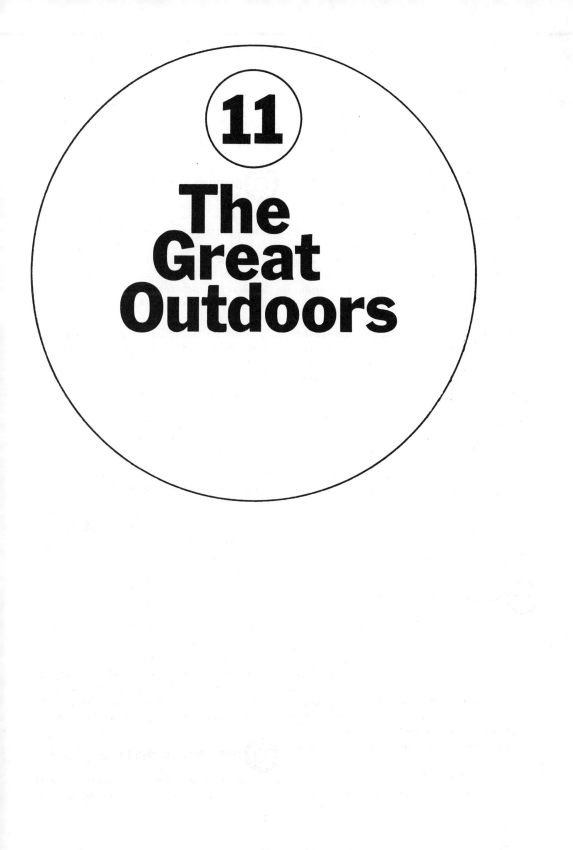

11

The Great Outdoors

Let's fantasize for a moment and suppose that those flying saucers we've heard so much about actually contain little green men from Mars. Furthermore, let's suppose that, with their superior weapons and intelligence, they are able to make prisoners of us all, right here on earth.

Now it so happens that these nasty little creatures, for some reason known only to the Great Cosmic Intelligence, impose the following life-style on us: Every person over the age of eighteen is to spend the majority of his waking hours—for the rest of his life—in a windowless chamber, performing such tasks as filing and typing, assembly work, washing dishes, removing pits from peaches, and counting ball bearings.

Sound like a harsh sentence? Well that's the sentence millions of American men and women have imposed on themselves—the price they think they must pay for room, board, and other creature comforts.

Naturally, you believe a better life exists; otherwise, you wouldn't be reading this book.

If you're one who enjoys the outdoors and would prefer to earn your daily bread under the sun rather than under fluorescent lights, come along with us and let's look for something you might enjoy doing in the great outdoors.

Recreation

WEALTH IN THE WATER

Last we heard, some smart entrepreneur was turning a fast buck in the Caribbean by making a deal with a tourist cruise ship line to give its passengers amateur snorkeling lessons for a fat fee.

If you live in the southern coastal states —or would like to try your luck in the Caribbean—a lot of promotion and a little equipment can make you a fat cat in the snorkel racket too!

For further information:

Sports Illustrated Skin Diving and Snorkel-

ing, Sports Illustrated and Barry Allen. Philadelphia, J. B. Lippincott, 1973.

Complete Illustrated Guide to Snorkel and Deep Diving, Owen Lee. Garden City, New York, Doubleday, 1963.

SLIDING PROFITS

Make arrangements with a nearby shopping center to construct a giant slide, big enough to accommodate five or six people at a time, in a corner of their parking lot. Since they'll benefit by the fact that the slide will attract customers to the center, it'll be to their advantage to give you the space rent-free or at a reduced price.

Aside from the initial construction cost, you will have little to worry about in the way of maintenance. Your sliding subjects will keep the mechanism well polished. Provide burlap sacks to prevent friction between your customers' legs and the slide.

Do get personal liability insurance in case of accidents. Promote your attraction as the Biggest Slide in the World (or in town).

BE A BALLOON KING!

Buy a few hundred balloons, plenty of string, and a helium gas tank from a wholesale novelty company. Then, after getting permission from the proper authorities, set yourself up in a suburban shopping center, city square, fair, carnival, at a parade—anywhere kids are likely to congregate.

Charge twenty-five to fifty cents a balloon. As you sell each one, blow up another with helium from the tank to replenish your stock. The helium will keep the balloon up in the air. Or you can fill your balloons with air and attach them to long thin sticks. Of course, the more novel your product, the more you'll sell.

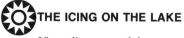

THE ICING ON THE LAKE

If you live near a lake or pond in an area where winters are icy and uneventful, rent some lakeside property and build a modest shack which can be slid out into the ice. Dig holes in the ice at intervals inside the shack and introduce your community to ice fishing.

Charge by the hour or by the fish caught. You can sell your chilly customers coffee and hot chocolate. Rent them fishing poles and bait as well.

Be sure the ice is solid, watch small children around the fishing holes, and get a good liability insurance policy before starting.

A VERY AMUSING BUSINESS

You say your name isn't Walt Disney? Well, never you mind, because anyone—if he's a bit of a promoter—can start and successfully operate an amusement park.

Start off small by leasing several acres of land in an attractive area outside of town. Next, advertise in trade journals for concessionaires. You'll need Ferris wheels, merry-go-rounds, and the standard games, but also try to find people with unique rides and attractions to whom you can lease space.

For further information:

Amusement Business, 1719 West End Avenue, Nashville, Tennessee 37203 (a weekly trade journal).

HOUSEBOAT HONEYMOONS

What could be more romantic than a honeymoon aboard a houseboat on a crystal-clear, secluded lake nestled in the mountains? If you can arrange this situation for honeymooners, rent out your houseboats fully stocked with provisions, by the week or month. Advertise in national magazines such as *Modern Bride* and *Bride's Magazine,* available at newsstands.

CAMPGROUND CASH

If you're fortunate enough to own spacious wooded country property with a brook running through it, you've got a ready-made campground.

Open it up to the public by erecting a large sign out front. Advertise in camping-equipment stores and in the daily newspapers. Charge your customers three dollars or so per night for each vehicle. For extra income, sell groceries and snacks.

SURVIVAL SCHOOL

If you enjoy roughing it, take a class in wilderness camping, foraging and cooking, and read a few reference books on the subject.

When you feel confident in your wilderness survival ability, organize weekend trips for those desk-bound nine to fivers. The going rate is no less than $40-50 per weekend for the privilege of sleeping on the ground, building fires by rubbing sticks together, and eating cattails and wild nuts. As a post-graduate course, you might teach techniques for hunting and protection against wild animals. Arrange transportation to and from your wilderness, and be sure not to feed your people any poisonous mushrooms.

For further information:

Survival in the Outdoors, Byron Dalrymple. New York, Dutton, 1972.

How to Stay Alive in the Woods, Bradford Angier. Riverside, New Jersey, Macmillan, 1966.

Survival in the Wilds, Robert Shockley and Charles Fox. Cranbury, New Jersey, A. S. Barnes, 1970.

MIDGET "500"

Build or buy some small models of famous race cars. Then get permission from a shopping center to set up a miniature track in a corner of their parking lot. For fifty cents or a dollar each, kids will don goggles and race around the track in their cars.

Since this will be a promotion for the shopping center, you might just get this concession rent-free, keeping whatever you take in as· profit. Don't forget to take out a good liability insurance policy.

For further information:

> *Midget Motoring and Karting,* Kenton McFarland and James Sparkes. New York, Dutton, 1961.

OPERATE A MARINA

Build a marina or lease an existing one in a coastal harbor or on the shore of a large lake. If you haven't a sizable bankroll to invest initially, start off small, expanding your facilities as your business grows.

Your services will include renting, cleaning, and berthing boats; selling gas; doing repair work; and organizing fishing parties. Add to your profits by selling ice, beer, and food.

RUN A DUDE RANCH

If you have farm property that would accommodate several families, you might consider operating a dude ranch. In addition to accommodations and good country cooking, you'll be expected to have a few horses for riding, cows to milk, and chickens to feed if your guests feel up to these activities.

Advertise in nearby city newspapers and, if you want national publicity, take out a small display ad in one of the national travel or vacation magazines. You might also have brochures printed up and distributed through your local and state chambers of commerce.

SAILING LESSONS

This enterprise is especially suited to those living in Florida or southern California.

Many individuals think of sailing as something mysterious—an activity only for the chosen few. The fact is that anyone, old or young, can learn to sail. If you have a boat and know the ropes, start your own sailing

school by advertising around docks and in the "Boats for sale" column of your newspaper.

For additional revenue you can teach sail-making, navigation, boat maintenance, and related subjects. You can also send prospective boat buyers to dealers who agree to pay you a commission for doing this.

For further information:

> *The Art of Sailing,* Percy Blandford. New York, St. Martin's, 1971.

> *Complete Beginner's Guide to Sailing,* A. H. Drummond, Jr. Garden City, New York, Doubleday, 1971.

BICYCLE RENTAL

If you live near a large park or a little way out of town you should do well with a bicycle rental agency. This can be done from your home. Charge $1.50 or $2.00 per hour, with a special discount for families. As a safeguard, ask for identification and a deposit before renting out your equipment.

Start small by buying a few used bikes and painting them attractively. They can generally be found through the classified ads of your local newspaper or at neighborhood garage sales. Many police departments also hold once-a-year sales or auctions at which stolen bicycles whose owners have not been identified are sold dirt cheap.

HILL-BILLING

Are you able to buy or rent a good-sized piece of hillside property? If so, you can make money summer and winter with the old-fashioned sport of tobogganing. Clear a steep runway for the stout of heart and a more moderate runway for the smaller or less adventuresome customers. Get yourself a fleet of toboggans. In the summer, use fallen leaves or straw as a track lubricant for dry runs. In the winter, you can rely on snow.

Before starting, get yourself a good personal liability insurance policy.

 **OPERATE A SKI LIFT**

Buy or lease property in a mountainous area and build a ski lift and lodge. Or get together with an individual or a hotel chain and have them build and operate the lodge while you build and run the lift.

Another method would be to sell memberships of $100 each to avid skiers for lifetime free use of the lift. One hundred skiers signing up would give you $10,000 working capital, which you might use as a down payment, securing a bank loan for additional capital.

 **CONDUCT NATURE CLASSES**

Many people, if given the opportunity, would like to learn more about the plant and animal life around them. Whether you live near the seashore or a swamp, a river or a rock formation, you can earn some nice change by conducting field trips into these areas.

If you're a little rusty on your flora and fauna, brush up on them at your library. Then work through nature organizations, schools, churches, recreation departments, children's camps, and scouting organizations in promoting your services.

For further information:

New Field Book of Nature Activities and Hobbies, William Hillcourt. New York, Putnam's, 1970.

Nature Study and Science, I. Finch. New York, Longman, 1971.

 **GREEN FROM GREENS**

Most golfers are happy for any opportunity to improve their game. That's why, if you have an acre or two of land, you'd be successful as the operator of a putting green. Naturally, you'll need to turf your property and keep it in good condition.

Advertise your green at sporting goods stores, golf pro shops, country clubs, and in the sports section of your newspaper.

SKEET SHOOTING

If you own or have access to a large piece of land outside the city limits, set up a skeet-shooting operation for local sportsmen.

Start out with manually operated traps, then progress to more sophisticated equipment later on.

Advertise your shoots in sporting goods stores and gun shops, on road signs, and in the newspaper and Yellow Pages.

CAMPING-TRIP ESCORT

Scouting organizations aren't the only groups that go on camping trips. Hundreds of private individuals make their living by escorting groups of boys or girls on weekend or week-long trips that might include hiking, swimming, fishing, nature talks, and campfire singing.

Plan your trips well in advance, then advertise in the paper and personally contact parents through schools, churches, PTAs, Little Leagues, and other such organizations.

For further information:

Nature Recreation: Group Guidance for the Out-of-Doors, William Venal. Gloucester, Massachusetts, Peter Smith.

The Camper's Handbook, John Power. New York, Scribner's, 1973.

The Complete Book of Camping, Heywood Gould. New York, New American Library, 1972.

RECREATIONAL VEHICLE RENTAL

Buy some small campers and trailers in the off-season. Get bargains by dealing with private parties, whose names you can find in the classified ads.

Then promote your rental service by leaving word at sporting goods and camping stores. Advertise in the Yellow Pages. During the season you'd be wise to put ads in the sports section of your local newspaper.

DRIVING RANGE

Driving ranges are prospering all over the country.

If you have a large piece of land all you need is a small stand from which to rent out balls and clubs. For additional profits set up a nearby archery or rifle range.

Of the Earth . . .

WILDFLOWER POWER

Where once horticulturists labored for years to produce a brighter tulip or a bigger rose, now garden owners are more than happy to grow the unadulterated, but still beautiful, flowers native to their area.

You can cash in on this new interest by gathering and selling seeds and cuttings of local wildflowers. Market them through garden centers, plant nurseries and garden magazines as ecology-oriented, truly natural seeds.

LUCKY MONEY

If you don't mind spending your days looking for needles in haystacks, try growing a field of clover, then seeking out the hard-to-find four-leaf specimens and marketing them.

They are incorporated into such items as cuff links, pendants, greeting cards and plastic paperweights. Contact jewelry and novelty manufacturers, greeting card publishers, and anyone else you think might have a need for your product.

SELL GRASS

You won't get "busted" selling *this* type of grass.

Grow a nice carpet of turf on your property, then cut it up and sell it to "lawnless"

new-home buyers by the square foot. For an extra fee, deliver and plant the sod.

Contact new-home buyers by going door to door.

RICHES FROM ROCKS

Because of the extreme temperatures, most homeowners in desert communities have "lawns" of rock rather than grass. Recently, however, because of the low maintenance involved, these gardens, usually composed of many different types of rocks, as well as of cactus and other hardy plants, have also become popular in nondesert areas.

Offer your rock-gardening talents to homeowners and builders. Since rock gardens can be used to enhance foyers, lobbies, and courtyards, owners of apartment complexes and industrial plants would likewise make good prospects.

For further information:

> *Rock Gardening,* Lincoln Foster. Boston, Houghton Mifflin, 1968.

> *Basic Book of Rock Gardens and Pools,* W. E. Shewell-Cooper. New York, Drake, 1973.

RUBLES FROM ROCKHOUNDING

Rockhounding combines sunshine, fresh air, exercise, travel, adventure *and* profit into an activity the whole family can enjoy.

First become familiar with rocks and gemstones by studying books on the subject. Then comb the land for salable specimens. Sell your treasures to collectors, craftsmen, lapidaries and jewelers. Advertise them in hobby, craft, and lapidary magazines such as *Gems and Minerals,* P. O. Box 687, Mentone, California 92359 and *Lapidary Journal,* P. O. Box 80937, San Diego, California 92138.

For further information:

> *Rockhound's Manual,* Gordon Fay. New York, Barnes & Noble (orders to Harper & Row), 1973.

Rockhound, P. O. Box 328, Conroe, Texas 77301 (a magazine published every two months).

KEEPER OF THE GREEN

As a gardener you'll need a small arsenal of tools such as a power lawn mower, pruning shears, hedge clippers and the like.

A large supply of customers is, of course, of the utmost importance. Get these initially by spreading the word to friends and neighbors, going door to door, and distributing leaflets throughout better-class neighborhoods. On a long-term basis, Yellow Pages advertising and—the best and least expensive of all —word-of-mouth advertising will help immeasurably.

For further information:

Gardening: A Basic Guide, Daniel Foley. New York, Barnes & Noble (order through Harper & Row), 1973.

Grounds Maintenance, Edwin Anderson. Indianapolis, Indiana, Theodore Audel (order through Bobbs-Merrill), 1971.

A GRAVE MATTER

Most modern cemeteries keep their grounds well-manicured, but many of the older ones do not. Very often, those who have lost loved ones return to the graveside weeks or months after the funeral only to find litter, weeds and turned-over tombstones.

Comfort these bereaved individuals by offering to provide a periodic service of cleaning up the gravesite and leaving a nice bouquet of flowers. Get names of potential customers from obituary columns and county records.

CURRENCY FROM COMPOST

There is a big demand among organic gardeners for compost to use as mulch for their crops. This material is made by piling sand, dead leaves, grass clippings, kitchen garbage, manure, sawdust, ashes and other organic material into a large pit. The compost pile is turned once a month or so.

It'll take the better part of a year, but eventually you can "harvest" your compost. Package it in five- and ten-pound bags and sell it to plant nurseries and garden centers, as well as to individual organic gardeners.

For further information:

Complete Book of Composting, J. I. Rodale. Emmaus, Pennsylvania, Rodale Books, 1960.

A HEDGE ON INFLATION

If you like working with greenery and have an artistic flair, put the two together by sculpting hedges into shapes of people, animals, cars, boats, planes, houses or geometrical designs.

Take some pictures of your more imaginative work to show as samples. Then simply walk down any residential street, offering your services to hedge-owners.

A WEALTH OF WEEDS

How would you like to start a business with absolutely no investment in inventory? You can do this by collecting and selling weeds. Dried seedpods, thistles, cattails, long grass, eucalyptus, and other weeds can be gathered free in the country. Add color by spray-painting some of them, then make them into simple arrangements, tying bunches together with colorful ribbon or placing them in vases.

Sell them to retail stores as window displays, to florists, and to gift and novelty shops.

For further information:

Dried Flower Arrangements from Garden, Bush and Seashore, Nancy Millard. New Rochelle, New York, Sportshelf and Soccer Associates, 1974.

Dried Flowers for Decoration, Violet Stevenson. New York, Drake, 1972.

RENT GARDEN SPACE

This is an ideal enterprise for a retired or partially disabled person.

If you own a large lot in the vicinity of a high-rise apartment building, divide your lot into small plots and rent them out to apartment dwellers as garden space. These individuals would either care for their own gardens or you could look after them yourself for an extra fee.

To get customers simply print up some handbills and leave them in lobbies of nearby apartment buildings.

SELF-SERVICE TREE LOT

Get some seedlings from a local nursery or seed supplier and plant them on your property. When they reach a few feet in height, open your lot to the public, letting people dig out their own trees. Replant as needed.

Promote your unique enterprise heavily, perhaps by donating some of your trees to the city and by being interviewed by the local newspaper or TV station.

SOIL SALE

Fertile soil is hard to come by in the city. Used by home gardeners in window boxes and flowerpots, this material is necessary for healthy greenery.

If you have access to some good earth, mix it with fertilizer, package it in various-sized heavy plastic bags, and sell it to hardware stores, nurseries, supermarkets, and garden centers.

OPERATE A FLOWER STAND

Flowers are an item that an individual may not think of buying all year. Then one day he rounds a corner and—zappo! He's confronted with a beautiful display of flowers and has just *got* to take a bunch of roses home to the wife or girl friend.

It happens all the time, and you can profit here by finding an empty lot on a busy thoroughfare or space in front of a large office building for your stand. After agreeing with the property owner to pay him a small monthly rental, contact a local wholesale florist for your stock.

For further information:

> *Success in Selling Flowers,* Stanley Coleman. New Rochelle, New York, Sportshelf and Soccer Associates.
>
> *The Retail Florist Business,* Peter Pfahl. Danville, Illinois, Interstate Printers and Publishers, 1973.

LAWN SPRINKLERS

If you're the slightest bit knowledgeable about plumbing you should have no difficulty in learning to install lawn-sprinkler systems.

The most opportune time to install this type of system is before the lawn is put in. Therefore, you'll want to work with home builders on a subcontracting basis. Also, dig up new customers by canvassing well-to-do neighborhoods just as the warm weather starts. In addition, be sure to spread word of your service to local nurseries and garden centers.

A SOIL TESTER

For under ten dollars you can buy a soil testing kit from a garden center or nursery. This kit will enable you to check soil for such things as pH level and mineral content, thus giving individuals valuable information regarding their soil *before* they plant that vegetable garden or bed of roses.

Get your customers through garden centers and nurseries, and by distributing handbills throughout residential neighborhoods.

For further information:

> *Introductory Soil Testing,* Shamsher

Prakash. New York, Asia Publishing House.

Introductory Soil Testing, Thomas H. Thornburn and Edward E. Bauer. Champaign, Illinois, Stipes, 1962.

LANDSCAPE DESIGNER

Just as many homeowners turn to an interior designer for fixing up the interior of their home, many also need advice and help in planning when it comes to "exterior decoration."

Needless to say, you'll have to be somewhat of an authority on many varied types of greenery. In addition, the owner will expect rough sketches of any landscaping you propose, so you should possess a modicum of drawing ability.

To get started, contact garden clubs, nurseries, and owners of new homes. If you can contract with a builder of new homes to landscape his models, or even his entire tract, you'll be off to a flying start.

For further information:

Gardening and Home Landscaping: A Complete Illustrated Guide, Jack Kramer. New York, Harper & Row, 1971.

Betty Ajay's Guide to Home Landscaping, Betty Ajay. New York, McGraw-Hill, 1970.

GARDENING LESSONS

Whether you choose to call yourself a "plant professor," a "gardening guru," or a "shrub savior," it's possible to make a comfortable income by teaching your gardening skills to others.

Planting of bulbs, sowing of seeds, identification of various flowers and plants, use of gardening equipment, caring for food gardens, and greenhouse gardening are just a few of the many possible subjects you might offer.

To get started you could offer your course through the Y or local garden club. After

you're in full swing offer to be interviewed for a feature article in the local newspaper.

FIREWOOD

If you own some heavily wooded property you could develop a nice income for yourself by cutting and selling firewood. Personally owned property, however, is not the only source of this material. Often the U. S. Forest Service will open up sections of national forests to the public, allowing them to cut timber.

Naturally, you'll need a chain saw and a truck. Sell your material directly to the public or to supermarkets, hardware stores, and other suitable outlets.

Services

DOOR-TO-DOOR CAR WASH

All you need for this endeavor is a bag of rags, dishwashing liquid and car wax, gumption, and elbow grease. Go from door-to-door in the suburbs, asking if car owners would like their vehicle washed and waxed. You can use their hose and wash the car right in their driveway.

At $2 for a combination wash and quick-wax job, you can easily make $20–30 a day. You may want to go into this business with a partner to keep you company and relieve the monotony.

SUNKEN TREASURE

If you don't mind wading knee-deep in muck, fending off an occasional water snake, and cutting your feet on broken glass once in a while, you can make easy money by retrieving golf balls from ponds on or adjacent to golf courses. Just wade right in with a sack and feel for the balls with your bare feet. If you'd like to get more deeply immersed in the business, get yourself some snorkeling or scuba equipment and dive for the balls.

Naturally, whether the pond is actually on the golf course or not, you'll need the property owner's permission. Sell your balls to pro shops and sporting goods stores.

FEATURE FANCY FENCES!

Fences, in one form or another, have been around since the first cave man could mutter "keep out" to his neighbor.

Why not study up on fence styles and construction? Then offer to erect fancy fences such as picket, lattice, grapestake, split rail, wrought iron, and chain link, as well as those employing a Grecian, Renaissance, or Early American motif.

You needn't limit your services to homeowners. Farmers, apartment house owners, and industrial plants would also make good prospects.

For further information:

Fences, Gates, and Bridges: A Practice Manual, George Martin. Brattleboro, Vermont, Stephen Greene Press, 1974.

How to Build Fences and Gates, Editors, *Sunset* magazine. Menlo Park, California, Lane, 1971.

BEACH BONANZA

Here's a chance to get plenty of fresh air and sunshine—and fill your coffers at the same time!

People go to the beach for fun. You can add to their enjoyment by setting up a stand in which you would rent out such items as chairs, umbrellas, floats, beach balls, rafts, and surfboards.

Naturally, you'll need to get prior permission from the owner of the property, perhaps giving him a percentage. But with the right location, you should make oceans of cash.

LIGHT LOOT

Searchlights, which can be visible for distances of up to 150 miles, are used to attract

attention at grand openings, premieres, celebrations, and other such events. Renting out these colossal candles at such affairs can be a lucrative enterprise.

Buy your equipment direct from a manufacturer, whose name can be found in the *Thomas Register of American Manufacturers* at your library. Attract attention to your own service by setting up your searchlights, with large signs on them, in the business district on an evening when all the stores are open. Advertise in the Yellow Pages.

A BUS BENCH BARON

Too many cities and towns across our land offer no place for a person to sit, other than the hard ground, while waiting for a bus. You can remedy this tiresome situation by getting permission from the city fathers to erect bus-stop benches at no charge to them.

Of course, your reward will come as you sell advertising on the fronts and backs of your benches. If you need ideas on how these benches are built, consult a building contractor or travel to a nearby city which already has these welcome conveniences, taking note of how they are constructed.

CURB THAT NUMBER!

If you've ever tried to locate an address on a dimly lit residential street at night you know how frustrating it can get. Most residents realize this and are willing to pay a small fee to have their address painted on their front curb.

All you need for this venture are some number stencils, a can of white paint, and a brush. Go door to door offering your curb-painting service for fifty cents a throw. Fifty Yeses a day will keep the creditors away!

ANTENNAS FOR SALE

Most TV repair shops will sell and install antennas but, *oy vey,* what prices! By supplying and installing antennas at cut-rate prices you'll develop a high volume which will electrify owners of local TV shops.

Get business by leaving word at electronics supply houses (where you'll be buying your antennas) and contract with stores selling new TV sets to do their delivery and installation work for them. Advertise in the Yellow Pages and in the TV section of your newspaper.

BUCKS FROM BRICKS

Even if you've never laid a brick before, you can easily learn. Once you're armed with this talent you'll find innumerable outlets for your work. Outdoor divider walls, flower boxes, birdbaths, brick walks, terraces, patios, and porches are just a few.

Get started in this venture by designing and building some decorative brickwork for friends and neighbors. Then make up some attractive color brochures which you can mail out to homeowners, builders, hardware stores, and brick manufacturers.

For further information:

Bricklaying Simplified, Donald Brann. Briarcliff Manor, New York, Directions Simplified, 1973.

Art of Bricklaying, Edgar Ray. Peoria, Illinois, Charles A. Bennett, 1971.

ADDRESS THE PUBLIC!

Many organizations sponsor outdoor events and must rent public address equipment from commercial firms at commercial rates. If you own or have access to loudspeakers, microphones, amplifiers, and the like, you can rent out your equipment to these organizations at a fraction of the going rate—and still make a nice profit.

Spread word of your services to schools and churches, scouting, social, civic, and political groups.

For further information:

Public Address Handbook, Vivian Capel. Dobbs Ferry, New York, Morgan & Morgan.

Hi-Fi Loudspeakers and Enclosures, Abraham Cohen. Rochelle Park, New Jersey, Hayden Book, 1968.

HANDLING HANDBILLS

Fortunately or unfortunately, as the case may be, our land is flooded with billions of advertising handbills every year. It is handbill-distribution firms that oversee this frequent flinging of fliers, this perpetual pitching of printed paper.

If you're not an environmentalist, start your own handbill-distribution firm by contracting with local merchants—the larger the better, naturally—to distribute their advertising matter. Then hire high school or college students to do the legwork for you. Spot-check their work frequently to guard against wholesale dumping of the material.

PROMOTE PATIOS!

Patios are a lot simpler to construct than most people imagine. Just level off the area and lay concrete patio blocks down, filling the cracks with concrete. These blocks are available in a number of different colors through most building-supply outlets.

Get customers for your patio installation service through door-to-door solicitation or by subcontracting work through home-improvement firms.

For further information:

How to Build Walks, Walls, and Patio Floors, Editors, *Sunset* magazine. Menlo Park, California, Lane, 1973.

How to Build Patios and Sundecks, Donald Brann. Briarcliff Manor, New York, Directions Simplified, Inc., 1973.

CASH FROM CARPORTS

An excellent opportunity exists for you to profit from installing carports for garage-less homeowners. Requiring only 4 by 4s for support and small amounts of asbestos shingles, fiber glass, or aluminum, these shelters are easy to construct. You might even pay someone else to install them while you concentrate on sales.

Get customers through handbill distribution, newspaper advertising, and door-to-door solicitation.

☀ ALUMINUM INTO GOLD

You might call this a modern-day form of alchemy. It involves collecting such items as beer cans, TV dinner trays, foil, and other aluminum products from roadsides and fields, then turning this trash into cash by selling it to a recycling center in your area. You'll also find returnable pop bottles along the way which can be sold back to local supermarkets.

There are thousands of recycling centers across the country. Check the Yellow Pages for one in your area.

☀ MAKE CLOTHESLINES

Most developers of new homes nowadays conveniently neglect such frills as backyard clotheslines, yet many housewives, even though they own clothes driers, prefer to hang many garments outdoors in the sun to dry.

If you live in an area containing many new homes, you can profit by this dearth of drying doohickies, this paucity of post paraphernalia, this scarcity of suspension stock.

First figure your material and labor costs: Material includes posts, wire, and cement mix; labor includes welding the posts, cementing them into the ground, and stringing the wire between the posts. Then add on your profit. To get business, simply call on housewives at the door, offering your service.

☀ BILLBOARDS ON WHEELS

In our area, it seems that every second store that's located beyond the central part of

town has a portable billboard out front advertising the latest "special."

These signs, which are about 4 feet by 10, have wheels and interchangeable letters —allowing them to say anything, anywhere. Around the perimeter of the signboard are flashing electric lights. Called "attention getters," these signs rent for about $150 per month.

Get into this business by making up some of these units, or by having them made. Then sell businesses on the idea of renting these as business stimulators.

☀ CASH FROM CRACKS

Walk down the street of any residential district. On every block you'll see cracked driveways and chipped curbs. You'll find these a source of steady profit if you'll only knock on the homeowner's door asking for work repairing such residential eyesores.

You can also find cracks and potholes in the parking lots of supermarkets and department stores. Again, offer your patching proficiency.

Carry patching compound and blacktop sealant with you on your rounds, making repairs and collecting your money on the spot.

☀ LOTS OF PARKING

Even if you don't own a sizable lot close to a downtown metropolitan area, you can still make big profits by leasing such property and turning it into a parking lot.

Instead of paying rent, you might even get the owner to accept a percentage of the profits, thus limiting your initial investment to the cost of a few signs and perhaps a small booth at the entrance.

☀ PATIOS INTO PORCHES

You can turn open patios into mosquito-free porches simply by erecting wooden or ironwork supports and enclosing the patio with wire screening.

Naturally, the best time to sell this service is in the spring, to coincide with the arrival of flies, mosquitoes, and other winged nuisances. Promote business for yourself by door-to-door solicitation, newspaper advertising, and leaflet distribution.

For further information:

> *How to Build and Enclose a Porch,* Donald Brann. Briarcliff Manor, New York, Directions Simplified, Inc., 1974.

PAINT HOUSES

Whether you're a high school student, college student, or graduate of the school of hard knocks, you can make a good living for yourself painting houses. The business is out there. Lord knows, plenty of houses, as well as apartment buildings, are in dire need of a good paint job. But, as in most other enterprises, it's up to you to hustle up business for yourself.

To get started, simply drive down the street looking for likely prospects. When you spot one, knock on the door and offer your services.

For further information:

> *Civil Service Examination Passbook: House Painter (C354),* Jack Rudman. Plainview, New York, National Learning Corporation.
>
> *How to Paint Anything,* Hubbard Cobb. New York, Macmillan, 1972.
>
> *How to Do Your Own Painting and Wallpapering,* Jackson Hand. New York, Popular Science Books, 1968.

RV STORAGE LOT

Many communities have ordinances prohibiting the parking of trailers, campers, and other recreational vehicles on the street. If you have a large lot, you can offer parking facilities to owners of these vehicles on a monthly basis.

To get business, contact RV sales agencies, insert ads in the newspaper, and erect a large sign on your property.

POOL PROFITS

Pool maintenance involves periodic inspection of pumps, filters, connections, and drains; cleaning; and testing for chlorine content. In the fall the pool must be winterized—covered and otherwise protected against the approaching inclement weather.

To get business, call on pool owners in person, offering your services, or work through swimming pool contractors and suppliers.

Camera Cash

For tips on equipment, film, selling your work, and related reading material, refer to Chapter 9, "A Fortune in Photography."

GOBS OF GOLD

If you live anywhere near a large naval port be on hand as naval ships depart for and arrive from overseas. Using a Polaroid, offer to snap going-away pictures of sailors and their sweethearts.

In order to attract attention wear something gaudy, with a sign on your chest saying something like: "Pictures delivered in 2 minutes—only $2."

Also, you could visit the dock a few days beforehand and take some good-quality color pictures of the ship. Frame these and then sell them to the girls after the ship leaves.

For further information:

> *How to Make Better Polaroid Instant Pictures: Complete Guide to Successful Use of the Polaroid Land Camera,* Paul Giambarba. Garden City, New York, Doubleday, 1970.
>
> *Polaroid Photography,* Kalton Lahue. Los Angeles, Petersen, 1974.

☀ FESTIVAL FOTOG

Over 5,000 festivals, carnivals, and other celebrations are held each year throughout the United States.

Why not appoint yourself a "roving festival photographer"? You'll have fun at these events, as well as profiting by them through your sales of prints to chambers of commerce, civic and fraternal organizations, and other festival sponsors.

Unless you have the time and expense to spare you'll want to make prior arrangements with the various festival sponsors, securing their permission and getting their orders in advance. To find festival locations, write the tourism department of the state you're interested in.

☀ IN YOUR BACKYARD

It's true that most of the scenes, attractions, and events in your area are not newsworthy or valuable to local publications. But to distant sources they have "travel" value and may be much in demand.

Travel magazines, travel agencies, airlines, railroads, bus companies, steamship lines, and resort hotels are just a few of the organizations that may be interested in good-quality color material.

Check *Artist's Market* and *Writer's Market* for potential buyers.

☀ AERIAL PHOTOGRAPHER

This enterprise consists of hiring yourself a small plane and pilot and flying low over industrial plants, real estate developments, farms, and ranches—even whole towns—taking pictures as you go.

You can take the shots on speculation, attempting to sell them after processing and printing, or you can make agreements beforehand with the people involved.

In any case, you must get a relatively stiff price—thirty-five to fifty dollars—for each print in order to cover your costs.

For further information:

Photography from Light Planes and Helicopters (M-5). Rochester, New York, Eastman Kodak, 1974.

☀ SHOOT STORES

Walking through the business district or shopping center of your town, take a picture of the outside of every store. After processing and printing, return to each store, calling on the owner with an 8 by 10 print of his business.

Have the print mounted in an inexpensive dime-store frame, and offer the framed print to the store owner for ten dollars. If he balks, reduce your price to whatever you can get.

As you can see, ten or twenty of these sold every day can keep your bank account in excellent condition.

☀ PARADE PIX

Visit towns in your area at parade time. Before each parade begins go to the assembly area. Ask individuals in charge of the various groups if they'd be interested in seeing finished pictures of themselves, their float, and the parade in general.

Get their names and addresses and visit them with your enlargements or proofs after the parade. If you've gotten some good shots—especially close-up shots of individuals—you should get some sizable orders.

☀ ACCIDENT PHOTOGRAPHER

Right or wrong, this enterprise involves capitalizing on others' misfortune. For here you'll be speeding to auto accidents and other catastrophies for the purpose of taking photographs that will later be useful—and marketable—to insurance companies and attorneys.

You'll need a police radio in your house, as well as in your car, to alert you to the location of the accident. Upon arrival, take pictures of everything: skid marks, the point of impact, auto damage, as well as any resultant personal injuries or fatalities. Then get the names of the parties involved and their insurance companies. Leave your card and contact the insurers, letting them know that you have pictures of the accident.

 **CONSTRUCTION PHOTOS**

Contact architects and builders in your area. Offer them progress photos on new construction of homes, apartment buildings, and office buildings on which they're working.

Your job will consist of taking pictures of each successive phase of construction and, finally, a shot of the completed work.

REAL ESTATE PHOTOGRAPHER

Make arrangements with several real estate brokers in your town to take shots of their houses for sale, supplying them with an 8 by 10 photo of each one. This will save them much valuable time, as the prospective home-buyer will be able to see a number of different houses while sitting in the broker's office.

Keep your prices low, as you'll be working on high volume.

 **PHOTO GUIDES**

If you live in an area that is at all conducive to a series of from thirty to forty or more interesting photographic scenes you can turn these local sights into some tidy profits.

Compose your series out of a variety of local scenes such as a ship in the bay, city hall, a small forest outside of town, a local historical mansion—anything that might have tourist interest. Take your shots to a local printer, with whom you'll offer to go in 50-50 on the cost of producing and distributing a small photo guide to the area. These guides can then be sold to tourists through local bookstores, newsstands, gift shops, retail stores, and the local chamber of commerce.

12

Writing: If You Can Talk, You Can Write

You're having a casual conversation with a stranger. Somehow the question "What do you do for a living?" comes up, and you say, "I'm a writer." A moment of silence as the ripples of these three magical words fade in the air. Then your acquaintance confides that he's always wanted to write a book on the circus . . . the plight of our senior citizens . . . the sex life of the two-toed sloth—you name it.

The point of this oft-repeated, true tale: Amazingly, almost *everyone* has a book in mind, but almost *no one* writes one. Well, why not?

Almost every day of our lives we state our opinions, give advice and, in general, describe our experiences to others. If you can spin a yarn that keeps your listeners breathless for half an hour, how much farther is it to putting it all in writing and getting paid for it?

Maybe you're afraid to waste a lot of time on a manuscript that makes round after weary round of publishers, never to be accepted. Actually, this happens to a great many manuscripts simply because most neophyte writers don't realize that most editors prefer to receive a query letter or synopsis and sample chapters first, rather than a completed manuscript.

But authoring books is only one of many, many ways to "write your paycheck." It's possible to generate a steady income for yourself by writing newspaper and magazine articles, guides, bulletins, greeting cards, poetry —even bumper stickers! Of course, since a best-selling book is likely to pay you 1,000 times more than the average magazine article, you'll want to consider seriously the idea of tackling a book.

We struggled along writing newspaper and magazine articles for a few years. One day we sat down and figured out exactly how much we had been getting paid for our time. It came out to something like eighty-seven cents an hour! That's when we decided to write this book. Of course, had we been smart we would have *started out* by writing a book.

The very first thing you have to do as a writer is to assume a professional posture. Do this by investing forty to fifty dollars in having attractive business letterheads printed up on good-quality paper. Since publishers don't know you personally, they'll form their first impression of you from your stationery. You may want to include the words "free-lance writer," "magazine writer," or a similar descriptive phrase under your name. If not, your name, address and phone number will be sufficient. Don't get too fancy. Just keep everything neat and businesslike.

While you're waiting for the printer to fill your order get a copy of *Writer's Market* from your bookstore. Here you'll find a treasury of over 5,000 paying markets for books, articles, short stories, greeting cards, plays, and poetry, as well as valuable tips on such topics as how to approach editors and how to submit your material. You'll also want to keep abreast of the field by subscribing to such publications as *Writer's Digest* and *The Writer.*

Now you're all set to pick your subject matter. What interests you the most? Sports, automobiles, animals, crafts, travel—whatever your interest, you're sure to have an audience.

From here on it's simply a matter of "marrying" your interests to existing markets, and if editors like what you have to offer the checks will soon start rolling in.

The references listed below will help you get started in the field:

Literary Market Place, New York, R. R. Bowker, yearly publication. Gives valuable information on where to find everything in the literary field from agents to writers' conferences.

Ayer Directory of Publications. Philadelphia, Ayer Press, yearly publication. A comprehensive guide to newspapers, magazines, and trade journals in the United States and Canada.

The Beginning Writer's Answer Book, Kirk Polking and Jean Chimsky, ed. Cincinnati, *Writer's Digest.*

The Non-Fiction Book: How to Write and Sell It, Paul Reynolds. New York, Morrow, 1970.

What's Really Involved in Writing and Selling Your Book, Robert Adleman. Los Angeles, Nash, 1972.

Writing Popular Fiction, Dean Koontz. Cincinnati, *Writer's Digest*, 1972.

A Practical Guide for Authors, William Booth. Philadelphia, Richard West, 1973.

The Magazine Maze

Every year periodicals from *Adam* to *Zane Grey Western Magazine* accept thousands of articles and short stories from free-lancers on an infinite variety of subjects, with the writer being paid anywhere from zero to $3,000 or more for each piece.

In writing for magazines you must be careful to match your subject to the editorial content of the particular publication. Upon request, many magazines will send you their guidelines for writers as well as a sample copy of their publication. Study these carefully, noting such aspects as subject content, the general slant of the articles, length, photography, and so on.

It's been estimated that good photographs are 50 percent responsible for the acceptance of most magazine articles. Therefore, you'll want to document your manuscript with photos or other illustrative material whenever possible. If you're unskilled in photography it would pay you either to buy a camera and learn the fundamentals or to take on a camera-toting friend as a partner.

If you're a crackerjack writer, by all means submit your material to the top publications. An easier way for most people to break into print, however, is to make submissions to the smaller publications. The pay is considerably lower, but the field is far less competitive. In any case, unless otherwise indicated in the *Writer's Market*, always query by letter to see if the publication is interested and enclose a self-addressed, stamped envelope.

For further information:

A Treasury of Tips for Writers, Society of Magazine Writers. Cincinnati, *Writer's Digest*, 1965.

Writing the Modern Magazine Article, Max Gunther. Boston, *The Writer*, 1973.

How to Write Successful Magazine Articles, Camille Rose. Boston, *The Writer*, 1967.

WRITE A CONFESSION!

Confession stories can best be described as literary soap operas with a "hook," the hook usually being in the title. Examples are "The Devil Raped Me on a Mountaintop," or "How Can I Tell My Mother I'm a Closet Queen?"

Acceptable articles can run anywhere from 1,000 to 10,000 words. The pay is somewhat on the low side, averaging about four cents a word. The most frustrating part of this market, however, is the fact that confessions publishers invariably demand a completed manuscript rather than just a query or outline before committing themselves. So unless you've got a lot of time or confidence—or both—better look around elsewhere.

For further information:

Confession Writing, Florence Palmer. Cincinnati, *Writer's Digest*, 1974.

CELEBRITY INTERVIEWS

It takes a writer with a certain type of personality to wangle his way into the lives of famous actors, actresses, artists, authors, politicians, or sports celebrities. But if you have that personality—and you live near Hollywood, New York, London, or Paris—there's no reason in the world why you can't make a living at writing and selling articles based on interviews with these individuals.

Possible markets include daily newspapers and their Sunday magazine sections, the weekly tabloids, and TV and movie fan magazines.

GAG MAG

A good outlet for your witty ways, your humorous habits, your comical character, is to publish your own monthly gag magazine containing jokes, cartoons and other jocularities.

Initially, you'll have to get the ball rolling yourself. But once you gain a readership you'll be flooded with comical contributions.

A PUZZLING BUSINESS

Are you puzzled over the reasons for your numerous rejection slips? Try puzzling others—and profiting—by creating word puzzles for puzzle publications.

Cryptograms, skeletons, word quizzes, slidograms and clapboard puzzles are a few of the many variations on the familiar crossword puzzle needed by crossword publishers.

DON'T BE JUVENILE! OR SHOULD YOU?

There are several possible outlets for well-written fiction and nonfiction for the juvenile and teenage markets. Most magazines in this field are published by religious groups; consequently, articles submitted to them must emphasize character building and other virtuous goals.

The children's book market encompasses a broader spectrum of subject matter. Thus, you may find that this field offers you more opportunity.

For further information:

How to Write for the Juvenile Market, Marjorie Hinds. New York, Frederick Fell, 1966.

Writing Juvenile Fiction, Phyllis Whitney. Boston, *The Writer,* 1960.

POETRY PROFITS?

In all conscience, we really couldn't encourage you to expect to become rich by writing poetry. On the other hand, Rod McKuen and Leonard Cohen do it, so it's not an impossibility.

In addition to accepting verse, some publications need articles on poetry, as well as

biographical information on poets. Most payment, however, is either microscopic or in contributors' copies.

For further information:

The Poet and the Poem, Judson Jerome. Cincinnati, *Writer's Digest,* 1973.

SPORTS, OF COURSE!

The sportsman-writer is indeed in an ideal position. He can pursue his pastime and at the same time make money at it. Some magazines such as *Sports Illustrated* and *Sports Afield* pay especially well.

So if you have expertise in fishing or football, bicycling or bow hunting, put it to use. And don't forget: Photos will not only bring you a bigger check, they'll help sell the article as well.

For further information:

Modern Sportswriting, Louis Gelfand and Harry Heath, Jr. Ames, Iowa, Iowa State University Press, 1969.

RETAIL TRADE JOURNALS

These publications are primarily distributed to retailers. Subject matter usually centers around successful merchandising techniques.

Almost any retailer in your town has a good story to tell about how he built up his business or promoted a particular item. Why not get it into print and get paid for it?

For further information:

Business Journalism, Julien Elfenbein. Westport, Connecticut, Greenwood Press, reproduction of 1960 edition.

MANUFACTURERS' TRADE JOURNALS

Manufacturers also have their own publications. *Plastics Technology* has a need for articles on plastics processing, and *Asbestos* requires pieces on the processing and manufacture of asbestos-based products.

If you're knowledgeable about manufacturing methods and keep up on new developments in industry, try your hand at this type of writing.

For further information:

Writing for Technical and Professional Journals, John Mitchell. New York, Wiley, 1968.

PROFESSIONAL JOURNALS

Professional journals, sometimes referred to as technical journals, have a constant need for pieces on scientific or technical subjects. New systems designs, scientific discoveries that bear directly upon the particular industry, and new uses for chemical by-products are typical subjects covered in these publications.

If you have a technical bent, and can lucidly describe new technical developments, this field might be for you.

For further information:

Writing for Technical and Professional Journals, John Mitchell. New York, Wiley, 1968.

SPONSORED PUBLICATIONS

The purpose of these publications is to publicize the ideals, objectives, projects and activities of the sponsoring organization. Examples are *Chevron USA,* the official publication of the Chevron Travel Club, and *V.F.W. Magazine,* for members of the Veterans of Foreign Wars.

Keep an eye out for local developments within various organizations, as well as for other potential articles which may be of interest to the members.

FARMING—DAIRY—POULTRY— LIVESTOCK

If you're up on the latest developments in crop raising and soil management; the feeding and breeding of dairy herds; egg, chicken, and turkey production; or livestock management, these subjects are possible money-makers for you.

Writing on these subjects, as in all nonfiction writing, however, make sure that your facts are accurate and that the subject matter of your article conforms to the editorial content of the publication that you're submitting it to.

For further information:

Reporting Agriculture through Newspapers, Magazines, Radio, Television, William Ward. Comstock Publishing Associates, Ithaca, New York (order through Cornell University Press), 1959.

Agricultural Technical Journalism, Rodney Fox. Westport, Connecticut, Greenwood Press, reproduction of 1952 edition.

HOUSE ORGANS

Contrary to what you might be thinking, we are not going to talk here about residential anatomy or musical instruments.

House organs, less confusingly referred to as house magazines, are company-sponsored publications circulated to employees, dealers and customers. These publications are almost exclusively interested in product-application articles: stories about tires being used in a big auto race, a tractor being employed in a new agricultural experiment, a crane being utilized in the construction of a new skyscraper.

Where to sell your articles? Over 4,000 major house organs are listed in the *Gebbie House Magazine Directory,* published every few years by the National Research Bureau, Inc., Burlington, Iowa. This directory can be found in any large library and almost all of the publications listed in it use good freelance material.

Writing for Newspapers

Writing for newspapers is another of several possible ways to establish yourself as a writer. Whether you submit material to your hometown newspaper or to one of the national weekly tabloids, you can bet your typewriter that if you've got something to say—and can say it well—editors will be happy to pay you for your work.

Newspapers have an insatiable need for news and feature articles on every conceivable subject, be it Mrs. Murphy's tea party or a local plane crash.

In getting started you may want to work as a "stringer," or correspondent. Write to the editor of your local newspaper informing him that you'd like to cover local events for his paper. If you've had any writing experience mention that also.

As in the magazine field, it will be to your distinct advantage to submit photos along with your articles, so mention in your letter the fact that captioned photographs will accompany your articles whenever possible.

If your interest lies in writing a daily or weekly column on a particular subject, enclose several sample columns for the editor's perusal, along with a cover letter outlining how his paper would benefit by publishing your column.

If the columns or news stories you'll be writing will have national appeal you'll want to contact news services, as well as newspapers across the country, offering your services and stating your qualifications. Address your letters to individual editors, and always enclose a self-addressed, stamped envelope.

The *Editor and Publisher Yearbook,* available at your library, contains a comprehensive listing of U. S. and Canadian newspapers, along with the names of their editors.

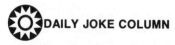

DAILY JOKE COLUMN

Everybody loves a good joke. That's why it has always surprised us that newspapers never have this type of column with which to offset some of the grisly front-page stuff. Well, maybe you can do something about it.

Get some first-class jokes from joke books or from your friends. Make them up into a few sample columns to send editors, explaining that you'd like to supply their readers with a daily dose of such jocularity. When they get through rolling in the aisles they may just give you the go-ahead!

OUT OF THE MOUTHS OF BABES . . .

Here, after getting the go-ahead from the editor of your local newspaper, you'll edit a daily children's question-and-answer column.

Get permission from local school principals to interview the kids in class. Use a tape recorder for their replies and take a flash camera along, snapping a picture of each child. The picture will appear next to the child's answer in your column. Get more answers than you actually need to each question, selecting only the wittiest for publication.

A SPORTS COLUMNIST

If you're fanatic over football, batty about baseball, and hooked on hockey, you'll fit in fine as a sports columnist for local newspapers.

To get started, write up some sample columns, photocopy them, and send them off to area newspapers along with an individual cover letter to each. Explain that you'd like to write for them on a daily basis and state your qualifications.

For further information:

Modern Sportswriting, Louis Gelfand and Harry Heath. Ames, Iowa, Iowa State University Press, 1969.

ON THIS DAY . . .

With the nostalgia craze sweeping the nation, a daily newspaper column relating the news as it happened 5, 25, or 100 years ago should generate considerable reader interest.

Get your facts from historical references, such as those listed below, at your library.

Dictionary of Dates, Robert Collison, ed. New York, Philosophical Library, 1961.

Encyclopedia of World History, William Langer, ed. Boston, Houghton Mifflin, 1972.

TEEN TALK

Many teenagers need advice on such topics as skin care, dating, etiquette, part-time job opportunities, and how to handle parents.

If you're a teenager, or in tune with the younger generation, perhaps you can help these kids by editing a daily column covering such subjects. Here the kids will ask the questions and you'll do your best to answer them.

NEW-PRODUCTS COLUMN

Whether your interest is amplifiers or airplanes, boating or beauty care, cars or cooking, there are sure to be lots of others in your town—in your state—throughout the country—interested in the same subject.

To keep abreast of new products get on the mailing list of manufacturers of items relating to the field in which you're interested. Then you'll be well-equipped to keep the public up-to-date through a daily newspaper column.

BE SYNDICATED!

A newspaper syndicate is an organization which takes a column, comic strip, feature piece, or other material and supplies it to newspapers, sometimes internationally, in exchange for a fee. The syndicate takes a percentage of the fee, then passes the rest along to the writer. Art Buchwald's column is syndicated, as is the comic strip "Blondie."

Although it's more effective for a beginner to submit his work to newspaper editors himself, you might prefer to send your material to a syndicate and let them take over the responsibility of marketing your work.

A complete list of newspaper syndicates, along with the titles of columns and features

which they handle, appears in the *Editor and Publisher Syndicate Directory,* 850 Third Avenue, New York, New York 10022.

For further information:

"Newspaper Syndication," by Gordon Greb, in *The Writer,* January 1974, pp. 18–21.

KITCHEN KORNER

This would be a good name for a newspaper column in which you'd provide valuable shopping and cooking tips, as well as giving recipes. In addition to drawing upon your own knowledge for your column, you could also use helpful information sent in by your readers.

CHILD CARE COLUMN

Actually, in producing this column you would act as editor rather than writer. It would be a "reader-participation" column in which you would publish questions from readers concerning the raising of children and other readers would in turn write in giving their advice and relating their experiences.

THE QUESTION MAN (OR LADY)

Here you'll edit a daily newspaper column in which you'll ask questions of people on the street. Naturally, the more provocative and controversial your line of questioning, the more lively and interesting the responses will be.

At the time of asking the question, you'll also snap the interviewee's picture, which will appear along with his answer in the column.

ANIMAL ARTICLES

If you're somewhat of an authority on such subjects as canine culture, feline feeding, canary care, piscine peculiarities, and hamster habits, try marketing your knowledge by writing a daily animal column.

DAILY STREET-NAME COLUMN

In our town there is a Blossom Street (named after the tobacco blossom); a Lady Street (named after George Washington's wife); and a Marion Street (named after Francis Marion, the Swamp Fox of Revolutionary War fame).

No doubt your town has interesting facts behind many of its street names. A newspaper column featuring a historic sketch of a different street each day should be of interest to many local residents.

THE WEEKLY TABLOIDS

If your forte is writing about such subjects as the love affairs of celebrities, wasteful spending in government, the occult, or bizarre life-styles, then the weekly tabloids may be just the market for you.

The largest, highest-paying, and most likely to pay a writer what he has coming is the *National Enquirer,* sold in supermarkets and newsstands everywhere. Some of the others pay moderately well, but the third-rate tabloids pay little or, worse yet, will simply refuse to pay you anything even after publishing your material. Be careful.

KRAFT KOLUMN

Why not combine your handicraft ability with your writing talents to produce a stimulating and instructive newspaper column on new ideas and techniques? Handicrafters are always on the lookout for new craft ideas, which are often hard to come by.

NEWSPAPER FEATURE WRITER

Call the feature editor of your local newspaper and find out if they accept feature articles from free-lancers. If they do, practically all you have to do to get a story is to walk out your front door. Interview the newsboy on the corner about his job. How about an article on the brand-new fleet of buses the city just bought? And, oh yes, don't overlook that ninety-year-old man who square dances every week.

Since newspapers pay extra for photographs, you'll want to bring along a camera with which to shoot these interesting subjects, sending in the prints with your story.

For further information:

> *Feature Writer's Handbook: With a Treasury of 2000 Tested Ideas for Newspapers, Magazines, Radio, and Television,* Stewart Harral. Norman, Oklahoma, University of Oklahoma Press, 1966.

> *Features with Flair,* Brian Nicholls. Portland, Oregon, International Scholarly Book Service, 1972.

WRITE AN ART COLUMN

Write up some sample columns on such events as art exhibits, the addition of a new wing to the local art museum, or the appearance of a well-known artist in town. Submit these to the editor of your local newspaper, offering to write daily columns for his paper.

THE GREEN THUMB

That's what you might call your newspaper column giving the latest tips on plant care, soils and fertilizers, building a greenhouse, and related topics.

If you can write clearly and entertainingly on this subject, try "planting" a few sample columns with newspaper editors and see if the idea grows on them.

SHOPPER'S COLUMN

Here you'll purchase space in your local newspaper for which you'll write a column on homemaking, cooking, children, clothing, sports—any subject of wide interest. Along with the chitchat, however, you'll mention new products available or on sale at local stores. Naturally, you'll collect five dollars or more from each store for mentioning them, the proceeds of which will pay for the ad and bring you a nice profit to boot.

THE CAR DOCTOR

This would make an excellent title for a newspaper column giving car owners advice on simple auto repairs and maintenance. One day your subject might cover tune-ups; the next day you could have your readers installing a new radio antenna.

You might ask readers to submit questions for you to answer in your column.

FREE-LANCE CONSUMER REPORTER

No doubt about it: The consumer revolution is upon us. Furthermore, you can profit by it. How? By running a column for your local newspaper in which disgruntled consumers can voice their complaints. Your job would be to write these up in column form, straighten out the difficulties with the firm involved, and then make a report within the column as to the outcome.

HUNTING AND FISHING COLUMN

If you're "reel" smart and a gun guru to boot, you might put your knowledge to good use by writing a daily hunting and fishing column for newspapers in your area.

Subjects might include where the big ones are biting and who bagged that big buck the other day. You'll also want to give tips on such subjects as the care of equipment and new products on the market.

LARGE-PRINT NEWSPAPER

People with vision problems, including many elderly individuals, would benefit greatly by receiving a large-print weekly newspaper.

Your paper would contain a condensation of the week's news, as well as want ads, comic strips, and other features. As with any other newspaper, you'll make your money on subscriptions, classified ads, and display advertising.

Bulletins—Guides—Services

PLOTS-A-PLENTY

Many novelists are experts at telling a story once they have a clear idea of the plot. Unfortunately, the ability of an otherwise talented author to think up fresh plots doesn't always measure up to his yarn-spinning talents. If you're primarily an "idea" person rather than a writer you might consider concocting story plots for these individuals.

You could either charge authors a flat fee or agree to share in the royalties of the book. Advertise in national writers' publications such as *Writer's Digest* and *The Writer*.

ODD PRODUCTS CATALOGUE

Where can one find such items as a live luna moth, a glass eye for a stuffed shark, or a sterling silver spittoon? In your catalogue of odd products, of course!

A good name for this publication, which you would print up and distribute yourself, might be the Orange Pages (as opposed to the Yellow Pages).

To get started, go to your local telephone company office, then comb through their directories of large cities for manufacturers and distributors of the unique—the rare —the bizarre. Send each a form letter offering inclusion in your catalogue for a specified amount. Figure your printing and distribution costs beforehand so you'll know what to charge each listee.

FREE-LANCE EDITOR

Most large companies have weekly or monthly publications, called house organs, which keep their employees informed of company events and employee activities. However, many medium-sized and small concerns have not.

Contact companies in your area and offer to organize a company publication for them for a fee. Have them get an employee from each department to forward news to you every month. Then edit the material, and arrange to have it printed and delivered to the company at its own expense.

By keeping your rates within reason, you can work with several different companies each month, bringing in a tidy income for yourself.

For further information:

Complete Guide to Editorial Freelancing, Carol O'Neill and Avima Ruder. New York, Dodd, Mead, 1974.

Editing the Company Publication, Garth Bentley. New York, Harper, 1953.

APARTMENT BULLETIN

Many apartment complexes, mobile home parks, and retirement communities have gotten so large and contain so many facilities, that they're virtually cities in themselves. And every city has its newspaper. So . . .

You could inexpensively mimeograph, or print up on a hand press, small monthly or semi-monthly bulletins relating to community affairs in your complex. A bulletin of this type containing newsworthy items about facilities, management, activities of the residents, and articles wanted and for sale would surely be worth 25 cents or so to residents.

You needn't limit yourself to one complex or community. You can publish a bulletin for each, endowing every bulletin with a different name. In fact, you might even convince the management to pay the printing costs for purposes of good public relations. Or sell outside advertising. Any way you do it, it's a good potential money-maker.

SOAP OPERA NEWSLETTER

With this enterprise, you and a few of your friends will each watch a different TV soap opera every day. Then you'll all make up short daily synopses of the shows you've watched. This information will be put into the form of a weekly newsletter and mailed to subscribers around the country, thus helping the many avid watchers of these shows to keep abreast of new dramatic developments.

Advertise your newsletter in national fan and women's magazines.

PUBLISH A BABY BULLETIN

Create a small newspaper or bulletin for the parents of newborn babies. It will contain tips on child care, humorous experiences of new parents, home-buying information, and advertisements of products and services by children's apparel shops, baby food manufacturers, toy stores, diaper delivery services, and other baby-related firms.

Your profit, of course, will come from the sale of these ads. You'll be responsible for selling and laying out the ads, editing the material, and printing and distributing the bulletin free of charge to parents of newborn babies. Find these in the daily listings of new births which most newspapers publish.

SUMMER JOB DIRECTORY

Every summer millions of high school and college students are unleashed from their desks and subsequently flood employment offices and businesses across the land seeking work.

An annual directory listing available summer jobs in resort areas, state and national parks, private industry, and government should prove to be a best seller among these students.

BE A GHOST-WRITER

Believe it or not, a great many individuals from prime ministers to paupers, from presidents to peons, have difficulty in coherently and convincingly putting what they want to say into words.

As a ghost-writer your job would be to write speeches, articles, essays, theses, and the like for politicians, businessmen, students—or anyone else. Of course, you yourself must be fluent and well-versed in your subject matter.

Get rolling in this lucrative field by advertising in business publications and in city and college newspapers.

ENGAGEMENT BULLETIN

In any big city at any given moment there are thousands of couples engaged to be married—a lucrative market for an alert promoter!

This enterprise involves printing up an "informational bulletin" with articles, hints, advice, and advertisements by firms dealing in wedding-related products and services. Here your profit would come from selling advertising to wedding consultants, bridal registries, printing companies, florists, caterers, limousine services, wedding chapels, and resorts catering to newlyweds.

Naturally, you'll be responsible for laying out the format of your bulletin, as well as having it printed up and distributed. Get the names of newly engaged couples from your local newspapers, then get their addresses from the phone directory or city directory.

RICHES FROM RESUMES

Many job seekers lose out on jobs they would otherwise get simply because they cannot write a convincing resume. If you can persuade these individuals of your ability to sell their talents in a resume, they'll be glad to pay for your services.

Start by placing ads in the "Help wanted" column of your newspaper. To get your service off the ground offer a money-back guarantee if the individual does not get a job within thirty days.

For further information:

Why and How to Prepare an Effective Job Resume, Juvenal Angel. New York, World Trade Academy Press (order through Simon & Schuster), 1972.

Personal Resume Preparation, M. P. Jaquish. New York, Wiley, 1968.

BULLETIN FOR THE HANDICAPPED

Here you'll produce a weekly or monthly bulletin devoted exclusively to the needs and problems of the handicapped. Material could include inspirational articles, and information on new products, job opportunities, governmental programs, and social security benefits—all insofar as they relate to the handicapped.

Advertise subscriptions to your bulletin in national and foreign publications. Initially, you'll have to come up with article material yourself, but once you get rolling you'll receive plenty of contributory articles and information from your readers.

BE AN AUTHOR'S AGENT

Unless you've done some writing of your own, worked as an editor, or have otherwise had some connection with the publishing industry, it would be to your advantage to go on to something more basic. An agent's success comes only after much related experience in the field.

An author's agent receives manuscripts from writers on every conceivable subject. These, if they are worthwhile, will then be submitted to a publisher who has a need for that particular type of material. Therefore, a thorough knowledge of literary markets is a must.

The agent makes his money when a manuscript is accepted for publication—usually receiving 10 percent of the author's royalties.

Because most manuscripts submitted to them are unsalable, agents may also charge a "reading fee" of anywhere from five to fifty dollars per manuscript.

To get started, advertise in writers' magazines such as *Writer's Digest* and *The Writer.* In addition, be sure to obtain a listing in the *Writer's Market,* 9933 Alliance Road, Cincinnati, Ohio 45242.

NEWS BULLETINS

Americans, by nature, are a very "news-hungry" people. But when traveling abroad, American tourists for the most part are cut off from the media due to the language barrier.

This enterprise involves your taping an English-speaking news broadcast from a shortwave radio every morning, and then, by typing and mimeographing the highlights of the previous day's news, producing several hundred "bulletins." These are delivered to hotels and restaurants for distribution to their English-speaking clientele free of charge. You are paid a flat fee by these establishments for your services.

PUBLISH A TOURIST GUIDE

This enterprise involves publishing a small guide, to be given away free to tourists, listing hotels, motels, restaurants, nightclubs, shops, and other businesses that rely on tourist trade.

You job will be to convince local businessmen of the value of buying advertising in such a guide. Once you can do that, your next step will be to make arrangements with a printer to print up your guide on a weekly basis. You'll be required to help the merchants write copy and lay out their ads, and to see that the guide is distributed to establishments frequented by tourists.

WRITE AD COPY

Advertising agencies across the land turn out millions of ads every year for newspapers, magazines, radio, and TV. While some of these ads are staff-written, many are assigned to free-lancers.

Put together some samples of your best work and take them around to advertising agencies, asking for assignments. If they like what you have to offer, you may "ad" a lot to your income.

For further information:

How to Write a Good Advertisement, Victor Schwab. New York, Harper & Row, 1962.

How to Write Advertising that Sells, Clyde Bedell. New York, McGraw-Hill, 1952.

SPORTSMEN'S BULLETIN

In an area where hunting and fishing are popular activities, avid sportsmen have a continual need for up-to-date information on who's bagging what, who's catching what —and where. You can make a good income for yourself by publishing a weekly or bimonthly bulletin giving the latest sports dope for the area.

You'll make your money by selling ads to gun dealers, tackle and bait shops, sporting goods and camping stores, restaurants, and liquor stores. It will be your responsibility to edit the publication, as well as have it printed and distributed.

TEENAGE DIRECTORY

Telephone directories, city directories, and directories of various organizations all represent valuable sources of prospective customers for many firms selling their products direct to the consumer. Since teenagers represent a valuable potential market for many firms, a teenage directory should be an extremely salable commodity in any community.

Compile your directory by distributing cards to school kids to fill out, perhaps giving each one a small trinket as an inducement. Or hold a city-wide drawing for teenagers, getting each one to fill out a name and address card beforehand. Sell your directories to local merchants, sales and research organizations, libraries, and to the kids themselves.

 GRANT AND SCHOLARSHIP INFORMATION SERVICE

Grants and scholarships are a lot more available than most college students realize. You can capitalize on this situation by offering information on these sources of aid.

Research the field by consulting publications such as those listed below. Then write up your own bulletin, listing grants and scholarships according to fields of interest. Market your bulletin by advertising in school papers.

For further information:

Annual Register of Grant Support, 1973–1974, Jerry Reitman and Jean Aroeste, eds. Chicago, Marquis-Who's Who Books, 1973.

Scholarships, Fellowships, Grants & Loans, Lorraine Mathies. New York, Macmillan Information, 1974.

Cash For College, Robert Freede. Englewood Cliffs, New Jersey, Prentice-Hall, 1975.

CLUB BULLETINS

Many organizations, large and small, would like to publish a weekly or monthly bulletin but, through inertia, have never gotten around to it. Reawaken their interest by offering a complete bulletin service.

Once the organization has forwarded its news to you, you will be responsible for mimeographing, photocopying, or printing it up, as well as distributing it to the various members.

From Fillers to Fame

FILLER FORTUNES

A filler is a short piece, anywhere from 10 to 750 words, which is used to fill in any

blank space at the end of a magazine or newspaper article. These can be on any subject under the sun. You must conform, however, to the editorial content of the publication you're writing for. To get filler ideas, look over the publications you're interested in.

Fillers pay anywhere from $10 to $300–400, depending on the type of material and the publication accepting it.

For further information:

Writing and Selling Fillers and Short Humor, A. S. Burack. Boston, *The Writer,* 1974.

How to Make Money Writing Short Fillers and Articles, Marjorie Hinds. New York, Frederick Fell, 1967.

 GREETING CARDS

If you've got a creative flair for verse or for coming up with fresh ideas, then writing greeting cards may be right down your alley. Greeting card companies use a prodigious amount of material and pay handsome rewards to writers who can produce for them.

Get started by making up a batch of ten to fifteen verses or card ideas and shipping them off to a card publisher. Since the greeting card business is fairly specialized, however, you have to be sure to send your work to the right publisher.

For further information:

The Greeting Card Writer's Handbook, Joseph Chadwick. Cincinnati, *Writer's Digest,* 1968.

How to Make Money Writing Greeting Cards, Lorraine Hardt. New York, Frederick Fell, 1968.

THE REGIONAL BOOK MARKET

A book does not necessarily have to have national appeal in order to be a success. Many books dealing with regional attractions have been published and successfully sold. A well-written book dealing with the history and legends of the Okefenokee Swamp would sell well in Florida. The history and culture of the Indian tribes of Arizona might make a salable book in that state.

Look around your state for a subject that might have regional appeal, then submit your ideas to a publisher.

CHILDREN'S PICTURE BOOKS

Another potential money-maker in the book market lies in producing a heavily illustrated picture book for children.

In submitting this type of material to a publisher, type your text on a white sheet of 8½ by 11 paper, along with each illustration. Your illustrations may be in rough form, since publishers usually have their own artists who would do the illustrating if the book were accepted.

For further information:

The Art of Art for Children's Books, Diana Klemin. New York, Clarkson Potter (order through Crown), 1966.

BE A PLAYWRIGHT!

Successful Broadway playwrights aren't the only ones profiting from their work. Other markets for plays are Off-Broadway theaters, university and community theaters, and play publishers and producers.

Remuneration can be in the form of a flat fee, royalty payments, or a percentage of the box-office gross.

Unless you're good enough to start at the top, begin your playwriting career by submitting your work to local community and university theaters.

For further information:

Profitable Playwriting, Raymond Hull. New York, Funk & Wagnalls, 1968.

Playwriting (A111), Bernard Grebanier. New York, Apollo Editions.

Playwriting: The Structure of Action, Sam Smiley. Englewood Cliffs, New Jersey, Prentice-Hall, 1971.

HOW TO WIN AT . . .

If you're a bear at blackjack, a demon at dice, or a rogue at the races, you probably know enough about the subject to write a book about it.

Through the years well-written books of this type have consistently sold well. Write up an outline and a sample chapter and submit them to a book publisher. You may have a winner!

SWAP SHEET

A swap sheet is a tabloid-sized newspaper consisting wholly of classified ads. These papers flourish in most large and medium-sized cities and are a boon to anyone who wants to buy or sell anything from used toys to automobiles. If your community doesn't already have one you're in virgin territory. You'll need a bankroll of at least a few hundred dollars for this one, though, as printing costs are fairly high.

First get some estimates on printing from local printers. After finding someone willing to take on the work at a reasonable figure, start combing the want ads of your local newspaper for people who have articles for sale. Call them and offer them a free ad in your new paper. If they sell the item, they can send you 10 percent of the selling price. If they don't sell, there's no charge. After you get going you can charge by the word or line.

Hire a friend or a college student to distribute the papers to newsstands, markets, and drugstores. Sell them for twenty-five cents each and give the dealer ten cents a copy.

THESAURUS OF ADVERTISING PHRASEOLOGY

This might be the high-sounding title of your book in which you'd list catchy phrases that advertising agencies, copywriters, and small businessmen could use in their ad copy. A book of phrases such as "doubly delicious," "unboundingly beautiful," and "startlingly significant" would not only save these parties much valuable time, but would serve as a catalyst to their own creativity as well.

Naturally, compiling a definite book of this type would entail massive amounts of time and labor. But once completed, it could very well become a classic in its field.

BUMPER STICKERS

As long as cars have bumpers there'll always be a desire for bumper stickers. If you can come up with some witty sayings you can easily cash in on this market. If you're somewhat short on originality, find your material in joke books at your library or in bookstores.

Commission a printer to produce your stickers in large quantities, thus cutting your costs. Distribute your witticisms to auto parts and hardware stores, variety and novelty stores.

SELL YOUR SALESMANSHIP

If you're anywhere near being in the category of a hotshot salesman why not merchandise this ability by writing a book on the subject? You could either specialize in a particular field, such as insurance or real estate, or write a "how-to-sell-everything-under-the-sun" kind of book.

A tip: With the recent upsurge of interest in the occult, something entitled "How I use my psychic powers in closing sales" is sure to be a best seller.

ETHNIC GREETING CARDS

Habla Español? Parlez-vous français? Sprechen Sie Deutsch? Well, if you do, you can combine your linguistic ability with your wit and design ethnic greeting cards. If you're short on artistic talent, get together with an artist on this project.

For further information:

The Greeting Card Writer's Handbook, Joseph Chadwick. Cincinnati, *Writer's Digest,* 1968.

LEGITIMATE PLAGIARISM

A glance through any big city library's government publications file will fill you in on the tremendous wealth of practical information available through the U. S. Government. Put this together with the fact that government publications are owned by the American people, and as such cannot be copyrighted. Anyone, including you, can reprint the material for their own use or to sell to others.

Sound interesting? Now check through the file for items you feel would interest a large group of people, print up your own edition, and step right into the business of legitimate plagiarism!

SCREENPLAY BY . . .

How would you like to see *your* name on a movie screen? Well, it's possible—if you've got talent and the ability to promote your work. However, the competition is rough. You must submit your work through an agent and—you guessed it—California is really the *only* suitable environment for a screenwriter.

To keep informed of trends within the industry it would be worth your while to consult copies of *Daily Variety* or *Hollywood Reporter,* both available at large newsstands.

For further information:

The Writer and the Screen: On Writing for Film and Television, Wolf Rilla. New York, Morrow, 1974.

Audiovisual Script Writing, Norton Parker. New Brunswick, New Jersey, Rutgers University Press, 1968.

13

Car and Truck: Putting Your Wheels to Work

Ever since somebody came up with the idea of building a platform on top of that newfangled contraption called a wheel, man has been able to use the wheeled vehicle as a source of livelihood.

When you think of it, there aren't really very many ways in which one *can't* make a living in some way connected with vehicles. Aside from manufacturing them, washing and waxing, painting, repairing, upholstering, chauffeuring, buying and selling them, and teaching others to do any of the above, some people even earn their bread by wrecking them!

So if you have a propensity for working with cars, trucks, buses, motorcycles, and the like, take a ride on the paths to prosperity listed herein.

Transportation and Delivery Services

BABY DELIVERY SERVICE

No, this enterprise is not for obstetricians! A better name for it would be baby *supply* service. For that's what you'll be delivering—baby supplies: everything from safety pins to cribs and playpens.

After promoting your service vigorously through media advertising, handbill distribution, and newspaper feature articles, you'll have mothers calling you from all over town expecting—and getting—twenty-four-hour service on deliveries. Buy your goods through local wholesalers.

PERSONAL SIGHT-SEEING SERVICE

Learn everything you can about the sights and attractions in your area. Then print up some attractive brochures advertising that you conduct personalized tours. Ask to place them on the front desks of leading hotels, motels—anywhere tourists are likely to see them.

Keep your rates low and do a good job. When your customers go back home they'll recommend you to friends who may be planning a trip to your city.

ERRAND SERVICE

Ever had to pick up a package downtown but didn't have the car? You would have gladly paid fifty cents or a dollar to have someone else run the errand for you.

Chances are there are hundreds of people in your city that would take advantage of this service if you were to offer it. All you have to do is let people know it's available. Better yet, if you arrange to have a radio-telephone installed in your car, your customers can call you while you're on the move, and you can service them that much faster.

To get started, advertise in the classified section of your local newspaper or leave leaflets on windshields of cars parked in the lots of suburban shopping centers.

JITNEY SERVICE

What's a jitney? It's a small, passenger-carrying bus operating over a regular route.

First find some area in your community that lacks adequate bus transportation, especially during the rush hour. Then, if you can convince local licensing authorities that a service of this type is needed in your community, start operating over a regular route, charging each passenger about what a bus would.

BABY FORMULAS

In many cities and towns firms specializing in mixing and delivering babies' formulas consistently enjoy much success. There's no reason why you, too, can't profit by this enterprise by mixing simple formulas according to doctors' prescriptions and then delivering a fresh batch daily to each customer.

When you're ready, get customers through

pediatricians, baby furniture shops, and maternity wards of hospitals, as well as by advertising in new suburban housing developments. Before starting, be sure to check local health regulations and secure a good liability insurance policy.

 AUTO TRANSPORT SERVICE

Many individuals moving from one part of the country to another want to fly or take the train to their new location. But what to do with their car? An auto transport service fills this need by finding people who are willing to drive these cars to their destination.

As operator of such a service you'll charge customers anywhere from $50 to $250 or more for transporting each car, depending on the distance to be driven and the type of car. You'll bond your drivers, perhaps giving them a small gas allowance.

Find both customers and drivers through the want ads and the Yellow Pages.

 HELP THE HANDICAPPED

There is a man in Boston who has built up a very lucrative business by transporting the handicapped. His "taxi" is an ordinary van equipped with a hydraulic lift on the back, enabling him to lift the individual *and* the wheelchair into the van at the same time.

Should you decide to enter this field, get your customers by notifying nursing and convalescent homes, doctors, and hospitals of your service. Before starting, however, check local licensing regulations. This enterprise may have to adhere to the same licensing procedures as a regular cab company.

 DRUG DELIVERY SERVICE

In any town the large majority of drugstores don't make deliveries because of the expense involved in buying a truck and hiring a driver.

As the operator of a drug delivery service

you'll offer to contract with *all* drugstores in town to provide free delivery on prescriptions and other drug items. You'll work either on a percentage of the money collected or on a flat-fee-per-call basis. The drugstores would benefit by increased business and better public relations.

 CHAUFFEUR SERVICE

Many people, especially those who can't drive, have a need for a part- or full-time chauffeur. Furthermore, people sometimes like to put on the dog and be chauffeured to social events such as parties and theater premieres.

As operator of a chauffeur service your task would be, on the one hand, to screen and hire competent personnel, and on the other, to drum up business for your service. To find clients, advertise in the wealthier residential section of town, and in yacht and country clubs.

Business Services

OH, RUBBISH!

Even though most cities provide rubbish collection for their residents for a nominal fee or no fee at all, private rubbish companies continue to flourish everywhere. Why? Because we are the most prolific garbage-producing country in the world, and public facilities just can't keep up with the flow.

A dump truck is best for this business. Get your customers by going door to door, as well as by calling on such institutions as hospitals, apartment buildings, hotels, restaurants, and industrial plants. Charge whatever the going rate is in your area.

FROM RAGS TO RICHES

There's even money to be made from rags! Here's how you do it: Contact friends, neighbors, relatives, and go door to door, if necessary, collecting as many rags as possible. Launder them, then cut them up into twelve-inch square pieces and wrap them in bundles of two dozen each.

Next, call on service stations, garages, industrial plants, and anyone else who uses rags. Offer a weekly rag service, whereby you will pick up their dirty rags and deliver fresh, laundered ones. Base your fee on the quantity of clean rags delivered each week.

BE AN AUTOMATIC CAR WASH TYCOON

One of the easiest ways to make money is by selling a merchant on the idea of letting you install self-operating equipment on his property. In this case we're talking about installing coin-operated car washes on service station lots.

Your only expense here is the cost of the original equipment, which, for the most part, you can have financed. After installation, your only concern will be maintenance and repairs. You'll drop by once a week or so, emptying the coin box, paying the business owner a small percentage of the take, and pocketing the rest.

To find your equipment, refer to the *Thomas Directory of American Manufacturers,* at your library.

CLEAN UP ON GARBAGE CANS

Don't laugh! There *are* people in this world making a living as professional garbage can cleaners—and you can, too!

In addition to a pickup truck you'll need a steam jenny, which you can buy used or reconditioned. Suppliers can be found by looking in the Yellow Pages under "Steam cleaning equipment." Then build yourself a route composed of large restaurants, hotels, factories, and industrial plants. Since you'll only be charging your customers two dollars or so per month for each can, you'll have to develop a high volume of steady customers in order to make a decent living.

LOTS OF LINENS

Hotels, motels, and better restaurants are excellent prospects for a service in which you'd provide new batches of freshly laundered linen each week. By using your service, these establishments would save much in labor and on the cost of new linens, detergents, bleaches, water, etc.

To get started you'll need one or more trucks and a large commercial washing machine. For business, personally call on the above establishments offering your services, and advertise in the Yellow Pages.

A SOUND BUSINESS

Fit out your car or light truck with a tape player and external loudspeaker. Then, working for businesses, political parties, church bazaars, county fairs—or anyone else who is in need of such promotional services—drive your sound truck through densely populated areas of town.

Some communities, however, have passed "anti-noise" ordinances, so better check local regulations before starting.

MAIL DELIVERY SERVICE

With government mail service getting progressively more expensive and less reliable every year it's now possible for private individuals to break into this business successfully—and profitably.

Start by contracting with large local firms to make regular mass mailings in your area. Compute your rates on a per-hundred or per-thousand basis, with rates decreasing as quantities of mail get larger.

Depending on your volume, you'll need a number of delivery vehicles as well as a crew of dependable personnel. For cheap labor hire retired people and college students.

PAY DIRT

Would you believe there is even a market for dirt? You bet there is, when it is sold as landfill. Furthermore, building contractors at excavation sites will many times give away this fill just for the hauling.

Sell your dirt to new homeowners and builders.

VENDING MACHINE ROUTE

Nowadays vending machines offer everything from apples to zithers. Use your imagination and come up with some salable products. Then get permission from merchants to install your equipment on their premises, paying them anywhere from 10 to 25 percent of the gross profits from the machines. You'll be responsible for restocking and servicing the equipment on a regular basis.

To get started, check with several vending machine distributors on equipment prices. Many people start with a few small machines and gradually develop more locations, buying additional equipment as they go along.

For further information:

Adventures (Jingle Dollar) with Vending Machines, Coin Devices, and Rack Merchandising, Ray Burkett. Decker, Indiana, Ray De Vere Burkett, 1967.

Starting and Managing a Small Automatic Vending Business (SBA 1.15:13), Small Business Administration. Washington, D. C. Superintendent of Documents, U. S. Government Printing Office, 1967.

OPERATE AN INDUSTRIAL LAUNDRY

Uniforms, smocks, caps, linens, towels—these are just a few of the many items required by firms from dump yards to diamond manufacturers. Your job will be to supply these establishments with a new, freshly laundered batch of these necessities once or twice every week. Set up a few secondhand washers and dryers in your garage with which to do the laundering.

Break into the business gradually by concentrating on small firms such as service stations and cafés—that way you'll need only a small inventory. As your business grows, you can provide service to a greater number of firms, eventually extending your services to institutional establishments and large manufacturing plants.

RECYCLE NEWSPAPERS

If you can arrange with large apartment complexes to haul away their old newspapers on a weekly or semimonthly basis you can profitably sell truckloads of the stuff to paper-recycling outfits.

You might also promote paper drives for schools, churches, scouting organizations, and other groups interested in fund raising. You'd then pay these groups a nominal amount for the papers, and sell them to a paper recycler for profit.

MOBILE STATIONERY STORE

Many small and medium-sized offices have a need to place frequent orders for small amounts of office supplies. How handy it would be for them to pick up the phone, order the goods, and have delivery within twenty-four hours.

Your office-supply delivery firm would provide this service. Stock up on the most frequently ordered items, buying them through a wholesale stationer. Spread word of your firm by direct mail to all local businesses that might be attracted by your service.

PAINT AUTOS

The spray painting of automobiles is a messy and somewhat time-consuming task that is best performed by a specialist. The need to sand and prime before applying the color coat adds to the labor involved. But with a little experience anybody can learn to turn out satisfactory work.

If you have a large, dust-free garage or shed, start out by doing jobs for friends and neighbors, and by soliciting work from used-car dealers, cab companies, and other outfits that utilize fleets of cars and trucks.

SCRAP METAL

Inoperable stoves, refrigerators, washing machines, and car bodies are just a few of the many items that, most of the time, are given away just for the hauling.

You can find junk of this type by making the rounds of appliance dealers and by offering to clean out basements and attics for people. You'll also want to scavenge the streets just prior to rubbish pickup day. In addition, scrap metal and abandoned autos are often found lying next to roadsides and in open fields in the country.

Turn these useless hunks of metal into gold by selling them to scrap metal dealers, whose names you can find in the Yellow Pages.

Personal Services

CULTURE FOR THE COUNTRY FOLK

If you like books and traveling, why not combine the two by loading a panel truck full of appealing titles and hitting the road?

You'll have to travel far and wide to find areas without bookstores and public libraries. But once you do you can either sell your books outright—new or used—or start a rental service, in which case you'd return to the same towns on a regular basis.

For further information:

Beginning in Bookselling, Irene Babbidge. New York, Academic Press, 1971.

How to Run a Paperback Bookshop, Sidney Gross and Phyllis Steckler. Ann Arbor, Michigan, R. R. Bowker, 1963.

EXOTIC SEAT COVERS

In any large town you'll find a number of shops that custom-make auto seat covers. Most, however, cater to conventional tastes and thin pocketbooks.

Get the jump on these firms by designing and fitting seat covers of bearskin, leopard, rabbit, tooled leather—even mink! Obtain

customers through car dealers, auto parts stores, and country clubs, and by advertising in the more affluent section of town.

LOOT FROM LIMOUSINES

Here you'll need a fleet of limousines to start with. They needn't be new, but they must be immaculate in physical appearance.

Your service will consist of renting out your limos for weddings, parties, premieres, visits by out-of-town dignitaries—even for funerals. For an extra fee you might also provide chauffeurs.

When you're ready to go, spread word of your service through social and civic organizations, bridal registries, and newspaper ads.

A MOVING PROPOSITION

You needn't have a huge van with which to jump into the moving business. On the contrary, you can even start out with a minibus, making several trips if necessary, or you can rent a large truck for the bigger jobs.

The reason that many "mom and pop" operations of this type are successful is that not only can you give *personalized* service, but your rates will be far lower than those of the giant, established companies.

To find customers, contact local real estate brokers for names of people about to move, paying each broker a small commission if necessary. Newspaper and Yellow Pages advertising should also bring you customers.

For further information:

Do-It-Yourself Moving, George Sullivan. New York, Macmillan, 1973.

MOBILE DISCOTHEQUE

Outfit a van with a phonograph and records, speaker system, refrigerator, bar, and colored lights, and rent it out for outdoor parties.

Find customers by advertising in the newspaper, on the radio, and by distributing handbills to high school and college students.

AUTO FAIR

Here's a good way to profit by simply bringing used-car buyers and sellers together. First seek out a suitable location such as a drive-in theater or other large, vacant piece of property. After securing permission from the owner (he'll want some sort of fee), advertise for people who have used cars for sale to bring them to your lot on Saturdays and Sundays. You'll also want to slant your ads toward potential buyers.

Charge five dollars or so per car on sale each day. You'll find that after a few weeks of aggressively promoting this do-it-yourself used-car lot your profits will be "automatic."

CLEAN UP ON BASEMENTS AND ATTICS

Lord knows, there are certainly a lot of people around who wish they didn't have that basement or attic cleaning chore waiting for them in the near future.

As a "specialist" in this field you'll not only clear out their junk—you'll also haul it away to the nearest junkyard. Before doing so, however, search for items that might have value. Appliances, antiques, valuable paintings, and old china are just a few of the many articles people dispose of unthinkingly.

Get your customers by going door to door or by distributing leaflets in residential areas of town.

For further information:

Fortune in the Junk Pile, Dorothy Jenkins. New York, Crown, 1970.

CHECK-CASHING SERVICE

Fit out a panel truck or van with a "cashier's window" in it. Then make the rounds of well-established factories and industrial plants on payday, parking just outside the gate. Offer an instant check-cashing service, charging fifty cents or so per check.

Be sure to obtain adequate holdup insurance before starting. Also, you might want to have an armed security officer accompany you on your rounds.

DOLLARS FROM DRY CLEANING

Find a wholesale dry cleaner in your area who'll work efficiently and cheaply. Arrange to bring him your work. Next, distribute leaflets throughout large apartment buildings offering to pick up and deliver dry cleaning at reasonable prices.

Eventually you'll want to form a route for yourself, calling on and delivering to the same customers the same day of each week. For extra income you might also provide a laundry service.

AUTO PROFITS

You don't have to be an auto mechanic or a big-time car dealer in order to make money buying and selling cars. The secret is to buy your cars in reasonably good condition at low prices. Then, after performing some very minor work such as sewing up some upholstery or waxing the exterior, you sell high.

Buy your cars from auto auctions and through newspaper ads from people who are anxious to sell. To avoid advertising costs when selling, simply put a sign in the car's window with your phone number on it.

OPERATE A BEAUTY WAGON

If you're a hair stylist who enjoys gallivanting around the countryside, put the two together and operate a mobile beauty salon.

You'll need to outfit a van with a sink, hot and cold water, dryer, mirrors, etc. Then simply make the rounds of small towns, offering your services. Assure yourself of regular customers by visiting each town on the same day of every week. For extra revenue offer an assortment of wigs for sale.

For further information:

Introduction to Hairstyling, T. W. Masters.

New York, International Publications, 1969.

MOBILE COBBLER

Make the rounds of small towns in your area, picking up shoes for repair. If you appear in the same town on the same day of each week, your customers will know when to expect you. Take your work back to your shop, returning it to the customer the following week.

Getting to the sole of the matter, we could say that if you don't return with the shoes on time, you'll be considered a heel by your customers. But if you're dependable, you'll have your profits all laced up. (And don't take any rubber checks, to boot!)

For further information:

Practical Course in Modern Shoe Repairing, Chicago, Nelson-Hall, 1956.

HOME LINEN SERVICE

Homeowners with large families—especially those in the wealthier parts of town—are exceptionally good prospective customers for weekly delivery of sheets, pillowcases, towels, and washcloths.

Seek out customers here by going door to door offering your services.

DRIVING SCHOOL

As the automobile becomes more and more of a necessity each year driving schools grow in popularity and in profits.

If you're interested in entering this fast-growing field, the first thing you'll need to do is find out what state licenses are required, since some states do regulate driving schools.

To get into business you'll need a dual-control mechanism for your car, which you can get installed for under $100.

Next, it would benefit you greatly to take a course from an established auto driving school, in order to learn proper driving procedure and also pick up some good pointers on how best to teach the subject.

For further information:

In-Car Instruction: Methods and Content, W. G. Anderson. Reading, Massachusetts, Addison-Wesley, 1968.

HAULING SERVICE

Somebody has to haul away discarded refrigerators, TV sets, mattresses, and furniture. It might as well be you—especially if you get paid for it.

Since you're probably too young for a hernia, better get a husky helper for this job. Most of the items you pick up will be worthless, and you'll take them to the city dump. However, many times people will throw away valuable items—typewriters and toasters, even refrigerators and washing machines —that still work. These can be sold to secondhand dealers.

To get business, spread leaflets throughout your area and advertise in the Yellow Pages.

For further information:

Fortune in the Junk Pile, Dorothy Jenkins. New York, Crown, 1970.

USED TIRES

Many service stations and tire stores take in on trade tires which still have many miles of wear left on them. They will then either sell these at bargain prices, or they may even give them away if someone will haul them off on a regular basis.

After cleaning and applying tire paint to them you can sell them to people who'd rather not invest in new tires. Naturally, before selling them you'll inspect each tire thoroughly and discard those that are unsafe.

Get your customers by handbill distribution and by running regular ads in the newspaper classifieds.

Food on Wheels

ROLLING ROASTS AND TOURING T-BONES

Most small towns have no fresh meat markets and residents must travel to the nearest large town to buy their meat. You can ease their problem by outfitting a small truck with refrigerated display cases and making the rounds of small towns in your area, selling meat right from your truck.

Buy your meat wholesale. Work out a weekly route for yourself, calling on each town the same day of the week so your customers know when to expect you.

MOVIN' MINIMARKET

Milk, ice cream, fruit, and fish are sold by truck—why not offer a complete minimarket on wheels? Of course, you'll have to outfit your truck with shelves and refrigeration. But after you've built up a route of steady customers you'll look back and realize it was all worthwhile.

Travel the same route on the same day of each week so your customers will get to depend on you. Before starting, however, you'll want to check all local regulations regarding this type of enterprise.

MIDNIGHT SNACK DELIVERY SERVICE

Many college students burning the midnight oil get the hungries during the night and would welcome a ham sandwich or a slice of pie.

A partner is necessary in this venture. You would have to be on call from 10 P.M. till 2 A.M., with one of you delivering the goods and the other making up the orders and answering the phone at home.

To get started, publicize your enterprise throughout the campus, as well as in off-campus dormitories, fraternity, and sorority houses.

WATERMELONS GALORE

If you don't grow watermelons yourself make a deal with a local farmer to buy a daily batch. Load them into an ice-filled pickup truck early in the morning and head for a crowded beach or well-traveled and hot desert or country road.

Advertise your product with large signs, selling your melon by the slice, half, or whole.

SANDWICH ROUTE

This enterprise consists of making and selling sandwiches to food stores and taverns.

Start out by making a few dozen of the more popular varieties. A well-made hero sandwich is invariably gobbled up. Sell them on consignment, at a 25 percent discount; that is, if your sandwich sells for sixty cents, sell it to the store for forty-five.

Build your enterprise by making a quality product, and by daily replacing old sandwiches with fresh. Later on you can branch out into desserts such as slices of pie or cake, and cookies.

FREE-LANCE FOOD DELIVERY

In any fair-sized town there are dozens of hamburger, chicken, pizza, and fish 'n' chips joints which, individually, don't feel the need to provide delivery service to their customers. Taken as a group, however, there would be plenty of demand for home deliveries—and plenty of profits for the person making them.

Make the rounds of these establishments, offering to take care of deliveries on a fee-per-item-delivered basis. Then you'll want to encourage these businesses to aggressively promote their free delivery service to the public.

MOBILE CAFE

You can get your feet wet in this business by renting a fully equipped food truck and buying your food already prepared. Of course, if you decide to stay in the business you'll eventually want to cut down on your overhead by acquiring your own truck and preparing your own food.

When you're ready to go, call on one- and two-story office buildings, factories, and construction sites, offering them fresh sandwiches, hot cans of soup and chili, pies, cakes, candy, coffee, and soft drinks.

WAFFLE WAGON

One of Vivo's fondest childhood recollections is that of the waffle man. Twice a week, come rain or shine, he would be on Vivo's street with his truck dispensing waffle slices covered with powdered sugar.

You can start a similar operation by slightly modifying and installing a few waffle irons in an attractively painted panel truck or minibus. Pipe a musical tune through a loudspeaker to announce your arrival.

Charge twenty-five or thirty-five cents per slice, selling a whole waffle for about a dollar.

ICE CREAM ROUTE

Find yourself a used ice cream truck —they should be available in any large city. Buy your ice cream from a food wholesaler, varying your products as much as possible. Cover each neighborhood on the same day of the week, so the kids know when to expect you.

You won't get rich with just one truck, but you will make a lot of kids happy—and you'll never go hungry!

HOT DOGS ON WHEELS

Outfit a travel trailer, panel truck, or minibus with facilities for preparing and serving hot dogs, hamburgers, corn on the cob, and other such delicacies. To attract attention, paint your vehicle brightly and top it with a giant, scrumptious-looking hot dog on a bun.

Sell your wares at festivals, fairs, carnivals, and anywhere else people are enjoying themselves.

THE CASSEROLE CORNER

There exist shops specializing in hamburgers, fried chicken, and fish 'n' chips —why not casseroles? In fact, a casserole delivery service forms the basis of an extremely lucrative food operation in northern California.

Offer a large variety of dishes for your customer to choose from. It would also be of great promotional value to include a few unheard-of and outrageous varieties such as escargot casserole, caviar casserole, and peanut butter casserole.

Promote this unique service by leaflet distribution. If your products are good, word-of-mouth advertising will soon get you all the business you can handle.

For further information:

> *Casserole Cookbook,* John Roberson and Marie Roberson. Englewood Cliffs, New Jersey, Prentice-Hall, 1952.
>
> *Sunset Casserole Book,* Editors, *Sunset* magazine. Menlo Park, California, Lane, 1965.

FOOD SHOPPING AND DELIVERY SERVICE

In any metropolitan area there must be thousands of elderly and ill people who have difficulty getting to the supermarket for groceries. Add to this number housewives who are just plain *tired* of the weekly market-go-round and you've got the the ingredients for a very lucrative enterprise.

Your service consists simply of taking phone orders from these individuals, then doing the shopping and making deliveries to them. A fee of 10 percent of the bill, with a two-dollar minimum, is a fair rate.

For Mechanical Minds

ANTIQUE CARS

There are two ways to make money in this rapidly burgeoning field: one is to restore antique cars for other people, the other is to build and sell them yourself. Combine the two and, if your workmanship is flawless, you'll wonder why you didn't start in this field a lot sooner.

The best way to get started is to buy or build your own antique car, then join an antique car club. Soon the members will spread word of your automotive abilities for you. Also advertise in car-oriented national publications.

For further information:

> *Automobile Restoration Guide*, Stanley Nowak. New York, Sports Car Press (order through Crown), 1974.

> *Restoration of Antique and Classic Cars*, Richard Wheatley and Brian Morgan. Cambridge, Massachusetts, Robert Bentley, 1967.

AUTO-GO-ROUND

Calling on customers at home with your mobile auto repair and maintenance service, you'll offer such services as tune-ups, brake checking, and tire repair. You'll perform more involved work, such as transmission repair, at your home garage.

Promote your rolling garage service through auto accessory stores, and newspaper and Yellow Pages advertisements.

For further information:

> *Motor's Auto Repair Manual*. New York, Hearst, 1974.

> *Automotive Repair and Maintenance*, Robert Schipf. Littleton, Colorado, Libraries Unlimited—Colorado Bibliographic Institute, 1973.

ROVING BODY SHOP

With a little practice you can learn to eliminate dents in fenders, trunks, and hoods of cars in minutes. Carrying a few simple tools and a small supply of various-colored spray paints, make the rounds of supermarket parking lots and shopping centers. Offer to pound out dents, charging whatever you can get, while the car owner is shopping.

In order to look "official," wear some sort of uniform. If you sell yourself well, don't be surprised if your earnings reach fifty dollars per day or more.

For further information:

> *Basic Bodywork and Painting*, Spence Murray, ed. Los Angeles, Petersen, 1973.

> *Auto Body Repairing and Repainting*, Bill Toboldt. South Holland, Illinois, Goodheart–Wilcox Company, Inc. 1972.

AUTO DIAGNOSTICIAN

Sounds impressive, doesn't it? Here's how it works. You'll offer to meet your customer, the potential car buyer, at the location of the car he is contemplating buying. With simple test instruments, such as a vacuum gauge, radiator air pump, multimeter, and hydrometer, you'll check the operating condition of the car, giving your customer a report of your findings.

You might charge twenty dollars per car or offer to check any two cars for twenty-five. Advertise through auto parts stores and through ads in the used-car classifieds.

MOBILE FIX-IT SHOP

One advantage in having a business on wheels is that instead of sitting around a shop hoping for business you can be out in the fresh air rounding up as many customers as you need.

Fit out a van with workbench, tools, nuts, bolts, nails, and other accoutrements of the trade. Then canvass well-to-do neighborhoods, making repairs of all kinds—and getting paid for them—on the spot.

For further information:

How to Fix Almost Everything, Stanley Schuler. New York, Evans (order through J. B. Lippincott), 1963.

How to Fix It, M. J. Schultz. New York, McGraw-Hill, 1971.

AUTO CARE CLASSES

With the cost of auto repairs and maintenance rising faster than a nudist who just sat down on a barbecue pit it's no wonder that many individuals, especially women, are signing up for classes in this subject whenever they can find them. Here they learn such basics as how to change oil, do a tune-up, and change a tire. In addition, more advanced classes are sometimes available.

If you have a good-sized garage you can hold these classes at your home. Get your customers by advertising in beauty shops and ladies' apparel shops, through leaflet distribution, and in the newspapers.

For further information:

A Woman's Guide to the Care and Feeding of an Automobile, Carmel Reingold. New York, Stein & Day, 1974.

Car Maintenance and Repair (Motor Manuals Series: Vol. 4), Arthur Judge. Cambridge, Massachusetts, Robert Bentley, 1960.

MOBILE FARM MECHANIC

All farmers know the land, but many of them are all thumbs when it comes to repair of such machinery as tractors, pumps, motors, and dairy equipment.

Outfit a van with tools, spare parts, and test equipment and make the rounds of farms in your area, offering to make any necessary repairs of equipment on the spot. If you do good work, word will spread and you'll eventually have farmers calling *you* for your services.

For further information:

Self-Teacher in Farm Mechanics, I. L. Brakensick and Lloyd Phipps. Danville, Illinois, Interstate, 1961.

Tractor and Small Engine Maintenance, Arlen Brown. Danville, Illinois, Interstate, 1973.

BE AN AUTO WRECKER

By advertising in the newspaper and Yellow Pages you can usually get broken-down cars just for hauling them away.

After towing these collapsed conveyances back to your yard, strip them of all useful parts: engines, transmissions, radios, heaters, generators—anything salable. Then aggressively advertise and promote your cut-rate, used auto parts supply business throughout town. Sell the bare chassis as scrap metal.

MOTOR CAR MAINTENANCE

There are a whole slew of maintenance jobs that you can perform for car owners —even if you can't tell a piston from an exhaust pipe! Washing and waxing, installing headlights, repainting scratches, replacing antennas, and resewing upholstery are just a few examples.

Launch your maintenance business by contacting used-car dealers, by notifying auto parts stores, and by leaving handbills on car windshields. If you have a helper, you might also offer a free pickup and delivery service.

For further information:

How to Service and Repair Your Own Car, Richard Day. New York, Harper and Row, 1973.

The Complete Book of Car Maintenance and Repair; a Survival Manual, John Hirsch. New York, Scribner's, 1973.

14

The Selling Game

Did you know that earnings in the field of selling are higher than in any other field where a college degree is not generally required? In fact, some direct salesmen earn more than many doctors!

What accounts for these seemingly disproportionate high earnings? One reason is that the very foundation of our economy is built upon the production and marketing (and systematic obsolescence) of goods, as well as upon the sale of services. Another reason is that the power of persuasion is a skill that is not possessed or readily learned by a large percentage of individuals. On the one hand, we have a manufacturer or service company whose lifeblood depends on marketing its goods. On the other, we have a skilled technician ready and able to meet the challenge. What better milieu, then, for high earnings?

Assuming you've never sold before, how do you decide which segment of the selling field to enter? First ask yourself with whom you'd like to deal. Businessmen, homeowners, doctors, boards of directors, buyers —the choice is considerable. Would you prefer selling a product or a service? Tangibles or intangibles? Indoors or out? In person or over the telephone? Would you like to travel in your work? Will you need extensive training? Would you work on a commission or must you have the security that a salary provides?

Once you've answered these questions, you've but to settle on a product or service with enough potential to support you in the manner to which you're accustomed. *You'll* have to be the judge of that.

Where to find products? The newspaper classifieds are usually filled with opportunities for salesmen. You'll also want to consult copies of *Specialty Salesman* and *Salesman's Opportunity,* available at large newsstands. However, we must caution you to evaluate your product potential carefully. Many companies take on distributors or salesmen for products that continually do well for the company involved because of the many sales outlets these products enjoy, yet the individual salesman dies on the vine. One way to avoid this is to get an honest appraisal of the situation from an impartial distributor or salesman of the product, if you can find one.

In some cases, not only can you buy products directly from the manufacturer but, if you're shrewd, you can secure an exclusive local, regional, or national distributorship for his products, marketing them through your own sales organization. When you've found a product that suits your fancy, find its manufacturer by consulting the *Thomas Register of American Manufacturers,* available at your library.

If you're a neophyte in the sales field, however, it would probably be best to get some training first through an established sales organization. Most successful salesmen have learned the ropes in this manner.

In selling, two of the many ways to get prospects and customers are through door-to-door solicitation and the use of the telephone. Before attempting to solicit business by means of house-to-house canvassing, however, check local regulations. This activity may require a license or it may be prohibited altogether.

Before hiring commission salespeople to help you sell your product over the telephone check with the U. S. Department of Labor. You may be required to pay your employees a minimum wage, as prescribed by federal law.

But whether you're interested in selling abacuses or airplanes, brushes or buildings, combs or corporations, there's bound to be something in the selling field that'll make you—and your banker—very happy.

For further information:

Thirty Days to Big Money Selling: for the Salesman Who Wants More Money Now, W. Edwards. Englewood Cliffs, New Jersey, Prentice-Hall, 1972.

How to Make Big Money As an Independent Sales Agent, Edwin Bobrow. Englewood Cliffs, New Jersey, Prentice-Hall, 1967.

How to Earn Top Dollars in Direct Selling, Anthony Canning and Dorothy Waring. New York, Frederick Fell, 1968.

Sell and Grow Rich, Fred Kissling. Lexington, Kentucky, Lexington House, 1966.

Selling to Businesses

BRIGHTEN UP YOUR LIFE

Manufacturers have spared no imagination in bringing us light bulbs in every conceivable color, shape, and design. Write to concerns that produce these novel products, requesting commission schedules, catalogues, and samples. Then visit hotels, restaurants, offices, factories, and retail stores, selling them on the idea of brightening things up for themselves and their customers.

RING UP THE PROFITS ✓

An inexpensive ring is the type of item that lends itself especially well to impulse buying. Use this fact to your advantage by purchasing rings direct from manufacturers in wholesale lots and selling them at a discount to ladies' and men's apparel stores, department and jewelry stores, gift and variety stores.

GREENBACKS FROM PAPERBACKS

Contact paperback publishers, whose names you can find in *Literary Market Place,* at your library, and wholesalers, arranging to buy large quantities of paperback books at a discount. You'll also need some display racks, which you can get used from a store-fixture supplier.

Then offer to install your paperback racks, which you'll maintain periodically, in such establishments as hotels and motels, drug and variety stores, supermarkets, and gift shops.

ANTI-SHOPLIFTING DEVICES

The soaring shoplifting rate has prompted merchants to install antishoplifting devices, much to the enrichment of those who manufacture and sell such items as one-way mirrors, closed circuit TVs, and time-lapse cameras.

Contact manufacturers of shoplifting prevention devices, offering to make wholesale purchases or to sell their products on a commission basis.

BE A VENDING MACHINE LOCATER ✗

Make arrangements with vending machine distributors in your area to be paid a commission, ten to fifteen dollars, for each machine you arrange to have placed in a business location. Then contact owners of businesses, selling them on the idea of having these machines installed. They'll be risking nothing, as the machines are usually installed on a "share-the-proceeds" basis between proprietor and distributor.

Likely prospects are restaurants for jukeboxes, service stations for snack machines, and large offices for coffee machines.

PRINTING EQUIPMENT BROKER

It's likely that some printers in your town have old equipment lying around that could be turned into cold cash. Call on them offering to sell their surplus equipment on a commission basis.

Find buyers by contacting other printers in the area, by direct mail advertising, and by advertising in publications for the printing trade such as *Printing Magazine,* 475 Kinderkamack Road, Oradell, New Jersey 07649.

MERCHANDISE RACKS

Any time you offer a merchant an item that he can make money on, the odds are he'll want to do business with you. Your job here is to tailor products in display racks to the needs of individual merchants in your area. For instance, a drug or variety store might go for a display of wooden greeting cards. An auto accessories dealer might buy a rackful of small map lights as a floor display. You'll supply the racks as well as the products.

To get started, simply seek out unique products and contact the manufacturer or distributor, requesting a wholesale price list and samples. Then take these samples around to prospective buyers.

For further information:

Adventures (Jingle Dollar) with Vending Machines, Coin Devices, and Rack Merchandising, Ray Burkett. Decker, Indiana, Ray De Vere Burkett, 1967.

A WAGON JOBBER ✗

In the old days enterprising "peddlers," as they were called, loaded up their buggies with everything from beans to beds and traveled from town to town selling their wares to merchants. Nowadays it's more stylish to use an automobile and, if you live in a large town, you can transact all your business without ever leaving the city limits.

Ball-point pens, key chains, watchbands, necklaces, billfolds, flashlights—there are thousands of possibilities. Keep your eye out for salable products, then contact the manufacturers of these items and arrange to buy them in wholesale lots. Resell them later to merchants at a profit.

For further information:

Jobbers Distributing Co., Inc., P. O. Box 1863, Durham, North Carolina 27702 (catalogues of products—$2.00).

SHOE SHINE MACHINES

It seems that the shoe shine boy has gone the way of nickle movies, quarter steaks, and good burlesque shows. In reality, though, he hasn't disappeared at all. He's simply been reincarnated as the electric shoe-buffing machine, that small buffing unit which, at the flip of a switch, will turn those scuffed shoes almost into mirrors.

Insurance and real estate offices, stock brokerage firms, large department stores —any business that demands a neat sales crew—will be fertile pickin's for your new-fangled shoe-buffing contraption.

AIR CHARTER AGENCY

Contact several companies specializing in air charters. Make arrangements to send them customers in exchange for a commission. Then contact social and travel clubs, entertainers, politicians, business organizations, ski clubs and other sports organizations. Work with them on arranging fast, dependable charter service to their destinations.

For additional profits you could also solicit customers for shipment of air freight.

SELL STATIONERY

For this sales operation you will utilize a WATS line—a service the telephone company provides enabling the subscriber to make unlimited long-distance calls after paying one basic monthly rate. Your salesmen will thus be able to call purchasing departments of large corporations in other cities, offering substantial discounts on large orders of stationery supplies.

Buy your merchandise from a wholesale stationer.

For further information:

How to Increase Sales and Put Yourself Across by Telephone, Mona Ling. Englewood Cliffs, New Jersey, Prentice-Hall, 1963.

Products

IT'S A SHOE-IN!

In a box factory, where one of the authors used to work, a co-worker became a distributor for a large shoe manufacturer as a sideline. By the end of a few weeks of his constant haranguing, his sales pitch had so convinced his fellow workers that their feet were being irreparably damaged by wearing store-bought shoes that he'd sold over 100 pairs! After that, he quit the factory and became a full-time shoe distributor.

So you see shoes can, indeed, be a money-maker for the aggressive salesman. The following companies will supply catalogues and samples:

Mason Shoe Manufacturing Co., Chippewa Falls, Wisconsin 54729, and

Bronson Shoe Co., 710 West Lake Street, Minneapolis, Minnesota 55408.

PEDDLE PEEPHOLES Ⅹ

For two dollars you can buy from hardware stores a little gadget that fits into the front door of a house. It allows the person standing on the inside to see out, without the caller being able to see in. Installation takes only about five minutes, requiring just one small hole to be drilled in the door.

Arm yourself with a batch of these and an electric drill. Then simply call on local homeowners, offering to install the peepholes for eight to ten dollars. Seems like an easy way to make some quick cash.

AN ALARMING SITUATION Ⅹ

Automobile burglar alarms are relatively inexpensive, easy to install, and *excellent* insurance against break-ins. If you've ever been around when one of these alarms has gone off, you know it's loud enough to scare the tux off a penguin a mile away.

Contact local electronics equipment outlets as a source of supply, or check the *Thomas Register of American Manufacturers,* at your library. Sell these items to auto-parts stores, service stations, and garages, as well as to individual car owners.

SELL SEEDS—REAP PROFITS Ⅹ

You can buy large quantities of seeds and bulbs from wholesale seed distributors at sizable discounts. Package these items attractively, then hire mobs of school kids to sell the products door to door, paying them a small commission. Better yet, offer prizes such as baseball gloves, bikes, and transistor radios, depending on the amount each child sells.

PRODUCT PROMOTER

Fortunes have been made on such items as antishoplifting mirrors, magnetic flashlights, and hand driers for public restrooms. At one time all these items were completely unheard-of. It took an alert promoter to foresee the potentialities of such items and to act on his beliefs.

Continually keep your eyes open for new possibilities. Publications such as *Specialty Salesman* and *Salesman's Opportunity* contain thousands of new product ideas. When you're ready, contact the manufacturer and get an exclusive territory. Then arm a sales crew with your money-maker and send them into the field.

BOOTY FROM BRUSHES

If you're having a close brush with poverty and bristle at the idea of not being able to pay your bills, get a handle on the situation by combing your neighborhood for brush customers. You won't make a million dollars selling brushes door to door, but many individuals are able to support themselves in this work.

To get started, contact the Fuller Brush distributor in your area.

BAUBLES FROM BIBLES

One of the more popular ways to sell Bibles—and certainly one of the most lucrative—is door to door. Invariably the thick, heavily illustrated, expensive versions sell the best, mainly because an aggressive Bible salesman just won't take no for an answer.

The real money here, however, lies in developing your own sales crew who will do the dirty work while you sit in your air-conditioned office filling out bank deposit slips.

Find Bible publishers in the *Literary Market Place,* at your local library.

PROTECTION MONEY

With the crime rate soaring to ridiculous heights, and house break-ins near the top of the list, it's no wonder that home burglar alarm systems are selling faster than beer at a popcorn festival.

Buy equipment through manufacturers advertising in electronics magazines and listed in the *Thomas Register of American Manufacturers,* at your library. Find prospects through door-to-door solicitation and direct mail advertising, personally calling on interested parties with a well-prepared presentation of your product.

For further information:

> *Protect Your Property: The Applications of Burglar Alarm Hardware,* Richard Cole. Springfield, Illinois, Charles C. Thomas, 1971.

SALES CREW MANAGER

First find some products for the home. Just about anything will do! Unusual lamps or pictures, bedspreads, throw rugs, decorative drinking glass sets, and place mats are just some of the possible items. If you can find something unique—something not normally found in the stores—so much the better.

Get the products from wholesale distributors, which you can locate through the Yellow Pages.

Next place an ad in your local newspaper for door-to-door sales people. Select four or five men and women, arm them with sales books and samples, and take them out in your car to a suburban area. There they'll canvass door to door with the samples, for which they'll take orders. Follow them in your car and, since you'll have the merchandise in your truck, you'll be able to make delivery and collect the money that same day. Pay your people 20 percent of the selling price.

FIRE EXTINGUISHERS

In order to motivate people to buy fire extinguishers you'll have to practically scare the pants (or the skirts) off them. So the first thing to do is to spend half a day at your local library digging up grisly statistics relating to national fire casualties in general and fatalities in your hometown in particular.

Then get on the phone with a preplanned sales pitch and try to set up appointments at which you'll demonstrate your equipment to *both* husband and wife.

Get your extinguishers direct from a manufacturer.

WATER SOFTENERS

Hard water, which exists in many communities, is difficult to clean with because of its inability to dissolve soap. Besides leaving rings around tubs and sinks (and collars), it uses about twice as much soap as soft water. Home water softeners solve these problems by restoring the proper mineral balance to the water.

If you live in a hard-water area, get your feet wet (in *soft* water) by going to work for a distributor of water softeners. Find names of such firms in the Yellow Pages.

HONG KONG TAILOR AGENCY

Hong Kong tailors have an excellent reputation for tailoring quality custom-made men's suits—at about half of U. S. prices! What most people don't know, however, is that these suits can be ordered by mail.

Get names of Hong Kong tailors by writing the British Embassy, 3100 Massachusetts Avenue NW, Washington, D. C. 20008. Then write the tailors explaining that you'd like to be an agent for them. They'll send swatchbooks of sample material for you to show your customers. In exchange for your commission, you'll be responsible for collecting a deposit, taking measurements, and forwarding the orders to Hong Kong.

HOUSEHOLD GOODS

Many times individuals or families find it necessary to sell their household belongings prior to moving but don't really want to be bothered with the chore.

Take over this task for the homeowner, holding a two- or three-day "marathon sale." You'll be responsible for promoting the event through the newspapers and neighborhood signs. Charge your clients 25 percent of the proceeds from the sale.

Find likely prospects through real estate brokers and by advertising in the paper.

PEDDLE AT PARTIES

Millions of dollars' worth of merchandise—everything from art objects to zircons—is sold through party plans every year.

As a company representative your task consists of getting ladies to invite their friends into their homes for an evening of sociability as well as for the purpose of watching you demonstrate your products. A token gift is given to the hostess for her cooperation and refreshments are served to the guests. Naturally, you'll take orders for your products and also round up more volunteer hostesses.

A number of companies sell their products in this manner. They are all listed in a free publication called the *Membership Roster*. For your copy, write Direct Selling Organization, 1730 M Street, NW, Washington, D. C. 20036.

CAUSE FOR ALARM

If you can convince people that they can save their lives and property by buying home fire alarm systems from you, you'll have yourself a hot item.

To get started, write manufacturers of this equipment for facts and figures. Then drum up prospects through newspaper ads, direct-mail advertising, and door-to-door canvassing.

CATALOGUE SALES AGENCY

Most everyone is aware of the fact that merchandise can be ordered through Sears and Montgomery Ward catalogues. But these are only two of hundreds of firms that deal in catalogue sales.

Start your own catalogue sales agency! First write to various firms that sell their products in this manner. Tell them of your plans and ask them about a commission arrangement. They'll provide free catalogues, order blanks—even samples—upon request.

Where to obtain catalogues? Get the book called *Catalogue of Catalogues: The Complete Guide to World-Wide Shopping by Mail*, by Maria De La Iglesia. New York, Random House, 1972.

SECURITY BARS

Most homeowners are jittery because of the steadily increasing number of residential break-ins. What better time to sell iron security bars for windows?

If you're trained in ironwork manufacture you can produce this product as well as sell it. Otherwise go to work on a commission basis for a company specializing in this field. Find such firms in the Yellow Pages under "Iron work."

ENCYCLOPEDIAS

Your best bet here is to work for one of the larger, better-known firms such as *Britannica* or *Americana*. Sales agencies for these firms exist in all major cities.

You'll get valuable on-the-job training with these outfits but, as in all commission sales, it may take you a while to start bringing in a decent paycheck—better have a small bankroll to see you through the first month or so.

Services

 **AUCTIONEERING**

To get started as an auctioneer you can rent a large shed in an industrial area or, if the weather is nice and you live in the country, you can just hold your auctions in an open field.

Let it be known, through newspaper and handbill advertising, that you're in business. Invite people to bring in anything from tricycles to automobiles. Hold your auctions on weekends, and have some benches for your customers. You could even make a few extra dollars by selling hot dogs and soda pop.

Charge a 10–20 percent commission to the seller on the selling price of every item sold. If you're good, and you promote the business properly, you should sell $1,000–$2,000 worth of merchandise every weekend.

For further information:

> *Auctions and Auctioneering*, Ralph Cassady, Jr. Berkeley, California, University of California Press, 1967.

 **TRAVEL AGENT'S SCOUT**

As a scout for various travel agents in your area you will send these firms business in exchange for commissions paid to you.

It will help to have a lot of acquaintances in your community, as well as to have done some traveling of your own. To drum up business you might put on some slide or color film presentations dealing with various foreign countries. These are available at little or no charge through many airlines and steamship companies.

Start by contacting local travel agents and finding out what they are willing to pay for your services.

 **SELLING SCHOOL**

If you're the type that can sell ice cubes to Eskimos, parkas to desert dwellers, and an in-person TV interview to Howard Hughes, would-be salesmen will pay a lot to learn your methods. Why not help them by starting a school on selling?

Plan your courses by using the materials listed below. Then advertise in publications such as *Specialty Salesman* and *Salesman's Opportunity*.

For further information:

> *Textbook of Salesmanship* (instructor's manual and text), Frederic Russell, *et al.* New York, McGraw-Hill, 1974.

> *Basics of Successful Salesmanship* (instructor's manual and text), W. M. Thompson. New York, McGraw-Hill, 1968.

 **SALES CORRESPONDENCE COURSES**

Perhaps a less time-consuming and more profitable way to teach your selling skills, your talking talents, your motivating methods, and your persuasive prowess would be to make up and market a correspondence course on the subject.

Using the references listed below as a guide, write up some of your own material, including study guides and quizzes. Then advertise your course in publications such as *Specialty Salesman* and *Salesman's Opportunity*.

For further information:

> *Textbook of Salesmanship* (instructor's manual and text), Frederic Russell, *et al.* New York, McGraw-Hill, 1974.

> *Teaching by Correspondence*, Renee Erdos. New York, Unipub, 1967.

BUYERS' DISCOUNT CLUB

Consumers would pay ten dollars or so per year for a membership card in your discount club. This card entitles the member to a 10–15 percent discount on any merchandise being sold by merchants who agree to become a part of the plan.

To start, contact all types of local retail

merchants, explaining your plan. The merchant invests nothing—and therefore risks nothing—by cooperating. When a fairly large number have agreed to participate, print up membership cards and promote their sale aggressively.

NEWSPAPER SUBSCRIPTIONS

Create a job for yourself by making an arrangement with a local newspaper to solicit subscribers for them by phone. Get the paper to give some special incentive to new subscribers, such as offering them the first two months for the price of one.

Then open up a small office, install several phones, and hire a crew of phone sales personnel to sell subscriptions throughout the area. Pay them a small commission or the minimum wage.

For further information:

How to Use the Telephone in Selling, J. L. Wage. New York, Beekman, 1974.

MAGAZINE SUBSCRIPTIONS

Selling magazine subscriptions is a relatively effortless way of making a living. Prospects are everywhere, and if you can motivate whole organizations to subscribe to publications that would be beneficial to them, you can garner pocketsful of commissions en masse.

To get started, contact wholesale subscription brokers such as International Circulation Distributors, 250 West Fifty-fifth Street, New York 10019, or check your Yellow Pages under "Magazines—subscription agents." These concerns will provide you with price lists, order blanks, and sales tips.

GARAGE SALES

Because garage sales seem to exude a neighborly, old-fashioned atmosphere, attending them has become a popular weekend family activity.

You can capitalize on this trend. During the week scour the want ads, secondhand stores, thrift shops, attics and basements for antiques, furniture, china, costume jewelry, appliances—anything that might have value.

Advertise your garage sales in the newspaper classifieds, and by putting up notices throughout the neighborhood. Better check existing regulations first, however, as some communities have recently started curtailing these enterprises.

For further information:

The Better Garage Sale Book, Jean Young and Jim Young. New York, Bantam, 1974.

How to Hold a Garage Sale, James Ullman. New York, Scribner's, 1973.

The Advertising Game

MATCH THIS ONE!

It's been proved! Restaurants, gas stations, clothing stores, and other small businesses could all benefit greatly from matchbook advertising. You can likewise benefit by selling it to them. Commissions on reorders will further add to your coffers.

The following matchbook manufacturers will help you get started in this hot item: Superior Match Company, 7530 S. Greenwood Avenue, Chicago, Illinois 60619, and Monarch Match Company, 2300 Monterey Road, San Jose, California 95150.

BAG YOUR FORTUNE

Thousands of minigrocery stores and variety and drugstores give away millions of bags every year—plain paper bags.

If you could buy bags in wholesale lots, sell advertising space on them to large chains, then distribute the bags to local merchants for less than the bags presently cost them, there's no question that you'd strike it rich.

ADVERTISING SPECIALTIES

This involves selling business firms on the idea of distributing to their customers calendars, pens, pencils, key chains, and other novelties with the firm name imprinted on the item.

The larger, more affluent companies will buy items like gold-plated globes of the world, sterling silver letter openers, and elaborate paperweights. One of the authors knew a man in San Francisco who made a small fortune when a large plumbing-equipment company placed an order for 500 small, imprinted plastic transistor radios made in the shape of bathroom toilets!

You can get ideas and names of distributors for hundreds of these specialty items by reading a copy of *Salesman's Opportunity* or *Specialty Salesman,* both of which are available at large newsstands.

BOOTY FROM BOOK COVERS

Here you'll make money by giving away book covers to the bookstores of elementary schools, high schools, colleges, and universities. How? By first selling ads to local merchants and having them printed on the book covers.

To get stock, order quantities of heavy, colored paper sheets from a paper distributor.

SIGNS OF THE TIMES

Ever since man began trading one type of goods for another he's realized that attractive outside advertising is like money in his pocket. Hence, the sign salesman has always prospered and will continue to do so.

Send for manufacturers' catalogues, price lists, and illustrated brochures. Then simply make up a sales portfolio and walk down the street of any business district, calling on those merchants whose business could be improved by the installation of one of your signs.

CABLE TV ADS

Most cable TV stations originating their own programming have unused channels that could be put to good use. One profitable use for a vacant channel is to set up a revolving wheel and camera combination. Ads are placed around the perimeter of the wheel. A timer holds each ad in front of the camera for ten seconds, then moves on to the next ad, with taped music being played in the background. In this manner, firms can advertise their products to viewers.

Contract with a local cable TV station to set up one of these systems. Then go into the business community selling ad space.

SALES PORTFOLIOS

Companies dealing in insurance, real estate, office machines, swimming pools, and home improvements are just a few of the innumerable types of direct-sales organizations that would benefit by paying you to design convincing sales portfolios for their salesmen.

To start, simply make up a sample portfolio. Then call on sales firms and offer your services.

TELEPHONE BOOK COVERS

These are plastic folders made especially to fit telephone books. You'll distribute them free to telephone subscribers. Where's the profit here? Before distribution, you'll sell local merchants ads which will be printed on the folders.

Get your folders from a wholesale stationer.

Insurance—Real Estate—Securities

LIFE INSURANCE

Thousands upon thousands of men and women are making above-average incomes in this field. Don't overlook it in your quest for a lucrative enterprise.

To get started, simply contact life insurance agencies in your area for the lowdown. Although you'll be working on straight commission after getting started, if you're young and glib of tongue you should be able to find a company that will pay you during training and give you a weekly "draw" for your first four to six weeks in the business.

For further information:

> *How I sell 25,000,000 Dollars of Life Insurance Year After Year,* Karl Bach. Radnor, Pennsylvania, Chilton, 1973.

> *Opportunities in Life Insurance Sales,* Lee Rosler. Louisville, Kentucky, Vocational Guidance Manuals, 1974.

MORTGAGE INSURANCE

One especially lucrative form of life insurance is decreasing term insurance, or mortgage insurance. Here the insurance company insures the homeowner only for the amount remaining on his mortgage, during the term of that mortgage—hence the name "decreasing term."

Names of homeowners are provided through banks and savings and loan associations holding the mortgages. Because the salesman never has to walk into the prospect's home "cold" it's an ideal setup.

To find out more, call a few of the larger lending institutions in your area and ask them the name of the insurance company servicing their mortgage holders. One of the larger and more reputable insurance companies in this field is Family Life Insurance Company, Park Place, 1200 Sixth Avenue, Seattle, Washington 98101.

DISABILITY INSURANCE

Some companies specialize in selling disability, or health and accident, policies rather than life insurance. Although long-term earnings are generally lower here than they are in life insurance, many health and accident companies provide their salesmen with "leads"—names of people who have inquired about the company's policies. Naturally, this saves the salesman valuable time by eliminating the necessity of prospecting for customers.

You can find the more aggressive companies—where the better opportunities lie—by referring to the newspaper classifieds.

REAL ESTATE RICHES

Houses, apartment buildings, stores, lots, farms—even skyscrapers—are sold by real estate agents. It's a highly lucrative profession for a lot of people, as it can be for you.

First visit a few brokers' offices and decide which aspect of the business you'd like to enter. When you've chosen a broker to work with, he'll assist you—sometimes financially—in preparing for the exam that most states require.

For further information:

> *Real Estate Selling Magic,* Gael Himmah. Walnut Creek, California, Gael Himmah Publishing, 1974.

> *How I Sold a Million Dollars of Real Estate in One Year,* George Gardiner. Englewood Cliffs, New Jersey, Prentice-Hall, 1969.

MORTGAGE BROKER

The business of the mortgage broker is to secure mortgages from lending institutions for individuals or companies. Through his expertise and contacts a competent broker many times can secure a loan that might otherwise have been rejected. He earns a percentage of each loan granted.

You can learn the business by going to work for an established mortgage firm, later branching out on your own.

STOCKS AND BONDS

The field of stocks and bonds represents one of the most lucrative activities in the entire selling field.

If you're young, degreed, and glib of tongue, you're much in demand by such firms as Merrill Lynch and E. F. Hutton & Co. Upon being hired, you'll be paid a salary while training, then rewarded handsomely after training by a salary, commission, or a combination of the two.

All states require that securities representatives pass a stringent examination before soliciting business.

MUTUAL FUND SALES

A mutual fund is a firm that owns securities in several different companies. Owning shares in a mutual fund gives the investor the advantage of diversification which he might not otherwise be able to afford.

Mutual fund salesmen are well paid but, as with stocks and bonds salesmen, they must participate in an intensive training program and pass a rigid state examination before going out into the field.

Two of the larger firms are Investors Diversified Services and the Dreyfus Fund.

15

Retail Shops-Services-Schools

Many people enjoy the stability and sense of accomplishment provided by having their own shop, store, school or other place of business outside the home.

A nonhome-based business offers some definite advantages. Your business will exude a more professional air and you'll be able to erect permanent signs, attractively display your goods, and post notices in your windows of price reductions or sales. Thus, much business can be generated from outdoor foot traffic with relatively little effort.

Moreover you'll never have to be concerned about being interrupted by authorities suddenly demanding that you cease operations because of your location in a residential district. And if your home happens to be inhabited by one or more raucous youngsters, dogs or relatives, having your own shop allows you to escape to the sanctity of its domain and pursue your vocation in relative tranquillity.

For further information:

Fundamentals of Retailing, Benjamin Butcher. New York, Macmillan, 1973.

Modern Retailing Management, Delbert Duncan. Homewood, Illinois, Richard D. Irwin, 1972.

Retail Business Management, K. Gillespie and J. Hecht. New York, McGraw-Hill, 1970.

Retailing Management, William Davidson. New York, Ronald Press, 1966.

The Book Bonanza

TWOFER ONE

This might be a good name for your paperback book exchange, in which you'll give customers one paperback book for every two they bring in. Of course, you'll sell your paperbacks as well—at bargain prices.

You'll need a large stock of books to begin with. These you can get cheaply by buying out another shop or by advertising for them in the local classifieds. Promote your business

heavily by putting up notices in libraries and on college bulletin boards, and through advertising in newspapers and Yellow Pages.

For further information:

Beginning in Bookselling, Irene Babbidge. New York, Academic Press, 1971.

METAPHYSICAL BOOKSTORE

If you live in a fair-sized community, especially one in which there is a college or university, you stand a good chance of profiting by opening up a bookstore dealing in the occult.

From astrology to voodoo, your books would encompass the entire field. As a sideline you could sell incense, Ouija boards, pendants, and the like.

For further information:

Beginning in Bookselling, Irene Babbidge. New York, Academic Press, 1971.

RICHES FROM RELIGION

Since the time of Moses, or at least since the invention of the printing press, stores dealing in religious books and related goods have prospered.

You might start small by specializing in religious books for children. Then gradually expand by offering Bibles, missals, hymnals, prayer books, rosaries, gift items—even robes and church furniture.

MONEY FROM MAGAZINES

Here's an enterprise in which you can pick up your inventory for next to nothing. Scour out old magazines in hotels, waiting rooms, bus terminals, railway depots. The trick is to make deals with the custodians of these places by which they would save old publications for you and you would pay them a few cents a pound in return.

When you've got a fair supply open a small shop in the business district. Don't expect to sell your old copies of *Family Circle* for more than five or ten cents each. Where you'll make the big money will be on such publications as *Playboy* and *National Geographic,* which should sell for about 75 percent of the original selling price.

OPEN A TECHNICAL BOOKSTORE

Most large cities have bookstores specializing in technical subjects. However, many medium-sized towns do not. Here is an excellent opportunity for the book-oriented entrepreneur.

Find publishers of technical books in the *Literary Market Place,* at your library. Write to these firms telling them that you wish to be a dealer. They'll send you catalogues and price lists.

In addition to catering to the retail trade contact local stores, factories and industrial plants. Let them know they can order technical books through you.

For further information:

Beginning in Bookselling, Irene Babbidge. New York, Academic Press, 1971.

Cash From Clothing

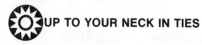

HAT HEAVEN

This might be the name of your one-price ladies' hat shop. With hundreds of hats available at $2.98 each, a woman could spend hours trying on hats—then walk out with half a dozen for under $20!

Find a manufacturer that'll sell to you direct, thus eliminating the middleman. A good source is the *Thomas Register of American Manufacturers,* at your library.

UP TO YOUR NECK IN TIES

There's a certain attraction for the public in stores that sell all their merchandise at the same price—necktie stores included.

Because your profit on each tie will be low

this enterprise requires that you have a store in a high-volume area such as downtown or in a shopping center. Order your ties from manufacturers and wholesalers in large lots, thus cutting your costs.

Promote your product heavily, especially at first, perhaps by announcing a two-for-the-price-of-one sale or by having a grand opening with live entertainment.

GAG T-SHIRTS

T-shirts for boys and girls, men and women, offer an ideal background for amusing adages, political phrases and religious relevancies.

Locating your shop in a tourist area, you'll offer to imprint T-shirts with whatever the customer desires. Also have stock samples to choose from. The material can be imprinted either by means of silk-screening or by the heat transfer method.

For further information:

Printing on Fabric, Ellen Bystrom. New York, Van Nostrand, 1971.

PANTS-A-PLENTY

This is the name of a store in the Midwest that deals exclusively in—you guessed it—pants. Their stock includes everything from Bermuda shorts to bell bottoms.

They buy their goods in wholesale lots as "factory seconds." This, combined with the low overhead they pay by being located on an off-street of the downtown area, enables them to sell their merchandise at extremely attractive prices.

BARGAIN CLOTHING SHOP

Locate clothing manufacturers and suppliers who can consistently supply you with large quantities of factory rejects —slightly flawed garments that can't be sold through the better clothing outlets.

Then open up a small clothing store in a

"workingman's" section of town and beat out the competition by selling your merchandise at rock-bottom prices.

Find names of clothing manufacturers in the *Thomas Register of American Manufacturers,* at your library.

MATERNITY THRIFT SHOP

Most people hate to spend any significant amount of money on items that will serve them for only a limited amount of time. Certainly maternity apparel falls into this category.

Capitalize on this fact by canvassing homes in areas containing older children where housewives are likely still to have their maternity clothes yet not be planning to have more children. Offer to buy these garments at low prices.

After washing and ironing these clothes, distribute handbills in *new* housing developments, offering your goods at bargain prices.

Specialty Food Shops

GOURMET DOUGHNUTRY

Such items as glazed and chocolate doughnuts are standard fare in the normal doughnut shop. But how about featuring in your shop doughnuts flavored with guava, Scotch, mint, or peanut butter? Why not vary the appearance as well, molding your products into pretzel or spiral shapes, or forming them into numbers or letters of the alphabet in order to appeal to children? There are innumerable possibilities. Start out by embellishing basic recipes found in any general cookbook. Then buy some used equipment, rent a small store in a good area, and you're in business.

BETTER NUT BUTTERS

Who decreed peanuts should have a monopoly on nut butter? Open your own nut butter specialty shop, featuring almond, cashew, walnut, brazil, macadamia nut butters, and sunflower or sesame seed butters as well.

Just grind the nuts or seeds in a hand mill or electric grinder, and add a little oil or water if necessary to improve the consistency. Your customers will go nutty over your better nut butters.

OH, FUDGE!

An old American favorite, fudge can be made in a variety of flavors. Start fudging around today! Break into the fudge fray by experimenting at home with recipes from general cookbooks till you come up with some quality products.

Market your fudge creations through your own attractively decorated specialty shop. You can also package your goods handsomely and distribute them to food stores, variety stores, restaurants, and fund-raising organizations. And don't eliminate the possibility of a fudge-by-mail business.

NUTS TO THEM

"Nuts to You" is actually the name of a business in northern Wisconsin. Specializing in nuts from around the world, they sell walnuts from California, pistachios from India, and macadamia nuts from Hawaii. Their shop is located on a well-traveled highway just outside of town, so it gets trade from travelers as well as from townsfolk.

You can open—and profit by—a similar operation. Contact a food importer in any large city to arrange for delivery of your stock. You'll also need a peanut roaster and some attractive display cases for your goods.

INTERNATIONAL FOOD SHOP

Before opening a store specializing in groceries from other lands it's best to take a survey of the ethnic minorities in your town.

Ask them about the availability of some of their favorite foods. If you find that there is a market for your goods and decide to open a store, make up an extensive list of your neighbors' needs.

Then place your order through a large food importer. These are most readily found in large East and West Coast cities.

# PEDDLE PIES

Pies are one of America's favorite desserts. If you can come up with a high-quality product you can successfully operate a "pie palace," a restaurant or take-out shop specializing in twenty to thirty to forty or more varieties. You can also sell your products to other eating establishments and specialty food shops.

If you're not a pie expert already, experiment using standard recipes, then improvise, coming up with some of your own original creations.

For further information:

The Pie Book: 419 Recipes, Louis De Gouy. New York, Dover, 1974.

The Pie Cookbook, Farm Journal Editors. New York, Nordon Publications, 1975.

# POPCORN PARADE

Have you ever heard of blueberry-, licorice-, or onion-flavored popcorn? How about a beer- or bourbon-flavored product?

Your biggest investment in opening a multiflavored popcorn business is a commercial-sized popcorn machine, which you should be able to buy, used, for under $200. After experimenting and developing several different flavors of this habit-forming snack food you can open up a specialty popcorn shop or stand. You might also package and distribute your products to theaters, supermarkets, and beer parlors—even liquor stores might be persuaded to buy a carton of the liquor-flavored variety for sale to their customers.

ICE CREAM PARLOR

You'll do best in the ice cream business if you offer a superior product served in a distinctive atmosphere. You might try creating unique flavors possessing unusual names such as kumquat pecan or papaya swirl. Design your parlor on a Gay Nineties or other attractive theme.

When you're ready, throw a grand opening, featuring a children's ice cream eating contest, and award a year's supply of ice cream cones to the winner. This stunt will surely get you some valuable newspaper coverage.

For further information:

Complete Book of Homemade Ice Cream, Milk Sherbet, and Sherbet, Carolyn Anderson. New York, Bantam, 1974.

Ice Cream and Ice Cream Desserts: 470 Tested Recipes for Ice Creams, Coupes, Bombes, Frappes, Ices, Mousses, Parfaits, Sherbets, Etc., Louis De Gouy. New York, Dover, 1974.

START A HOMEMADE FOOD SHOP

If you're an organizer you might consider getting a bunch of local ladies together and starting a homemade food cooperative.

Each lady would help stock the shop with her favorite homemade items. Cheeses, bread, ice cream, pastries, honey, fresh and canned fruits and vegetables, jams and jellies—the possibilities are endless.

Open your shop in the best section of town, selling only high-quality items.

CANDY KITCHEN

If you can come up with some novel ideas for candy treats you might profit by opening your own candy shop. Candy canes, taffy, peanut brittle, chocolates, fruit bars, decorative lollipops, marzipan, caramels, and mints are just a few of the infinite number of possibilities. For variety, try making your candy in different shapes.

You can also package your creations attractively and sell them through food outlets, gift shops, and fund-raising organizations.

For further information:

Homemade Candy, Food Editors, *Farm Journal,* and Nell Nichols. New York, Barnes & Noble (orders to Harper & Row), 1974.

Old-Fashioned Candymaking, June Roth. Chicago, Regnery, 1974.

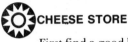CHEESE STORE

First find a good location for your store. It needn't be a large place, since even a large variety of cheeses takes up a relatively small area.

Next contact some of the bigger cheese importers. Visit your local library and find copies of the Yellow Pages for some large eastern and western cities, where such importers are based. Order a variety of cheeses, letting the importer guide you in selecting the most popular types. Place small orders at first, until you see where the demand lies.

HEALTH FOOD SUPERMARKET

Organic fruits and vegetables, raw honey, herb teas, and vegetarian cookbooks are just a few of the millions of dollars' worth of goods that health food markets sell in this country every year. It can be a lucrative business—especially if there is no store of this type around you.

Start by contacting wholesalers in your area, buying your produce direct from a local organic farmer if possible. You'll also want to make arrangements with a nearby bakery to supply you with bread according to your own nutritious recipe. Then simply find a suitable location and open your doors!

Assorted Shops

AD SHOP

We've all heard of a classified ad newspaper, but how about a classified ad *store?*

Open up a small shop in a high foot-traffic area. Display hundreds of 3 by 5 index cards containing information about items and services for sale and for rent. Individuals could either mail in the cards to you for display or they could drop them by. Charge $1 or so per card per week.

FOR TRUSTING SOULS

We believe that, although most people are eager to latch onto a bargain in their purchases, they'll be fair if given the opportunity. If you believe this, you might be able to profit by this unique merchandising idea.

Open up a small retail store. You can deal either in new goods or in used merchandise. It can be anything: Furniture, appliances, bicycles, jewelry—you name it. On each item, place a tag honestly stating what the article cost *you.* Then let your customers decide how much profit you should make on it, and pay you for it accordingly.

Your markup won't be as high as the department stores', but if you promote your business aggressively enough, word of your bargains will spread, and you'll make up the difference by generating a high sales volume.

A FORTUNE IN FRANCHISING

The franchise system, which covers a vast array of enterprises, offers an excellent opportunity to those individuals desiring to escape most of the headaches normally attendant on getting established in a new business. You'll be trained and provided with a fully equipped, ready-to-go operation, using the franchisor's trade name.

In exchange for these services you'll be required to pay a fee to the franchisor in proportion to his size and the demand for his franchises. In addition, you'll be required to buy all your materials from, or through, him.

There are advantages and disadvantages in buying a franchise. Study books on the subject first and, as with any prospective investment involving a large amount of cash, be extremely cautious in your dealings.

For further information:

The Franchise Boom, Harry Kursh. Englewood Cliffs, New Jersey, Prentice-Hall, 1968.

The Franchise Handbook: A Complete Guide to Selecting, Buying, and Operating, compiled by Jan Cameron. New York, Barnes & Noble (orders to Harper & Row), 1971.

Directory of Franchising Organizations. Pilot Industries, 347 Fifth Avenue, New York 10016 (an annual publication).

National Franchise Reports, 333 North Michigan Avenue, Chicago, Illinois 60601 (monthly bulletin).

FOUND A FLEA MARKET

In our estimation a large flea market is the next best thing to a three-ring circus. Clothes, furniture, appliances, toys, automobiles, bicycles, and every conceivable type of bric-a-brac are bought, sold, and traded in an atmosphere of raucous joviality.

Flea markets are usually held on weekends on the lot of a drive-in movie theater, in an open field, or in a large shed. If you own or can lease a spacious area near a fair-sized town, it's simply a matter of leasing out small spaces to vendors for five dollars or so per day each. Attract customers by having a free admission policy.

FLEA MARKET VENDOR

If you don't need the headaches (or the big profits) involved in operating a flea market, it's still possible to make a good livelihood as a vendor.

The trick here is to find a good wholesale source of supply for your products. Tools, decorative kerosene lamps, wall posters, small appliances, toys—they'll all sell well, but *only* if they can be bought and sold at bargain prices. In addition, during the week you can search out items like antiques and used clothes, selling them for a profit at a flea market on the weekends.

GO FLY A KITE!

Or, better yet, make them for others to fly. There is a man in San Francisco who has developed a full-time retail business making and selling kites of every conceivable shape, color, and design. He's even got a giant winged model that soars like an eagle!

Start by making a few "far-out" models in your home. Sell them to friends, neighbors, supermarkets, drug and variety stores, and gift shops. Word will spread, and later on you can branch out into your own retail outlet and perhaps into a lucrative mail-order business.

For further information:

Twenty-Five Kites that Fly, Leslie Hunt. New York, Dover, 1971.

Chinese Kites: How to Make and Fly Them, David Jue. Rutland, Vermont, Tuttle, 1967.

OPEN A GOURD MUSEUM

We wouldn't believe it if we hadn't seen it with our own eyes: A man in the Southwest makes a comfortable living by selling nothing but dried gourds!

The way he built his business was by advertising, through roadside signs, free admission to his gourd museum. Many unusual specimens, including one over six feet long, were on display, and most were for sale.

Start your museum by obtaining seeds from a local supplier and planting them in the spring. After the gourds reach maturity, cut and store them in a house or dry shed for a few months, in order to dry them out. Tying leather straps around the gourds while they're growing will produce some novel and interesting shapes.

When you've accumulated a large inventory, open a small shop next to a busy highway, heavily advertising your products through roadside signs. To increase your volume offer discounts for large purchases.

YOUR KEYS TO SUCCESS

If you can find yourself a high-volume location such as the mall of a suburban shopping center, or inside a busy department or variety store, you should be able to make a hefty income by running a key-duplicating stand.

To start, you'll need a key machine and a good stock of blanks, which should cost you less than $300. Buying a used machine will reduce this figure substantially.

Since your profit on each 50¢ key will be about 40¢, selling 100 keys per day will net you in excess of $1,000 per month, less, of course, your rent and other overhead.

 THE PIANO PARADE

First study up on piano repair and tuning. Then find used pianos through the classified ads, repairing and refinishing them when necessary.

Naturally, you'll have to be a bit of a horse trader, buying low and selling high. Sell your pianos through the same medium as you bought them—the newspaper classifieds.

Three firms offering home study courses in piano turning and repair are:

- Niles Bryant School, 3631 Stockton Boulevard, Sacramento, California 95820.

- American School of Piano Tuning, P. O. Box 707, Gilroy, California 95020.

- Capital Piano Tuning School, 3160 S.W. Sixteenth Court, Fort Lauderdale, Florida 33312.

For further information:

Complete Course in Professional Piano Tuning, Repair, and Rebuilding, Floyd Stevens. Chicago, Nelson-Hall, 1972.

 BE A NONBARBERING BARBER

Did you know that it's possible to own your own barbershop without ever having snipped a hair? You simply rent shop space, then get a licensed barber to manage the

business, hiring as much additional help as needed.

You'll want to set yourself up in a good location, however, preferably in a suburban shopping center or swank residential area. Furthermore, after you get going there's nothing to stop you from expanding your operation to include several shops in various parts of town or in nearby towns.

GIFT EXCHANGE

Here your business will consist of offering a service whereby customers can exchange unwanted or unneeded gifts for items that they truly want.

You'll give credit for the full retail value of each gift. The customer can then opt to exchange it for another of equal value or for one of greater value, paying the difference. He or she could even leave the gift, returning periodically until something suitable is found.

Your fee? Charge customers 20 percent of the retail price of the item they bring in for exchange.

ELECTRONICS EXCHANGE

TV sets, stereo equipment, tape decks, radios—these items are constantly changing hands. You can jump into the middle of this vast electronics playground by offering to buy, sell, and trade equipment. If you have doubts about the salability of certain items take them in on consignment, paying the owner a percentage of the selling price only after the item is sold.

Start by making deals around your neighborhood, buying and selling through the newspaper classifieds, and putting up notices in electronics supply houses.

NEEDLEWORK SHOP

If you're being "needled" to death by your creditors, let us provide here a few helpful "points."

As the proprietor or proprietress of a needlework shop your task will be twofold. One phase will consist of giving instruction in knitting, embroidery, crocheting, and other needlework crafts. The other will involve selling designs and materials to your students and to the general public.

If local zoning and licensing regulations permit, you might want to get your business off the ground by setting it up in your home, moving into a commercial area after you've grown.

CLEAN UP WITH VACUUM CLEANERS

You may not realize it but there is a big market in used vacuum cleaners, since a well-built machine will continue to work effectively for many, many years.

You can profit by repairing these units, as well as by buying and selling them. If you need training, enroll in a night course or study books on the subject, practicing on old machines until you get the knack.

RUN A HOBBY SHOP

If you've never gotten out of the model-building stage and you still enjoy working with model cars, planes, railroads, and the like, why not turn your enjoyment into a full-time business, selling supplies and holding classes?

Since most of your customers will be in the subteens and teens, it's most important to locate your business near one of the newer suburban housing developments where you'll have a large potential market to work with.

Advertise your grand opening heavily by distributing handbills throughout the neighborhood. On the big day have prizes, contests, balloons, clowns, magicians, model exhibitions, rock bands, and anything else that will attract attention.

For further information:

Craft, Model, and Hobby Industry Directory. Hobby Publications, Inc., 229 West Twenty-eighth Street, New York, New York 10001 (annual—lists manufacturers, wholesalers, and mass merchandise buyers of hobby/craft products).

Profitable Hobby Merchandising. Profitable Hobby Merchandising, Inc., Pleasantville, New York 10570 (a monthly publication).

Hobby Industry Association of America, 200 Fifth Avenue, New York, New York 10010 (a trade association).

GREETING CARD BOUTIQUE

We call this shop a boutique because, in addition to a complete line of conventional greeting cards, you'll offer hand-crafted and personalized varieties as well.

You'll buy your hand-crafted cards from local craftsmen. These specialties will consist of such unique items as wooden cards, leaf prints, or products with wildflowers impressed into the card itself. You'll also take orders for personalized cards, sending any necessary work off to a printer.

To get started, contact greeting card manufacturers and wholesalers. To obtain hand-crafted products advertise in the newspaper classifieds.

RUN A SWAP SHOP

As a swap shop operator you'll act as broker between seller and buyer, charging the seller 25 percent of all items sold. Accept for sale anything you think will sell. Clothing, bicycles, lawn mowers, furniture—if you have a large lot you could even accept automobiles for sale.

Get started by spreading the word to friends and neighbors. Distribute leaflets and put classified ads in the newspaper.

For further information:

Starting and Managing a Swap Shop or Consignment Sale Shop (SBA 1.15:15), Small Business Administration. Washington, D. C., Superintendent of Documents, U. S. Government Printing Office, 1968.

Eating Establishments

Eating is fun! Serving food can likewise be enjoyable, provided you continually challenge yourself to create new and unique ideas for your customers' pleasure.

Listed in this section are some types of restaurants known well to most of us, plus a few that nobody every heard of—all the better to attract wide publicity at opening time!

Of course, the basics of all restaurant operation are the same and, in case you're unfamiliar with these, we've listed below a few books which will get the ball rolling for you. Happy restauranting!

For further information:

So You Want to Start a Restaurant? Dewey Dyer. Boston, Massachusetts, Cahners, 1971.

How to Plan and Operate a Restaurant, Peter Dukas. Rochelle Park, New Jersey, Hayden.

Starting and Managing a Small Restaurant (SBA 1.15:9). Small Business Administration. Washington, D. C., Superintendent of Documents, U. S. Government Printing Office, 1964.

NOVELTY RESTAURANT

Victoria Station, a national restaurant chain, houses its eateries only in old, renovated railroad cars—still standing on an unused siding! A student in Texas serves his meals to fellow students from an old police paddy wagon.

Refurbished buses, jails, circus wagons, barns, streetcars, tents, churches, schools, firehouses, police stations, even caves and abandoned gold mines can serve as unique settings for eating establishments.

GOURMET CUISINE PARLOR

In every town there are always those who love to indulge their tastes in foods such as frog legs forestière, lobster thermador, and braised venison.

If you possess superb culinary skills why not try your hand at catering to these people? Your establishment needn't be large, but the decor (and the prices) must match the fine quality of the fare served.

To get started, advertise in places such as yacht and country clubs, museums and art galleries, in printed programs of classical performances—anywhere the well-heeled are likely to congregate.

For further information:

Gourmet: Favorite Recipes from Famous Los Angeles Restaurants, Jeanne Voltz and L. A. Burks. Garden City, New York, Doubleday, 1971.

Gourmet Cooking for Everyone, Guirne Van Zuzlan. Levittown, New York, Transatlantic Arts, 1969.

OPEN AN INTERNATIONAL RESTAURANT

As the owner and operator of an international restaurant your specialty would consist of several dishes native to each of five or six different foreign countries. You might offer such items as Mandarin duck, Hungarian goulash, boeuf Bourguignonne, enchiladas, paella—even pizza!

Of course, this looks like a complex operation, and it is. So unless you have prior restaurant experience it's best to start out with a few such dishes and expand your menu as you go along.

For further information:

Drake's International Recipe Cookbook, Drake Editors, *et al.* New York, Drake, 1974.

Famous Dishes of the World, Wina Barn. New York, Macmillan, 1973.

OPERATE A TEAROOM

This is mainly an afternoon business, catering mostly to ladies between shopping jaunts or just wanting a place to go to get away from the kids for a few hours.

You'll have a variety of teas, coffees, cakes, and cookies to offer your customers. The atmosphere should be pleasantly quiet, perhaps with some soft music in the background.

Locate your tearoom in an accessible area of town, possibly between several suburban shopping centers.

HOUSE OF OMELETTES

There are at least several hundred possible varieties of this popular egg dish to choose from. A menu consisting of thirty or forty different types of omelette would be a real treat for those who have wearied of standard breakfast fare.

For promotional purposes be sure to include on your bill of fare a few unique specialties, such as a caviar and perhaps a peanut butter omelette. (Ugh!)

For further information:

Omelette Book, Narcissa Chamberlain. New York, Knopf, 1956.

Art of Cooking Omelettes, Mrs. Romaine De Lyon. Garden City, New York, Doubleday, 1963.

DRIVE-IN SPECIALTY RESTAURANT

This is a specialty restaurant with a novel twist. Customers can sit in their cars and be served quality Oriental, French, Italian, or Mexican dishes.

Of course, you'll want the exterior of the restaurant, as well as the waiters' uniforms, to conform to whatever style of food you serve.

Since this field is relatively unexplored you'd best start out small, expanding the operation as your business grows.

For further information:

Starting and Managing a Small Drive-In Restaurant (SBA 1.15:23), Small Business Administration. Washington, D. C., Superintendent of Documents, U. S. Government Printing Office, 1972.

SOUP 'N' SALAD

As the owner of a soup and salad restaurant you would cater to people on diets or to those who just want a change of pace at lunch time.

Make your dishes unique, using attractive names such as Shamrock Soup and Rainbow Salad. Have several different varieties of soups and salads, rotating your selections each day. Charge a price for each item, as well as a combination price for soup and salad together.

If you conduct your enterprise with a flair even soups and salads can generate mass appeal.

For further information:

The World Book of Soups, Nina Frond. New York, Drake, 1972.

The Complete Book of Salads, Beryl Marton. New York, Avon, 1974.

COFFEEHOUSE

These enterprises flourish in the university sections of most large cities. Here students or other lovers of the informal life can converse over a hot cup of coffee or tea, play checkers or chess, study, or listen to a real live folksinger.

Open your establishment near a college or university. Have a few chess and checker sets for the customers. You should be able to get musicians to perform for you without pay —let them pass the hat after each performance. You might even consider charging a small admission fee of fifty cents or a dollar.

OPEN A REDUCERS' RESTAURANT

One different—but potentially profitable—restaurant gimmick involves opening an eatery strictly for those on diets or concerned about their caloric intake.

Offer a large variety of broths and salads, crackers instead of bread, tomatoes instead of potatoes. Eliminate sugar in desserts.

If your meals are tasty, as well as truly low in calories, those weight watchers will beat a path to your door.

For further information:

The Better Homes & Gardens Calorie Counter's Cookbook, Editors, *Better Homes & Gardens.* New York, Bantam, 1974.

Delicious Diet Cookbook: The Sensible Way to Slim, Lois Levine. New York, Macmillan, 1974.

BURGERS 'N' DOGS

To get started in this business, first find yourself a good location. Look for an area in which there are a lot of offices, or a factory. At lunch time stop into a café or burger stand near the area you're interested in. If customers are waiting in line, it's a pretty sure bet that, by offering good service—and perhaps a gustatory specialty or two—you'll do even better in the same area.

You won't get rich with a small stand of this type. You'll do well to earn $150–$200 per week profit. But if you're ambitious you can set your sights on a bigger and better establishment later on.

OPEN A FACTORY LUNCHROOM

Many factories have cafeterias, but a lot do not. In many cases a factory will install equipment at their own expense, then lease out the facilities to a private individual, who would then be responsible for operating and maintaining the business—as well as profiting from it.

Seek out industrial plants in your area with no such facilities and try to sell them on the idea. Before meeting with them, however, arm yourself with statistics on the plant and some solid reasons why they should finance such an operation.

GOODIES TO GO

One way to break into the food business on very little capital—under $1,000 if you're thrifty—is to open up a take-out food store.

Chicken, shrimp, fish 'n' chips, meat pies, spaghetti, chow mein, hero sandwiches—are all possibilities. Better yet, come up with a new, exotic food specialty of your own!

Find a suitable location, buy your equipment used, promote your enterprise aggressively—and you can't miss.

HEALTH FOOD RESTAURANT

If you've ever been in an honest-to-goodness health food or vegetarian restaurant you know that it's like entering a whole new world. Delicious soups and salads, "steaks" made entirely of organic vegetables, umpteen different types of teas, and whole grain breads are just a few of the many items served.

Start your own health food restaurant by serving up these wholesome meals in your home or by opening a small café. If your food and service are impeccable, word will spread and health enthusiasts will beat a path to your door.

For further information:

Organic Health Food Cookbook, Rosy Marcus. New York, Universal Publishing, 1971.

Vegetarian Cookery (5 vols.), Patricia Black and Ruth Carey. Mountain View, California, Pacific Press, 1971.

CHILDREN'S RESTAURANT

The emphasis here, of course, will be on delighting the children not only with food they like, but with the decor as well. Gaily painted walls, animal chandeliers, chairs shaped or painted in animal forms, and colorful tablecloths are just a few of the many things that will induce Junior to bring his parents to your unique eatery. A clown host and a Cinderella cashier are other good ideas.

Once you open your doors, promote your enterprise through any or all of the methods outlined in Chapter 3.

OPEN A DINNER THEATER

You don't need a million dollars to open up a dinner theater. Start by renting a small amount of space, decorating it tastefully, and having local musicians or a small theater group entertain during meals.

Who knows, by gradually expanding your capacity and upgrading your entertainment you may eventually headline Frank Sinatra, the New York Philharmonic, or the Bolshoi Ballet.

The Rental Field

BIKE GARAGES

Take advantage of the bicycling boom by leasing, by the month, guarded garage space to commuters who desire to bike to the commuter station every day.

Rent a small lot near a busy commuter station. Then build a shed to protect the bikes in inclement weather. Each customer will lock up his own bike for the day, but before taking it home in the evening he'll have to show a monthly pass with a number that corresponds to a decal on his bike. Good insurance against theft—and a good income for you.

CASH FROM CANOES

If you live anywhere near a lake you should seriously consider establishing a canoe rental concession. You'll need permission from one of the property owners on the lake, but if you offer him monthly rent or a small percentage of your receipts he should go along with you.

Next you'll need a fleet of ten to twenty-five or more aluminum or fiber glass canoes —they're the sturdiest type. A fair rental rate is $1.00 per hour or $3.50 per half-day.

Get your customers by advertising in the entertainment section of your local newspaper and by distributing leaflets around high schools and college campuses. Get your-

self a good liability insurance policy before starting this enterprise, in case of accidents.

MINIWAREHOUSES

Many individuals and families often find themselves in cramped living conditions due to a combination of heavy accumulation of household goods and inadequate storage space.

Miniwarehouses are beginning to spring up all over the country to ease the plight of these overburdened residents. The larger organizations own clusters of several hundred waterproof, theftproof chambers in various towns. Since each chamber has its own outside entrance with a lock, the tenant can put in or take out his goods any time of the day or night. Each chamber rents for from ten to fifty dollars per month, depending on its size.

If you have, or are willing to build a large structure that can be used for this purpose, divide it into secure cubicles. Then promote your "store-it-yourself service" through roadside signs and newspaper and Yellow Pages advertising.

MOTORCYCLE RENTAL

If you're handy at repairing motorcycles buy some older models, fix them up, and rent them out on an hourly basis to tourists, college students, and others. Before letting your bikes leave the premises, however, you'll want to get adequate identification and a deposit from each customer.

Be sure to secure a good liability and theft insurance policy before starting in business.

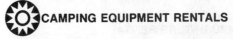

CAMPING EQUIPMENT RENTALS

Accumulate an inventory of used camping gear such as tents, sleeping bags, lanterns, stoves, and backpacks. Your best bet is to get these cheaply during the off-season through newspaper ads, secondhand stores, and store clearance sales.

Advertise your business in the Yellow Pages and in the newspapers during the season. Try to interest organizations in a group rental plan. Be sure to get identification and a small deposit before renting out the equipment.

SPORTS EQUIPMENT RENTAL SERVICE

Many skiers, archers, hunters, and other sportsmen don't indulge in these sports frequently enough to justify purchasing the necessary equipment. This opens up a big rental market.

The best time to accumulate an inventory of sports gear is during the off-season. At that time, make it a point to scour sport shops, secondhand stores, and classified newspaper ads for bargains. When you're ready to hang out your shingle, advertise in the sports section of your local newspaper.

SUPPLIES FOR THE SICK

Beds and bedpans, wheelchairs and walking canes: These will be the types of items you'll supply on a rental basis to the sick.

Accumulate an inventory of this equipment through hospitals and nursing homes—they frequently must sell off old items to make room for the new. Also scour secondhand stores and advertise in the newspaper classifieds.

When you're ready to go, spread word of your service through doctors, hospitals, and nursing and convalescent homes. Advertise your enterprise in the newspaper obituary section and in the Yellow Pages.

FURNITURE RENTAL

Many individuals and families, especially those who move frequently, would rather not buy their furniture. This situation opens up yet another opportunity for you to be your own boss.

Acquire an inventory of used furniture and appliances through garage sales, flea markets, and secondhand dealers. Then leave word of your furniture rental service with home and apartment rental agencies, paying them a commission on referred customers, if necessary. Also advertise in the "Homes and apartments for rent" section of your local newspaper, as well as in the Yellow Pages.

TOOL RENTAL SERVICE

Awls and axes, pliers and power drills, tin snips and tamping sticks! These are just a few of the scores of tools needed by people in your town every day. Many people simply won't invest in seldom-used tools—they'd rather rent them when needed. This is where you come in.

First accumulate a small but varied arsenal of the more popular but seldom bought tools. Advertise on supermarket bulletin boards, and in the newspaper classifieds and Yellow Pages. As your business grows, expand your inventory to include a greater variety of useful implements.

EXERCISE EQUIPMENT RENTALS

Although the sale of exercise equipment has become a multimillion-dollar business in our society, many overweight individuals hesitate to invest in such items as exercycles, treadmills, rowing machines, weight-lifting apparatus, slant boards, and other accoutrements of the pudgy set.

Purchase some of this equipment and rent it out by the month to these people. Potential customers are everywhere. Two excellent places to start promoting your service are health food stores and weight watchers' clubs.

Services

OPEN A DANCE HALL

To our way of thinking, this enterprise, if operated and promoted properly, is a sure gold mine.

Find an abandoned hall or warehouse outside a large city, where the rents are relatively low. Refurbish it attractively, turning it into, not a luxurious ballroom, but a dance hall with "atmosphere."

Specialize in a different type of dancing each evening. Latin, Israeli, Greek, Scandinavian, and rock 'n' roll are all good possibilities. For extra profits give lessons before the start of each evening's festivities, and sell snacks and refreshments.

FAMILY AMUSEMENT CENTER

There are many places a family can go for amusement of an evening or Saturday afternoon: movies, bowling, miniature golf, and so on. But why not start an amusement center with all these facilities in one place? You could show silent movies in a small room, have pinball and other amusement machines, slot car races, chess, checkers, Ping-Pong, and billiards, as well as midget versions of bowling and miniature golf.

Open your amusement center in a better section of town—one with a lot of kids. Promote your enterprise heavily, featuring a spectacular grand opening.

A MINIATURE GOLF COURSE? OF COURSE!

Since miniature golf is best enjoyed outdoors, this enterprise will be limited to about six months out of the year—unless you reside in a year-round playground such as Florida or southern California. Then, naturally, the profits will be rolling in all year.

A good location is of utmost importance in this business. The best locations are those near heavy concentrations of teenagers, such as beaches and amusement parks. Once you've selected your location, make the rounds of similar courses in your city or in nearby towns, in order to pick up some good ideas on design.

PRIVATE EYE

If you've ever envied the exploits of Mike Hammer or TV's Cannon you'll be pleased to know that you, too, can get paid for finding missing persons, uncovering blackmailers, shadowing suspects, and other similar tasks.

The minimum fee for most private detectives is fifty dollars per day plus expenses, so the pay is good. The best way to get started is to go to work for an established detective agency, branching out on your own after you learn the ropes.

Private detectives must be licensed and bonded in most states.

For further information:

The Investigator: A Practical Guide to Private Detection, James Ackroyd. New York, International Publications, 1974.

MASSAGE PARLOR

Today these enterprises flourish in most major cities and in many small towns across the land. It's simple enough to get started in the business. Just rent some small store space in a better area of town, furnish it tastefully, staff it with personnel, and you're ready to open your doors.

You can hire masseurs, masseuses, or both. Personnel can work on the opposite sex, but because of a preponderance of illegal operations within this industry, many communities are touchy about this arrangement and you may have licensing problems.

For further information:

Massage Book, George Downing. Berkeley, California, Bookworks, 1972.

Gunilla Knutson's Book of Massage, Gunilla Knutson. New York, St. Martin's, 1972.

CASH FROM COSMETOLOGY CLASSES

Cosmetology involves the cosmetic treatment of the skin, hair, and nails. Schools specializing in this subject graduate thousands of students yearly who, in turn, go on to high-paying jobs in the field.

If you have knowledge on this subject, plus organizational and teaching ability, you should consider starting a school of this type. Recruit students through high schools, beauty supply outlets, and newspaper advertising. You'll no doubt need a state license before starting in business.

For further information:

> *Cosmetology Teacher Training Manual,* J. Yahm. Bronx, New York, Milady Publishing, 1971.
>
> *Standard Textbook of Cosmetology,* Constance Kibbe. Bronx, New York, Milady Publishing, 1972.

DANCING FOR DOLLARS

If you're nimble of foot and a tiger at teaching, put these two assets together and start your own school of dance. Naturally, the more versatile you are, the better, since you'll be getting requests to teach everything from the waltz to the Watusi, the minuet to the mambo, the fox-trot to the fandango.

The best way to get customers initially is to get permission from a dance hall owner to hold classes on his premises. In addition, you could pick up some students by teaching at the local Y or evening adult school.

For further information:

> *The Teaching of Popular Dance,* Morton. Columbus, Ohio, Charles E. Merrill, 1966.
>
> *Introduction to the Teaching of Dance,* Elizabeth Hayes. New York, Ronald Press, 1964.
>
> *What to Teach in Dancing,* Alex Moore. New Rochelle, New York, Sportshelf and Soccer Associates, 1974.

DO-IT-YOURSELF AUTO REPAIR SHOP

With mechanics' fees inflating faster than the crop of a North America sage grouse at mating time, it's not hard to figure out the reason for the success of do-it-yourself auto repair shops.

In this type of operation you'll have a large garage or shed containing hoists or pits, workbenches, tools, and test equipment available for people who want to repair, maintain, or otherwise service their own cars. Charge an hourly, daily, or weekly fee, and be on hand to give any needed advice.

After you've set up shop, get your customers through auto-parts stores, high school auto shop classes, newspaper ads, and Yellow Pages advertising.

For further information:

> *How to Service and Repair Your Own Car,* Richard Day. New York, Times Mirror Magazine (order through Harper & Row), 1973.
>
> *The Complete Book of Car Repair,* John Hirsch. New York, Scribner's, 1973.

DO-IT-YOURSELF ELECTRONICS SHOP

Good electronics equipment is expensive. Many amateurs would like to have the use of meters, oscilloscopes, and the like, but just wouldn't need the equipment often enough to justify purchasing it themselves.

Here's where you come in. By setting up your own well-equipped electronics shop, you can profit by charging individuals an hourly, daily, or weekly fee for its use. As a sideline you can hold classes and sell your students tubes, resistors, and other components.

To get customers, notify electronics students in nearby trade schools and leave notices at local electronics supply houses.

ROOMMATE SERVICE

If you live in a large or medium-sized town this is a natural for you. Members of the young, single crowd are constantly on the lookout for someone congenial to live and share their rent with.

Simply place an ad in the classified section of your local newspaper under "Rentals to share." If yours is a college town you can also place an ad in the school paper or on the bulletin board.

Charge ten or fifteen dollars per applicant. Have each one fill out a form listing the type of roommate preferred, the rent he or she can pay, etc., and then start matching them up.

Done properly, this can be a gold mine for you!

BE A MEN'S HAIRSTYLIST

Why, we remember the time when, if a man ever said he was going to a hairstylist, he'd be considered more than a little "funny" by his friends. Times have changed, though, and today men's hairstyling salons often outdo their female counterparts in elaborateness—and price.

It's possible to start a business of this type without ever having cut a hair. Simply find someone skilled, licensed, and dependable to manage it for you. In addition to hairstyling, you could offer scalp treatments, facials, manicures, sauna baths, hairpieces—even dancing girls!

For further information:

The Complete Book of Men's Hair Styles and Hair Care, Miriam Cordwell and Marion Ruddy. New York, Crown, 1974.

Advanced Textbook of Barbering and Men's Hairstyling, Textbook Committee of Barbering. Bronx, New York, Milady Publishing, 1969.

ELECTRONICS REPAIR

You may not realize it but you needn't be a competent technician in order to enter this field. Even if you possess only elementary knowledge on the subject—such as the ability to check tubes and solder broken wires—you can make simple repairs of TV and stereo equipment and farm out the more complicated work.

Naturally, you'll pay wholesale for getting the equipment repaired, charging your customers the normal service rate. Your customers needn't know your methods of operation. Of course, when you become more proficient you'll want to do all your own work.

For further information:

Electronics for Everybody, Ronald Benrey. New York, Times Mirror Magazine (order through Harper & Row), 1970.

Electronics for the Beginner, J. A. Stanley. Indianapolis, Indiana, Howard W. Sams, 1968.

KARATE SCHOOL

This operation works best in a big city, where the large population will give you a substantial number of prospective students to deal with.

Since it's mostly the under-twenty-five crowd that's interested in this ancient art you'll fare best by doing your prospecting near high schools and on college campuses. To get students interested, offer "specials" to them.

You'll also want to promote your school by putting on exhibitions at high schools, colleges, fairs, carnivals, picnics, and other social events.

For further information:

Karate Training Methods, Paul Crompton. New York, International Publications, 1971.

Manual of Karate, Ernest Harrison. Hackensack, New Jersey, Wehman.

Practical Karate (6 vols.), F. Donn and Masatoshi Naka Yama. Rutland, Vermont, C. E. Tuttle, 1963–65.

AUTO RADIOS AND TAPE PLAYERS

You don't have to be an electronics wizard to repair auto radios and tape players. Furthermore, since you are performing a technical service you can command a healthy fee.

Learn the basics through evening adult classes or home study courses. You can get your first customers through friends and neighbors. When you're ready to hang out your shingle, spread the word through electronics supply houses and advertise in the newspaper classifieds and the Yellow Pages.

For further information:

Auto Radio Servicing Made Easy, Wayne Lemmons. Indianapolis, Howard W. Sams, 1969.

Practical Guide to Auto Radio Repair, G. Warrenheath. New York, Theodore Audel (order through Bobbs-Merrill), 1965.

Questions and Answers About Auto Tape Units, Leo Sands. Indianapolis, Howard W. Sams, 1973.

 REUPHOLSTERING

What's a furniture owner to do when his favorite easy chair starts coming apart at the seams? Throw it out? Not on your life! He'll probably turn to that "furniture physician," the reupholsterer, to get it back into shape.

Reupholstering, however, is somewhat trickier than it looks, so if you have no experience better study up on the books listed below or take a night school course in the subject.

You'll need a truck for pickup and delivery, plus a few part-time helpers.

To get started, use any of the applicable advertising and promotional ideas outlined in Chapter 1.

For further information:

Furniture Upholstery and Repair, Editors, *Sunset* Magazine. Menlo Park, California, Lane, 1970.

All About Upholstering, John Bergen. New York, Hawthorn, 1968.

LABOR UNLIMITED

In contrast to the conventional employment agency this enterprise involves providing clients with workers for such temporary jobs as mending a fence, cleaning a basement, mowing a lawn, or weeding a garden.

When you're ready for business, find students and retired persons through your state employment agency, college employment offices, and senior citizens' centers. Get clients through handbill distribution and by advertising in the newspaper classifieds.

16

Business Services: A Big Business

The area of business services encompasses thousands of potentially profitable enterprises. Furthermore, many of these ventures, such as convention planning, researching, collecting delinquent accounts, and managing grand openings, require little or no initial capital.

Once you're established as a "specialist" in your chosen field, word of your service will spread throughout the business community and, if your work is good, you'll find yourself getting new business automatically. In addition, most services lend themselves to repetition. A firm that needs offset printing done or envelopes addressed once will need the same service again.

As in any field, you'll want to advertise and promote your service aggressively. Personal calls, direct-mail advertising, telephone solicitation, business periodical advertising, and leaflet distribution are a few of the methods that can be employed. Naturally, you'll want to match your promotional methods to the business involved and type of service offered.

The following survey will give you an excellent bird's-eye view of the opportunities existing in the field of business services. We hope one of them will prove to be a winner for you.

Advertising and Promotion

GRAND OPENER

Some merchants may be whizzes at buying and selling merchandise but simply can't plan and execute an effective grand opening. As a "specialist" in grand openings and reopenings your task is to take over all aspects of these events, from advance publicity to the final cleanup.

Offer your services to members of the business community in person or by phone. Get names of businesses about to open through the city hall licensing bureau.

WALKING BILLBOARDS

This is the term you might use to describe T-shirts imprinted with the names of hamburger joints, motorcycle dealers, radio stations, resorts, and other businesses.

You'll sell your imprinted shirts in large lots to local businesses, which will in turn sell or give them away to the general public as a promotional item.

Buy your T-shirts from a manufacturer or wholesaler, imprinting the ads by means of silk-screening or heat transfer.

For further information:

Printing on Fabric, Ellen Bystrom. New York, Van Nostrand, 1971.

Textile Printing and Painting Made Easy, Ursula Kuehnemann. New York, Taplinger, 1967.

BE DEMONSTRATIVE!

Demonstrators are hired by the hundreds by such firms as small-appliance manufacturers, food companies, and toy makers. Their demonstrating talents are put to use in stores, and at trade shows and conventions.

Fill your till by providing these firms with competent, professional demonstrators. Solicit business from firms by direct mail and by advertising in trade publications. As agent you'll receive 15–25 percent of the fees paid your demonstrators.

WELCOME WEALTH FROM A WELCOME WAGON

Have coupon books printed up with a different merchant's name on each. Some will give free prizes; others discounts on merchandise. Your job as a welcome wagon hostess would be to welcome new arrivals into the community by calling on them and presenting each family with one of these coupon books.

In addition to distributing the books you

would arrange for their printing and for keeping track of new arrivals through real estate agents and apartment house managers. Your fee would be paid by the merchants involved.

Create this job for yourself by proposing the idea to local merchants' associations.

FREE-LANCE PUBLIC RELATIONS EXPERT

If you've had experience working for ad agencies or fund-raising organizations, writing newspaper releases, or working in radio or TV, you've already got initial contacts for setting up your own PR firm.

Now all you need is the confidence to go it on your own, and some good, old-fashioned pavement pounding to dig out those clients. Call personally on firms you feel could enhance their image and increase their sales through an effective PR program.

For further information:

Public Relations (A Teach Yourself Book), Herbert Lloyd. New York, International Publications, 1974.

Lesley's Public Relations Handbook, Philip Lesley. Englewood Cliffs, New Jersey, Prentice-Hall, 1971.

Public Relations News, 127 East Eightieth Street, New York, New York 10021 (trade journal).

ETHNIC ADVERTISING CONSULTANT

Many times advertising agencies want to slant their ads toward Blacks, Chicanos, Italians, Chinese, or other ethnic groups. If you're familiar with one or more of these groups, your expertise might be a highly salable commodity.

Send an "ethnic pitch" to advertising agencies in your area, stating your abilities and qualifications.

START A SHOPPER PAPER

In most areas the cost of advertising on TV and radio and in daily newspapers is ex-

orbitant. What merchants need is a small, weekly "shopper"-type paper, distributed throughout their *immediate* area, providing a concentrated, effective, and inexpensive form of advertising. Distribute your paper free to homes, making your profit from the sale of advertising space.

Contact local printers and get estimates on printing costs. When you've selected one, have him print up a "dummy"—a sample that you can show to merchants. Then start calling personally on local business owners, concentrating, of course, on selling them full-page ads.

BUILD BILLBOARDS

Because billboards are responsible for uglifying many natural scenic wonders throughout our land we hate to admit that they're money-makers for their owners. But it's true.

How do you get into the business? Scout out good locations along roadsides. Then contact the owners, offering to lease the property on a long-term basis.

After you've constructed your billboards, use them to advertise the fact that they're for rent. Be sure to check applicable federal and state laws before starting.

A FUND RAISER

Many organizations such as Scouting groups, Little Leagues, bike clubs, and ecology groups are always on the lookout for ways to raise money. As a professional fund raiser your job will be to organize revenue-producing activities for these groups, such as minicarnivals, stage shows, dances, parties, bingo games—anything that will attract the public.

For your services you can charge up to 25 percent of the gross receipts from the event. Obviously, a few events every month, each bringing in $1,000 or more, will bring you a tidy income.

For further information:

Techniques of Fund-Raising, David Conrad. New York, Lyle Stuart, 1974.

Fund Raising Techniques, E. Hereward. New York, Beekman, 1969.

MARKET RESEARCH

Companies spend enormous amounts every year trying to determine our tastes relative to their products or services. A vegetable canner, for instance, might want to know whether housewives prefer jars instead of cans as containers. A cigarette manufacturer might desire to gauge the public's reaction to a new filter.

Market research firms are constantly hiring interviewers to query the public. If you've never done this type of work before, go to work for one of these firms. After you gain experience, set up your own outfit, hiring others to do your interviewing while you seek out new accounts.

Office Services

A CASH-COLLECTING ENTERPRISE

If you've got the stomach for harassing your fellow citizens you'll find throughout the country loads of merchants stewing about money owed them by their customers. They have nothing to lose by letting you try to collect for them—and a lot to gain.

Contact local merchants by phone, mail, or personal visit, offering your services. Your fee will be anywhere from 25 to 50 percent of what you collect. In order to sharpen your money-extracting skills, find out how the experts do it by reading up on the subject.

For further information:

Credits and Collections, Richard Ettinger and D. E. Galieb. Englewood Cliffs, New Jersey, Prentice-Hall, 1962.

Making People Pay, Paul Rock. New York, Routledge & Kegan Paul, 1973.

BE A COPYCAT

The proliferation of "instant" copying outfits in the last few years attests to the high public demand for this type of service.

Considering the fact that you'll need at least one offset press, initial paper stock, and store space in a commercial area, this enterprise will require an initial investment of at least $1,000. However, once you get started and develop a steady trade through doing high-quality work and delivering it on time, the profits should start rolling in.

After you set up shop, print your own handbills and distribute them to businesses in your area. Yellow Pages advertising should likewise pull in a lot of trade for you.

For further information:

Starting and Managing a Small Duplicating and Mailing Service, Small Business Administration. Washington, D. C., Superintendent of Documents, U. S. Government Printing Office, 1963.

The Single Color Offset Press, I. H. Sayre. Chicago, Lithographic Textbook Publishing, 1970.

PART-TIME OFFICES

Many independent professional people such as salesmen and contractors don't have the need for a full-time office but, nevertheless, could use a part-time "home base" for making phone calls and writing up reports.

Open up an office to provide these individuals with desk space for one or more days per week, charging accordingly. Each desk would be equipped with its own phone, and for additional fees offer an answering service as well as mail and secretarial services.

CARDS TO CUSTOMERS = CASH TO YOU

Thousands of dentists, optometrists, insurance salesmen, accountants, and other professionals desiring to maintain goodwill send out birthday and Christmas greeting cards every year to patients and customers. You could build up a nice source of income for yourself by taking over this task for these busy individuals.

Print up some attractive, businesslike stationery for yourself. Then make mass mailings to professionals in your community, offering your services.

THE ADDRESS GAME

If you're very fast with a typewriter and *if* you can stand addressing 1,000, 2,000, 5,000 envelopes a day—day in and day out—then you may be cut out for the addressing business.

Beware, however, of firms that promise riches for addressing envelopes. Your best bet is to go out and get clients on your own. Retail stores, clubs, churches, and various civic and social organizations—anybody who mails literature in quantity—are all potential customers. For extra profits offer such additional services as folding, stapling, and stuffing.

FREE-LANCE SECRETARY

Initially your job will consist of anything you can get: taking dictation, typing letters, sending out monthly statements, typing manuscripts. Later on you can specialize in whichever type of work suits you best.

Print up and distribute handbills to business offices, stores, doctors' offices, college students, and anyone else you think may need your services.

For further information:

Modern Secretary's Complete Guide, Twyla Schwieger. Englewood Cliffs, New Jersey, Prentice-Hall, 1971.

The Successful Secretary's Handbook, Esther Becker and Evelyn Anders. New York, Harper & Row, 1971.

CLIPPING SERVICE

Having a newspaper clipping service is one way to work and keep up on the news at the same time.

Decide whether you want to offer clippings covering just your city, or the county and state as a whole. This is important because you'll have to subscribe to every daily paper in that area. You'll also need a photocopy machine for duplicating the clippings.

Start by contacting business firms in your area that you think might be interested in your service. Clipping-service fees usually run about ten dollars per month for the first fifty clippings, with ten cents being charged for each additional clipping.

For further information:

Counseling Notes: Clipping Service (CN-33), Small Business Administration. Washington, D. C., Superintendent of Documents, U. S. Government Printing Office, 1969.

TELEPHONE ANSWERING SERVICE

A lady in Portland, Oregon, started taking messages for her phoneless neighbors as a favor to them. Soon she began charging for her services. Today she has a large answering operation in which she employs fourteen operators.

You'll need over $1,000 to cover your initial expenses. But if you're aggressive in drumming up clients such as doctors, salesmen, electricians, plumbers—anyone on the move—you'll be amply rewarded.

For further information:

Fundamentals of Telephone Answering Service, The Bell Telephone System American Telephone and Telegraph, 195 Broadway, New York, New York 10007.

Counseling Notes: A Telephone Answering Service (CN-8), Small Business Administration. Washington, D. C., Superintendent of Documents, U. S. Government Printing Office, 1969.

☼ OPERATE AN EMPLOYMENT AGENCY

Here you're a matchmaker of sorts, trying to get prospective employees and employers together.

After you've established yourself in an office get a copy of the newspaper want ads. Call any employers who are advertising for help, and offer your services. Get your applicants by doing your own newspaper advertising.

Fees may be paid by the employer, the applicant, or both, and are almost always based on a percentage of the monthly or annual salary.

Some states regulate these types of firms, so check licensing requirements before starting in business.

For further information:

Starting and Managing an Employment Agency (SBA 1.15:22), Small Business Administration. Washington, D. C., Superintendent of Documents, U. S. Government Printing Office, 1971.

☼ FREE-LANCE INSURANCE CLERK

Today doctors are buried under an avalanche of insurance forms that must be filled out before patients or doctors can get reimbursed for fees paid or services performed.

If you're at all conversant with the procedures involved in handling these forms, offer your services as an insurance clerk. Your job would be to visit doctors' offices each week and handle any claim forms that need processing.

☼ A TELEPHONE STENOGRAPHER

Many small businessmen who have no need for a full-time secretary could use the occasional services of a stenographer. How handy it would be if they could call you on the phone, dictate a letter or two, and have the letter delivered or mailed back to them the same day.

Round up customers for your telephone dictation service by personally contacting small businesses and leaving a card.

For further information:

Reference Manual for Stenographers and Typists, Ruth Gavin and W. A. Sobin. New York, McGraw-Hill, 1970.

Stenographer-Typist: Practical Preparation, Arco Editorial Board. New York, Arco, 1968.

☼ TEACH OFFICE SKILLS

Shorthand, typing, taking dictation —these and other office skills can be taught by you, right in your own home, if you have ability along these lines.

A major expenditure will be the renting or leasing of a number of typewriters, chairs, and desks for your pupils.

Put ads up on high school bulletin boards and advertise in high school papers. Or, if you can get the names and addresses of students, you might send them each a brochure describing your classes.

☼ FREE-LANCE TRANSLATOR

If you speak a second language fluently, translate your talents into dollars by hiring yourself out as a translator to businesses who deal with foreign firms.

The United States Department of Commerce, Fourteenth Street between Constitution and E, N.W., Washington, D. C. 20230, can give you a list of domestic companies doing business with foreign firms. Write these companies stating your qualifications. Also join the American Translators Association, P. O. Box 129, Croton-on-Hudson, New York 10520. This professional society can keep you up to date on current work opportunities.

☼ TEMPORARY HELP AGENCY

Provide office help, sales and technical people, and skilled and unskilled laborers, all on a temporary basis, to offices, sales agencies, industrial firms—anyone who is in a pinch for help.

Launch an aggressive telephone campaign to offices and industrial firms. Also advertise in the newspaper classifieds for both clients and employees.

NOTARY PUBLIC

As a notary public your main duty will be to verify, with your signature, that papers brought to you have been signed in your presence. You'll also administer oaths and take depositions.

For a small fee you can be registered as a notary public by your state, although some states require you to post a bond or pass an examination as well.

Your best bet is to locate yourself near a business district. Flood business offices with handbills informing them of your service. Also advertise in the Yellow Pages.

For further information:

Notary Public, Arco Editorial Board. New York, Arco, 1966.

FREE-LANCE BOOKKEEPER

Work with business firms to design record-keeping systems and periodically maintain them. If you have knowledge of tax laws, so much the better. This skill should be a valuable selling point in obtaining new clients.

Spread the word to small businesses by calling on them personally. Contact larger firms by means of handbills or direct mail. Place an ad in the Yellow Pages.

For further information:

Bookkeeping for Beginners, W. E. Hooper. New York, Pitman, 1970.

Bookkeeping Made Easy, Alexander Sheff. New York, Barnes & Noble (orders to Harper & Row), 1966.

MAKE RUBBER STAMPS

Shops, offices, shipping companies, industrial firms—these are a few of the businesses that have a constant need for rubber stamps. Costing only about 40¢ each to make, these products sell anywhere from $1.50 up, depending on the size. If you can combine this large markup with a high volume of business you'll have profits aplenty.

You'll need a small vulcanizing press and a supply of type. For manufacturers, consult the *Thomas Register of American Manufacturers,* at your library. Then solicit business actively through personal contact, telephone, or direct mail.

Indoor Work

MUSICAL MONEY

Many libraries in large metropolitan areas have record collections dating back to the early days of the recording industry. Make arrangements to check out some of the more unique platters. Take them home and record them on tape. If you can't check them out, perhaps you can get permission to bring a portable tape recorder into the library, taping them in an unused room.

Then rent or sell your tapes to pizza parlors, coffeehouses, bars, ice cream parlors —any establishment where nostalgic music would be appreciated.

PROOFREADING PROFITS

Somebody has to catch typographical errors *before* they appear in print. Otherwise our newspapers, magazines, and books would be nothing but a glut of garbled garbage.

Hang out your proofreading shingle by contacting publishers in your area and by advertising in such publications as *Writer's Digest, The Writer,* and *Editor and Publisher.* Charge by the word or typewritten page.

For further information:

Proofreading and Copyediting: A Practical Guide to Style for the 1970's, Harry McNaughton. New York, Hastings House, 1973.

FREE-LANCE WATCHMAN

Most small businesses cannot afford to hire a full-time night watchman but might go for the idea of someone checking their premises several times each night.

Contact local businessmen, offering this service for a moderate fee. Homeowners about to go on vacation would likewise be excellent prospects. You'll need a two-way radio in your car in case of trouble.

MONEY FROM MODELS

Since advertising agencies, garment manufacturers, and photographers have a continual need for models, this enterprise enjoys an ever-present market.

Before starting, you'll need a "stable" of all types of models: men, women, old, young, short, tall, fat, thin, attractive, and not-so-attractive. To get them, simply advertise in the newspaper classifieds.

Next make up some attractive brochures, containing pictures of your most striking models. Take or mail these to prospective clients. You can also promote your agency by sponsoring beauty contests and fashion shows.

REWARDS FROM RESEARCH

Many writers and business firms require research data which they will gladly pay to acquire.

As a "research specialist" your job will be to gather information from libraries and other sources on any subject your clients request. Charge an hourly rate or a flat fee, depending on the project.

Get your business by advertising in writers' magazines such as *Writer's Digest* and *The Writer,* as well as in various business publications.

For further information:

Guide for the Beginning Researcher, Mabel Wandelt. Englewood Cliffs, New Jersey, Prentice-Hall, 1970.

Finding Facts Fast: How to Find Out What You Want to Know Immediately, Alden Todd. New York, Morrow, 1974.

FREE-LANCE TITLE SEARCHER

This enterprise involves searching property titles at the county records office, then preparing abstracts of them for attorneys specializing in real estate transactions. Although the work is fairly simple, some knowledge of the field is necessary in order to do a thorough and accurate job.

Simply contact attorneys, offering your services.

ARTISTS' MORGUE

Commercial artists and illustrators are in constant need of illustrations on which to base their work. For instance, if an artist were commissioned to draw an ad containing an illustration of a jellyfish, a Sherman tank, or a Venus's-flytrap and didn't quite know what one looked like, he'd lose valuable time by having to trudge down to the library or visit a zoo or museum to get the information.

By collecting and filing illustrations from old magazines, which you can pick up cheaply secondhand, you will eventually have a large inventory from which these individuals can select.

Get your clients through art agencies and artists' supply stores, and by advertising in trade magazines.

ANTISHOPLIFTING SERVICE

If you have a streak of spy in you, hire yourself out to department and variety stores, and other large retail outlets. Posing as a shopper in ordinary street clothes, you will watch for, and apprehend, light-fingered shoppers.

If you can cut stores' shoplifting losses, you'll be their most valuable "customer."

NIGHT WATCHMAN AGENCY

Even as holders of good theft insurance policies, most businessmen are constantly edgy over the possibility of a break-in. These are excellent prospective clients for a service in which you would supply night watchmen.

Get your watchmen by finding retired persons or college students through newspaper classifieds or your state employment agency. Get your clients through personal contact or telephone solicitation.

APARTMENT HOUSE MANAGER

At first glance it may not seem that an individual could support a family with this enterprise. But let's look at the facts: First, managers of large apartment complexes are usually given rent-free lodgings—the equivalent of anywhere from $150 to $300 salary per month. Second, many managers earn an additional 5 percent of the monthly rent receipts. Therefore, if you manage only a *small* high-rise of, say, fifty units renting for $200 each per month, you've got additional income of $500 per month. And managing fifty apartment units is *not* a full-time job.

In most big cities owners of apartment complexes are crying out for sober, dependable managers. Simply look in the newspaper classifieds—or insert an ad of your own.

For further information:

Managing an Apartment House Profitably, Jerry German. Jericho, New York, Exposition Press, 1973.

Guide to Apartment House Management, Mary Holt. Jericho, New York, Exposition Press, 1971.

CONVENTION PLANNING SERVICE

Large companies are constantly having conventions. These get-togethers are usually in a city or town far removed from the company headquarters, thus making it difficult to take care of all the necessary arrangements beforehand.

If you live in a big city and possess superior organizational abilities, set yourself up as a convention planner. Do this by writing large companies at their headquarters and offering your services. In order to look professional you should have a business letterhead.

Your work will consist of providing transportation, renting suitable facilities, planning and organizing the convention proceedings, securing accommodations for the participants, writing press releases, and making all other necessary arrangements.

REBUILD BATTERIES

Automobiles represent but a small fraction of battery-operated vehicles. Industrial batteries are used in a multitude of industrial, construction, and farm vehicles and appliances. Therefore, a huge market exists for rebuilding and reconditioning batteries.

There are many books available on the subject. Study these, practicing on old car batteries. When you've got the hang of it, contact industrial plants and large construction firms.

For further information:

Storage Batteries: Including Operation, Charging, Maintenance, and Repair, George Smith. New Rochelle, New York, Sportshelf and Soccer Associates, 1971.

BUILDING MAINTENANCE

Somebody's got to wash the windows and empty the wastebaskets of the Empire State Building, and it's certainly not going to be the owner! Instead, some building-maintenance firm has contracted to do this work and no doubt profits handsomely from it.

You can start a similar business in your town by contracting with small offices and office buildings. Of course, all your employees must be screened and bonded before starting.

Equipment: Sales—Rentals—Repair

THE TOILET TRADE

Construction sites, fairs and carnivals, and outdoor expositions are a few of the locations requiring portable toilets. Charging twenty-five to fifty dollars per month each, the companies who supply them profit nicely from their rental.

Build or buy a number of portable privies. Then contact building contractors and officials of fairs, carnivals, and other outdoor events.

Portable toilets need periodic emptying and cleaning. They are emptied by means of a pump truck, which you can rent, or a sewage disposal service can perform this challenging task.

USED-FURNITURE SCOUT

You've heard of Boy Scouts, talent scouts, and sports scouts—here we have the used-furniture scout.

Make arrangements with secondhand furniture dealers to act as a buyer for them. Find out what types of furniture they're interested in and what prices they're willing to pay. Then scout out bargains at flea markets and garage sales. You might also insert classified ads for used furniture in your local newspaper.

When you've found a suitable item, make an offer. If it's accepted, you'll pay cash and immediately call one of your dealers. He'll come out and pick up the furniture, paying

you 25 percent over and above what you paid the seller.

A PRINTING BROKER

Like a school of sharks feasting on the carcass of a dead whale, the business world feeds on a plethora of letterheads, printed envelopes, business cards, forms, memo slips, report sheets, and other printed matter.

Arrange with a local printer to drum up business for him in exchange for a commission. Have him supply you with a sample kit. Then call on offices, retail stores, industrial plants, and the like, soliciting printing orders from them.

THE BUSINESS MACHINE BUSINESS

The sheer volume of business machines sold in this country every year is assurance enough that you can make a small—perhaps even a large—fortune in this active field.

Typewriters, adding machines, calculators, copiers, duplicators—make it your business to buy, sell, and rent this equipment *used*. Prospective customers are everywhere: Among your clients might be offices, garages, service stations, and retail stores.

OFFICE MACHINE REPAIR

Even if you know nothing about repairing and servicing typewriters, adding machines, calculators, duplicators, photocopiers, and the like, it's a simple enough matter to learn. You can attend night classes, take a correspondence course, or even study some books and practice on your own till you're proficient.

Go from office to office and store to store, introducing yourself and leaving a card. If you make enough calls the law of averages will get you plenty of business.

On the Move

**A REAL SNOW JOB**

Unless you live within the Arctic Circle the snow removal business will be a seasonal job for you. Nevertheless, it can be a lucrative one.

Prior to the first snowfall, contact shopping centers, department stores, supermarkets —any business using a large parking lot. Propose a contract for the winter, based on rates lower than the competition's. As an extra service offer salting and sanding. Individual homeowners are also good prospects.

To find equipment, look in the Yellow Pages under "Snow removal equipment."

**GUILDERS FROM GUIDING**

Many times when an executive takes his wife along on a trip during which the husband must attend business meetings, seminars, or a convention, the wife will be left on her own in a strange city, unfamiliar with its attractions.

As a personal guide to such "stranded" wives your job would entail chauffeuring the ladies around town to various points of interest—fashion shows, art galleries, unique restaurants, and the like.

Write large corporations that are likely to schedule meetings and conventions in your area, explaining your services. A list of upcoming conventions can often be obtained through your state chamber of commerce.

A BANK MESSENGER

Most small businessmen cannot afford the high fees charged by commercial armored car services, but would be willing to pay a moderate fee for the security of having a reliable and trustworthy individual safely escort their daily receipts to the bank.

This enterprise entails building up a daily route for yourself, picking up deposits from the same firms at approximately the same times each day. As a commercial bank messenger, however, you would have to carry a gun, as well as be bonded and insured.

AN EMERGENCY CARPENTER

Any large metropolitan area has its share of fires, explosions, and vandalism. In order to prevent looting, retail stores that have had their windows smashed in such calamities need their storefronts boarded up pronto!

As an emergency carpenter you'll be available at all hours of the night and day to run out faithfully with hammer, nails, and boards, securing the property against looting.

To get business, mail explanatory literature to all insurance agents in your town. Although you'll occasionally be awakened from a sound sleep, you'll be nailing down some good profits for yourself!

CLEAN UP FROM CONSTRUCTION CLEANUP

After the last nail has been driven into a newly constructed home there remains much cleanup work to be done before the owners can move in. Debris must be hauled away; windows washed; excess paint, plaster, and cement scraped from windows, walls, and bathroom fixtures.

Approach building contractors, offering an after-construction cleanup service. Twenty-five to fifty dollars per house is not an excessive fee to ask. At these prices getting the go-ahead from a big contractor to clean all his new homes can net you a pretty penny.

**LOTS OF PAINT**

If, one day, you found yourself in a strange town with only a ten-dollar bill in your pocket, this is one enterprise that could start making you a steady income almost immediately.

Begin by checking out parking lots in the area. If you find a lot whose parking stripes are faded and dingy-looking (and most are), contact the person in charge, offering to restripe the lot for a fee. Then take your ten-dollar bill and buy some masking tape, a bucket of paint, and a brush, and get to work.

EXECUTIVE HOSTESS

Often large corporations transfer young executives and their families to distant cities where they are left more or less on their own to acclimate themselves to their new surroundings.

How much better it would be for these executives, as well as for their companies, if each family could rely on your guidance and assistance.

As an executive hostess you would arrange temporary accommodations, meet the family at the airport, help them find a permanent home, introduce them to others, provide valuable information on a multitude of things, and generally help them get settled.

Contact large firms whose home or branch offices are located in your area, offering a complete "resettlement service" for each new executive transferred there.

STEAM CLEANING

Special equipment, called a steam jenny, is required for steam cleaning auto engines, trucks, buses, and fronts of business establishments.

You can buy used or reconditioned equipment of this type for a few hundred dollars from a steam-cleaning equipment supplier found in the Yellow Pages. Then call on service stations, car and truck fleet owners, used-car dealers, and retail stores, offering your steam-cleaning skills on a regular, contractual basis.

OPERATE A MESSENGER SERVICE

Attorneys, ad agencies, insurance companies, accountants, and other service businesses have a constant need for rapid intracity exchange of forms, memos, reports, briefs, and other documents.

Rather than sending this information by mail, which would entail one or two days' delay, or by having a secretary drive across town, these firms would welcome the services of a speedy, dependable messenger.

Contact local firms and let them know your service is available. Incidentally, you'll have a much better chance of getting business if you can show you are bonded.

17

For Shut-ins: The Inside Story on Indoor Incomes

Has sickness or disability confined you to your home? Have you given up all hope of providing a decent, comfortable income for yourself?

Well, my friend, it may interest you to know that in this country there are thousands upon thousands of shut-ins who are successfully—year in and year out—generating adequate, sometimes phenomenal, incomes for themselves without ever setting foot outside their front doors.

How? Let's face it, in this world of competitive products, services, and ideas, it's the clever ones that survive the best. That applies to all of us. If you can come up with a winning mail-order item, produce large quantities of badges for local companies and conventioneers, or create exquisite tailor-made shirts for local boutiques, the fact that you're confined to the home will not hinder your money-making abilities one iota.

But, you say, most enterprises require marketing—visiting retailers, buyers, homeowners. Well, here you can hire a friend, relative, or even a professional salesman to perform this task, paying him a commission or taking him on as a partner. If you'd rather go it alone you can sell newspaper or magazine subscriptions by telephone . . . enter contests . . . sell your needlework designs to manufacturers by mail . . . run an income tax service . . . invest in the stock market. There are many ways to skin the revenue-producing cat!

So despair no further. The money is out there. It's just a matter of channeling it in your direction by putting your wits to work in providing a needed product or service.

Here's a list of over sixty money-making ideas. One of them should work for you.

Strike it Rich!

CONTESTS GALORE!

Every year throughout our land there are countless sweepstakes, drawings, and puzzle contests. In addition, many prizes are awarded by associations, foundations, and publishers in such fields as cooking, sewing, art, design, writing, and photography. It may surprise you to know that many people, after repeated sharpening of their contest-entering skills, are able to make a living in this field.

Be alert to announcements of contests through the media, entering them all—and don't forget about the Irish Sweepstakes!

For further information:

> *Fell's Official Guide to Prize Contests and How to Win Them,* Allen Glasser. New York, Frederick Fell, 1963.

> *Prizewinner,* Robert Spence Publications, Inc., 1315 Central Avenue, St. Petersburg, Florida 33733.

COIN MONEY

After 1964 all silver content in our coins was discontinued (except for half dollars of 40-percent silver, which were minted until 1969). This has precipitated one of the biggest treasure (or Treasury) hunts in the history of the U. S. Mint.

With the value of silver continuing to rise, coin dealers are now paying two and a half times face value for pre-1965 silver coins —regardless of the year or condition!

To get in on this "silver rush," simply get yourself a bag or barrel full of dimes, quarters, and half dollars from your bank.

While searching for silver coins you'll also want to keep an eye peeled for valuable *rare* coins.

For further information:

> *Red Guidebook of U. S. Coins,* R. S. Yeoman. Hackensack, New Jersey, Wehman.

> *Collecting Rare Coins for Profit,* Q. David Bowers. New York, Harper and Row, 1975.

REAL ESTATE

There are many ways to make money in real estate. One of the most popular—and profitable—involves purchasing run-down multiple-family residences in an area where property values are increasing. After improving the value of the property through repairs and renovation, you sell at a profit. It's as simple as that!

Furthermore, it's possible to get a large loan on property of this type. Moreover, the seller will often take back a second mortgage on the balance. Therefore, it's possible to start with under $2,000, pyramiding your profits each time you sell.

For further information:

> *How to Get Rich in Real Estate,* Robert Kent. Englewood Cliffs, New Jersey, Prentice-Hall, 1969.
>
> *How I Turned $1000 into Three Million in Real Estate—in My Spare Time,* William Nickerson. New York, Simon & Schuster, 1969.

THOSE BEAUTIFUL SECOND MORTGAGES

Many times buyers of new homes or income property will require more financing than is available to them under the first mortgage. Consequently, they'll turn to a second mortgage, even if the interest rate is relatively high.

Investors have made vast amounts of money by dealing in second mortgages—and you can, too. Of course, as in any investment, there is an element of risk involved. However, if you're cautious and know your business you can pyramid a molehill of a few thousand dollars into a substantial mountain of cash.

For further information:

> *Mortgage Your Way to Wealth,* Joseph Steinberg. Englewood Cliffs, New Jersey, Prentice-Hall, 1967.
>
> *Mortgage Lending: Fundamentals and Practices,* Willis Bryant. New York, McGraw-Hill, 1962.

Mail Order: Money in Your Mailbox

Ever since the invention of the postage stamp the mail-order industry has provided consumers with a convenient, effortless way to shop. Basking in the popularity of this shopping form is the vast legion of mail-order entrepreneurs who today form the nucleus of a multibillion-dollar-a-year business.

We've all heard of giants like Sears, Roebuck and J. C. Penney, but did you know that there are thousands of smaller firms —even one-man outfits—that are also prospering in this field?

For a person confined to his home the mail-order field offers a superior opportunity for a profitable livelihood. But how does one start? The most effortless and risk-free way to break into the mail-order business is through a system called drop shipping. Under this arrangement, no inventory is required. You simply advertise a product, and when the orders come in you send them to the manufacturer along with a remittance and your shipping label addressed to the customer. The product is then shipped directly to your customer, using your label. Thousands of mail-order items are successfully sold in this manner, with novelty and gift items being the most popular. To get started, write the manufacturer of the product in which you're interested, asking if he'll drop-ship his merchandise.

A more straightforward, but risky, way to begin is simply to find a product that appeals to you, buy a large quantity of it directly from the manufacturer—or, better yet, manufacture it yourself—and sell it by advertising in national magazines and newspapers and through direct mail.

As profitable as the mail-order business can be, there are, nevertheless, numerous pitfalls involved. Many of these can be avoided by studying books on the subject before plunging into the fray. You'll need to know, for instance, about such things as how to judge a product, sources of supply, where to advertise, test marketing, addressing systems, charge cards and COD orders, money-back guarantees, applicable federal laws, and how to sell your mail-order business.

The books listed below will enlighten you on these subjects. Study them carefully, and someday you, too, may be a mail-order mogul.

> *How I Made $1,000,000 in Mail Order,* E. Joseph Cossman. Englewood Cliffs, New Jersey, Prentice-Hall, 1963.
>
> *How to Start and Operate a Mail-Order Business,* Julian Simon. New York, Mc-Graw-Hill, 1965.
>
> *How Mail Order Fortunes Are Made,* Howard Sparks. New York, Frederick Fell, 1966.
>
> *How to Start Your Own Mail Order Business,* Ken Alexander. New York, Stravon Educational Press, 1960.
>
> *Small Business Digest,* P. O. Box 839, Long Beach, New York 11561 (a quarterly publication dealing with mail-order opportunities).

PRESENTS FOR THE POOCH

We have a friend who honestly would rather see his dog get a gift than get one himself. So . . . when his birthday or Christmas rolls around we make a trip to the local pet shop and pick up a rubber ball or bone, a fancy collar, or a canine sweater.

Many pet owners and their friends and relatives would subscribe to a pet gift service if it were made available to them. Here, in exchange for an annual fee, you'd agree to periodically send Bowser a new knickknack for his enjoyment.

Advertise your periodic pet present program in national pet magazines.

PERSONALITY PIX

There is a big demand for photos of movie and TV stars, musical personalities,

and sports figures—especially among the teenage set.

Capitalize on this market by securing such photos through fan clubs, agents, and publicity agencies. Then you can have large quantities cheaply copied from the originals, selling them, framed, through the mail at a profit.

Advertise in national fan magazines such as *Screen Stars* and *TV Star Parade.*

TOY-OF-THE-MONTH CLUB

For all those individuals faced with the perplexing problem of selecting gifts for other people's children, you can offer a solution: Subscriptions to your toy-of-the-month club. Here you'll send each lucky child a different unique small toy every month for a year.

Promote your toy subscription service via ads in national magazines.

GIFTS FOR GOURMETS

Over the years gourmet food packages have been one of the more successful mail-order items.

It's easy to get started. First contact a local food distributor and tell him you plan on selling gourmet gift packages through the mail. Get his wholesale prices. Then figure out your pricing. Since your advertising costs are considerable in the mail-order business, you'll want to keep your prices fairly high. This is all right—people normally expect to pay more for high-quality gift items.

Advertise in national magazines such as *Gourmet* and *Sunset.*

"HOW TO" BOOKS

As a group these are probably the most consistently best-selling items in the whole mail-order field. Subjects such as business, trades, hobbies, sports, psychological self-help, the occult, sex, and travel are all popular.

You'll get your books at large discounts from companies that have "overstock" —books that could not be sold through normal channels. Incidentally, in order to make repeat sales it's best to stick to one particular field of knowledge.

A few of the many companies dealing in overstock books are:

- Overstock Book Co., Inc., 519 Acorn Street, Deer Park, Long Island, New York 11729.

- World Wide Book Service, 251 Third Avenue, New York, New York 10010.

- Wholesale Book Corp., 902 Broadway, New York, New York 10010.

- Book Sales Inc., 110 Enterprise Avenue, Secaucus, New Jersey 07094.

HANDIES FOR THE HANDICAPPED

All over the world thousands of items such as self-opening umbrellas, tripod-base canes, and specially constructed underwear are successfully sold to handicapped individuals every year through mail order.

To find manufacturers of these products refer to the *Thomas Register of American Manufacturers,* at your library. Then print up and distribute mail-order catalogues and advertise in the classifieds of national publications.

VITAMIN CLUB

Vitamins have always been a good mail-order item. Your big sales point in selling these by mail will be a large discount to mail-order customers through a "club plan" whereby they contract to purchase quantities of vitamins on a regular basis.

Buy your vitamins at sizable discounts by ordering large lots through manufacturers. Find these in the *Thomas Register of American Manufacturers,* at your library. Advertise in women's, health, and retirement magazines.

CORRESPONDENCE COURSES

With a diligent effort, anybody can take some textbooks on a particular subject, add some study guides and quizzes, and presto! A correspondence course is born.

However, in order to market your course successfully you must select your sources of advertising carefully. Make absolutely certain that the readers of the publication in which you'll be advertising are likely to have an interest in the subject matter of your course.

For further information:

Teaching by Correspondence, Renee Erdos. New York, Unipub, 1967.

TIE SUBSCRIPTION SERVICE

Here you'll advertise stylish, monogrammed neckties through general interest and men's magazines. Offer a subscription service whereby the customer will receive a new tie monthly for a year, at a price of, say, $19.95. Get your ties direct from the manufacturer.

In addition to addressing your advertising directly to the prospective tie wearer, promote your subscriptions as gift items. Offer different colors and designs.

NEWSLETTERS

Real estate investments, the stock market, income taxes, legislation, business trends—these are just a few of many possible subjects on which you can write and sell a newsletter. Why, one of the authors even knew a man once who successfully published and sold a newsletter on nudist camp activities around the country!

Naturally, you'll advertise your service only in those publications that relate directly to the subject content of your newsletter.

For further information:

How to Make Twenty-Five Thousand a Year Publishing Newsletters, Brian Sheehan. Englewood Cliffs, New Jersey, Prentice-Hall, 1971.

CHEESE SUBSCRIPTIONS

As cheese lovers we place this item high on our list of welcome gifts. How nice it would be if some thoughtful soul arranged to have a different exotic cheese sent to us each month!

Cash in on the cheese market by operating a monthly gift-cheese subscription service. Advertise in food magazines and in the better general-interest magazines.

Buy your cheeses wholesale, through an importer. These are located in large coastal cities. Since you'll be selling mainly to the gift market, be sure to package your products attractively.

SELL PROTECTION

Pocket alarms, police whistles, electric prods, chemical sprays—these are just a few of the many types of personal protection devices that can successfully be sold through mail order.

Find distributors of these products by referring to the *Thomas Register of American Manufacturers,* at your library. Before starting, however, better check all applicable federal and state regulations regarding sale and shipment of these items.

FABRIC REMNANTS

Here's a novel idea for you. Contact textile mills and wholesalers in your area and offer to purchase odd lengths of fabric (mill ends) at a reduced price. Then place ads in magazines like *Stitch 'N' Sew,* Box 338, Chester, Maryland 01011 or *Textile Crafts,* P. O. Box 3216, Los Angeles, California 90028. You might also do well by placing a small display ad in the women's section of your local newspaper.

Dealing with People

WAKE-UP SERVICE

Alarm clocks are often ineffective in awakening those individuals who truly don't want to get up in the morning. However, it seems that the ringing of a telephone, for some arcane psychological reason, can raise the dead.

Get your morning wake-up service off the ground (or off the bed) by advertising in the newspaper classifieds and by distributing leaflets throughout large office buildings. Charge each customer five to fifteen dollars per month.

One pitfall of this business, however, is that if, one morning, *you* don't wake up, you're in deep trouble.

VOICE VIGNETTES

Businessmen are always on the lookout for a gimmick that'll bring them customers. Working with a friend, improvise short, witty thirty- or sixty-second radio commercials calling attention to a particular product or service. Get them on tape. Then call the owner of the business concerned, play him the tape over the phone, and ask if he's interested in buying it as a radio commercial. You might even make a deal with a local radio station, getting a commission on any radio time the merchant buys as a result of your efforts.

OPEN A YOUTH HOSTEL

The American Youth Hostels is an organization composed of thousands of young people whose interests center around bicycling, hiking, and exploring nature. Since many hostelers bicycle great distances, inexpensive accommodations, called hostels, have been set up all over the world. These are usually run by private individuals.

You can set up your own youth hostel in a large home, an apartment building, or even in a barn—anywhere a youngster can throw down a sleeping bag. For further information, and to be listed in their manual, contact American Youth Hostels, 132 Spring Street, New York 10012.

PERSONAL COUNSELOR

Individuals with personal and family problems can many times be helped simply by talking things out with another party. You needn't be a professional psychiatrist or psychologist—just interested and perceptive.

If this type of work appeals to you, spread the word through friends and neighbors. You might even initially volunteer your services to social service organizations, and then gradually build up your business by accepting clients into your own counseling sessions.

For further information:

Human Art of Counseling, Joseph Simons and Jeanne Reidy. New York, Seabury Press, 1971.

Art of Helping People Effectively, Stanley Mahoney. New York, Association Press, 1967.

ROOMING/BOARDINGHOUSE

You won't make a million by running a rooming- or boardinghouse, but you can free yourself from the nine-to-five routine—and that's what this book is all about!

Whether you merely take in roomers or decide on feeding them as well is strictly a matter of your own choosing. But in either case, unless you are a truly gregarious individual, or at least are able to tolerate others' foibles, idiosyncrasies, eccentricities, peccadilloes, and indiscretions, better look for another, less people-oriented enterprise.

To get customers, advertise in the newspaper classifieds and put notices up in the bus station.

ESCORT SERVICE

You can help lonely individuals—and create a money-making enterprise at the same time—by opening an escort service. Simply advertise for men and women to act as escorts for an evening, screening them carefully. Then advertise your escort service in the newspaper, and leave notices or brochures at some of the finer hotels in town.

Basic fees are usually twenty to thirty dollars per evening, plus expenses. Keep one-third of the basic fee for yourself.

OPERATE A GUEST HOUSE

If you have a roomy home on a well-traveled road, or in a town frequented by many tourists, consider operating a guest house. Rent out rooms for the night or by the week, mostly to tourists. Their reasons for staying at your place rather than at a motel will be twofold. First, your rates will be about one-half of those charged in a motel. Second, you'll provide a comfortable, homey atmosphere.

The only advertising you'll need is a sign in front of your home. Before starting, however, better check local zoning and licensing regulations.

PERSONAL MANAGER

As a personal manger your job is to help people who have overextended their credit to get back into good financial shape. Your clients turn their paychecks over to you each payday. You are then responsible for paying the rent and food bills and for arranging with creditors for eventual full payment of all outstanding debts.

You can either charge your client 10 percent of his outstanding debts for this service, or you can ask each creditor for a 10 percent commission on all monies repaid him. It's unlikely that banks and finance companies will consent to this arrangement. However, most retail merchants will jump at the chance.

Before starting this venture, better make a thorough check of all existing federal and state regulations pertaining to such activities.

For further information:

What to Do When Your Bills Exceed Your Paycheck: Everything You Need to Know About Getting Out of Debt, Sidney Sherwin.

Englewood Cliffs, New Jersey, Prentice-Hall, 1974.

DOMESTIC HELP AGENCY

You may not know it but the demand for reliable domestic help—cleaning women, cooks, maids, housekeepers—exceeds the supply. In other words, the customers are out there—it's the employees you've got to find. What better time to scour the labor market than in inflationary times like these?

To find your help, contact your state department of employment and, if necessary, advertise in the newspaper classifieds.

Services

MOVIE MONEY

Any large city contains film libraries that sell movies. Although some of the more recent movies are relatively expensive, many of the older cartoons and silents not only are inexpensive—but are more entertaining!

In your public library you can find film libraries listed in the Yellow Pages of big-city directories. Write these firms for catalogues. As you build up your own film library, start renting your films to local churches, schools, civic and community groups, and other organizations. In addition, you could make some extra profits by renting out projection equipment.

WRAP UP YOUR FORTUNE

Although department stores normally offer gift wrapping services, since the wrapping is mass-produced, the work is not as personalized as most people would like to have it. Furthermore, during holiday shopping time there's usually a long wait for service.

Start you own gift wrapping outfit, featuring fast, personalized work. In addition, you could also wrap packages for mailing; here your clients would be both private individuals and nearby small firms.

For further information:

Gift Wrapping, Adelaide Shaw and Josephine Shaw. New York, Arc Books (order through Arco Publishing), 1952.

PROFITS FROM PRINTING

You can open up your own print shop for under $100!

Buy yourself a small, hand-operated printing press. Then, working from your home, contact business firms, social and civic organizations, clubs, and individuals, offering to print up business cards, stationery, sales forms, tickets, and related items.

For further information:

Printing for Everyone, Gertrude Derendinger. New York, International Publications, 1960.

Basic Science: Printing, C. C. Ammonds. Elmsford, New York, Pergamon Press, 1970.

MR. FIXIT

Many small towns can still boast a "Mr. Fixit" who seemed more like a magician than a repairman because of his ability to take old, battered appliances or other pieces of equipment and have them operating like new in no time.

You don't need any capital to start a repair business, only a little mechanical and electrical aptitude.

To get started, distribute leaflets throughout the neighborhood, and advertise in the newspaper classifieds and the Yellow Pages.

For further information:

Fix Your Small Appliances (2 vols.), Jack Darr. Indianapolis, Howard W. Sams, 1974.

How to Fix Almost Everything, Stanley Schuler. New York, Pocket Books, 1970.

CUSTOM LAUNDRY

Many people are afraid to launder delicate fabrics, such as silk underwear and woolen sweaters, for fear of ruining them. Since commercial laundries work on volume, they cannot devote the necessary attention to these items.

This is where you come in. Since you'll be operating from your home, you'll be able to take the time to pamper panties and coddle capes.

Get your customers by spreading the word among friends and neighbors, and by distributing leaflets in nearby housing developments.

For further information:

Simple Laundrywork and Fabric Care, Marion Mennie. Plainfield, New Jersey, Textile Book Service.

Let's Talk Laundry, Frederick Dearmond. Springfield, Missouri, Mycroft Press, 1957.

RUN A REMINDER SERVICE

If you're at all like Cricket you have a tendency to forget occasions like birthdays and anniversaries—especially if you're long on relatives and a little bit short on memory. Well, dear reader, there are millions like you.

You can help some of these forgetful people by starting a service whereby you would send them a reminder through the mail, just prior to dates that are important to them.

Promote your reminder service initially by distributing leaflets and advertising in the newspaper classifieds. After you get rolling, contact your local newspaper and let them write a feature article on your unique service.

WEATHER REPORTS

This enterprise, which is currently being worked successfully in many areas throughout the country, involves buying or leasing telephone answering equipment which will provide a recorded message of the latest weather forecast for callers. Preceding each forecast, however, will be a short commercial announcement for a bank, department store, restaurant, or other firm. The fee you'll charge these sponsors will pay for your overhead, as well as provide you with a substantial profit.

Your job will be to obtain and record fresh weather information several times each day, as well as to round up sponsors for your service.

PLASTIC LAMINATING

Owners of such items as drivers' licenses, social security cards, birth certificates, and wedding licenses are often anxious to preserve these documents by protecting them in plastic. Organizations issuing I.D. cards are another large market for plastic lamination. Restaurant menus and credit card firms represent still more potential business. Craft items such as decorative bookmarks and coasters can be fashioned and laminated, then sold through gift and craft shops.

To get into business, you'll need a laminating machine. Find manufacturers of this equipment in the *Thomas Register of American Manufacturers,* at your local library.

COME INTO AN INCOME IN THE INCOME TAX BUSINESS

If you've got an above-average head for figures and forms, depreciation and deductions, you should do very well as an income tax preparer. Most of what you need to know is contained in the free booklets issued by the Internal Revenue Service.

Study up on these and, as soon as the first of the year rolls around, spread word of your service to friends and neighbors and advertise in the local newspaper. As your business and knowledge grow you can expand your services to include business firms, taking on extra help as needed.

WATCH REPAIR

You can learn watch repair by taking a correspondence course on the subject.

Start out by repairing watches for your friends and neighbors. If you do good work, word will spread. Soon you may find yourself with a full-time enterprise.

For further information:

Practical Watch Repairing, Don DeCarle. Hackensack, New Jersey, Wehman, 1964.

The Watch Repairer's Manual, Henry Fried. Princeton, New Jersey, Van Nostrand, 1961.

BOOKBINDING

A staggering quantity of books are sold in this country every year. After a few years a much-read book will start coming apart at the seams. These two facts add up to another potential money-making enterprise: bookbinding.

You can make money in two ways: rebind old and valuable books for individuals, and contract to bind new books for small publishers.

Get individual customers through bookstores and libraries. You can find a complete list of publishers in the *Literary Market Place,* at your library.

For further information:

Basic Bookbinding, Arthur Lewis. New York, Dover, 1952.

The Craft of Bookbinding, Eric Burdett. New York, Pitman, 1975.

REPAIR AGENCY

How convenient it would be if one were able to pick up the phone, summon a repairman for any problem under the sun, and have him appear promptly to perform the necessary repairs.

Provide this service by first making arrangements with local tradesmen whereby you will refer customers to them in exchange for a 10 percent commission based on their fee to the customers. Then you'll take calls from individuals needing repairs on anything from accordions to zoom lenses, in turn calling the appropriate repairman.

TAKE IN IRONING

Although you may find an occasional ironing millionairess, it's doubtful that you'll ever discover a millionairess ironer. Nevertheless, like all the other enterprises in the book, if you promote your talents aggressively you'll make an adequate livelihood.

Many housewives hate the chore and would gladly assign the job of ironing hubby's shirts to someone else. Therefore, handbill distribution in suburban neighborhoods is a good idea. To get members of the singles crowd as customers spread leaflets throughout singles apartment complexes.

IDENTIFICATION SERVICE

Hundreds of thousands of dollars' worth of valuable personal property could be saved every year if the owners only had some means of identification of their jewelry, guns, cameras, TV sets, and other valuables.

With a small engraving machine, which you should be able to find through the Yellow Pages, you'll engrave the owners' names and addresses on these valuable items. To get customers, leave notices at gun shops, camera and jewelry stores, and any other retail outlets that could possibly provide you with a good source of business.

Products

SHEKELS FROM SCARECROWS

Use your imagination to think up new, easy-to-assemble, effective scarecrow kits for the pest-ridden gardener and farmer. You may come up with a sophisticated version of the flashy aluminum pieplate-bedecked model, a noisy windmill or pinwheel contraption, or a collapsible wooden replica of the traditional straw man.

Have a good salesman market your unique product line through garden shops, garden supply centers of large department stores, farm supply outlets, and feed dealers. Advertising your products by mail order in the classified sections of national farm and garden magazines may also be a winner.

A SLIPPERY PROPOSITION

Soap is not difficult to make. In fact, up until the development of modern industrial methods it was invariably made at home.

By making your soap in different sizes, colors, designs, and scents, you can successfully market it through fine gift shops, boutiques, department stores—as well as through mail order.

Before getting started, however, better check federal regulations relating to cosmetics.

For further information:

Make Your Own Soap Plain and Fancy, Dorothy Richter. Garden City, New York, Doubleday, 1974.

Making Homemade Soaps and Candles, Phyllis Hobson. Charlotte, Vermont, Garden Way.

Soaps, Scents, and Sweet Substitutes: A Recipe Book, Beverly Plummer. New York, Atheneum (orders to Book Warehouse, Inc.), 1975.

TREASURES FROM TERRARIUMS

Terrariums—those handsome, bottled displays of miniature forests, deserts, and jungles—have recently become very popular as decorative items.

Your terrariums can be made to stand on a coffee table, hang from the ceiling, or be mounted on a wall. You might fashion a tiny

model for the windowsill or a giant version as a floor display.

Solicit orders from nurseries, garden centers, gift shops, and department and variety stores by showing samples of some of your more imaginative work.

For further information:

Successful Terrariums: A Step-by-Step Guide. Ken Kayatta and Steve Schmidt. Boston, Houghton Mifflin, 1975.

The Complete Book of Terrarium Gardening, Jack Kramer. New York, Scribner's, 1974.

BOOTY FROM BADGES

People wear badges for many different reasons. They're worn as name tags at conventions and social gatherings. Sports fans like to wear them imprinted with the name of their favorite ball club. School kids like comical faces on theirs. Political and religious badges are popular, as are humorous ones.

Get into the badge business by buying an inexpensive badge-making machine. Two manufacturers are: N. G. Slater Corp., 220 West Nineteenth Street, New York, New York 10011; and Badge-a-Minit, Box 618, La Salle, Illinois 61301. Find others in the *Thomas Register of American Manufacturers,* at your library.

Sell your badges to associations and clubs of all types, business and political organizations, and school and church groups.

PEDDLE PLANTS

Turn your green thumb into "green paper" by growing unique and novel varieties of plants and flowers that are not often found at other outlets. Venus's-flytraps, orchids, birds of paradise, and decorative hanging baskets are just a few possibilities.

In addition to selling your products direct to the customer try offering them to supermarkets and convenience stores, nurseries, and variety stores.

 **COSMETICS MANUFACTURER**

Sound too overwhelming? It's not. For you can create cosmetics right in your own kitchen.

Practice at home, studying books from the library or those listed below. After you've gotten the knack of it, package your product attractively in containers which you can buy wholesale. Then contact some retail dealers and get them to try your line. We must stress, however, that in this type of business creative and attractive packaging is every bit as important as the quality of the product itself.

Cosmetic goods also lend themselves well to the mail-order business, if handled properly.

Since the manufacture and sale of cosmetics are covered under the Food, Drug, and Cosmetic Act, it's best to check with the Food and Drug Administration, 5600 Fishers Lane, Rockville, Maryland 20852, before getting started.

For further information:

Cosmetics from the Kitchen, Marcia Donnan. New York, Holt, Rinehart, & Winston, 1972.

Here's Egg on Your Face: How to Make Your Own Cosmetics, Beatrice Traven. Old Tappan, New Jersey, Fleming H. Revel.

Successful Cosmetic Selling, Joan Degenshein and Naomi Stern. New York, Chain Store Publishing, 1971.

 **HOME BOUTIQUE**

Your boutique will specialize in ladies' apparel. Here you'll have the edge over large commercial establishments through your practice of giving personalized attention to your customers: A small selection of tastefully chosen clothing, set in a relaxed, cordial atmosphere, will appeal to a lot of shoppers.

To get your initial inventory contact clothing manufacturers and suppliers requesting that their salesmen call on you. Buy conservatively at first, until you can determine which items sell the best.

For further information:

Selling Fashion Apparel, Eleanor Mullikin. Cincinnati, South-Western, 1971.

 **BONSAI TREES**

Here is about the closest you'll get to money growing on trees. Bonsai are very old trees—some as much as several hundred years old—that have been naturally dwarfed by the wind and a lack of water.

Because of their age and the demand for them, bonsai can sell for hundreds of dollars. Is it any wonder, then, that importers of these miniature marvels profit nicely by their sale?

To get started, write to the Japan Trade Center, 1221 Avenue of the Americas, New York, New York 10036, for information on exporters.

For further information:

Step-by-Step Guide to Growing Bonsai Trees. Joan Melville. New York, Hippocrene, 1974.

Bonsai for Beginners, H. J. Larkin. New York, Arco, 1969.

The Sewing Circle

Needlework and sewing offer yet another excellent opportunity for the individual confined to the home. If you're a novice you'll want to learn the basics by studying up on the subject. Here are some books that will help.

Modern Sewing: A Text and Handbook, Frances Jones. Danville, Illinois, Interstate, 1972.

America's Sewing Book, Sandra Ley. New York, Scribner's, 1972.

Complete Book of Needlecraft, Ida Duncan. New York, Liveright (order through E. P. Dutton), 1972.

Anchor Manual of Needlework. Newton Centre, Massachusetts, Charles T. Branford, 1974.

SHOCKING SHIRTS

The mod men's shirt industry has a continual need for new and unique designs and colors. Use your creative ability to come up with new ideas, employing colorfully patterned material.

Custom-tailor your original creations to your own individual customers, or sell your premade goods to men's boutiques and department stores. You might also attempt to sell your designs by sending color photos of them to shirt manufacturers.

BANNER BUCKS

Thousands of banners are bought by high school and college students every year. Why not break into this business by creating some mod banners and selling them to parents of elementary school children, Little League players, and Boy Scouts as well?

Make up some attractive samples of felt, containing names of schools and their sports teams. Then take them around to some of the potential buyers listed above, soliciting orders.

For further information:

Banners and Hangings: Design & Construction, Norman Laliberte and Sterling McIlhany. New York, Van Nostrand, 1966.

 GO A-QUILTING

To most people the old-fashioned quilt evokes a warm, friendly remembrance of days gone by. Because of the time-consuming labor involved in their making, good quilts are relatively expensive. Nevertheless, quality products continue to sell well.

Sell your finished products to department and variety stores, gift and children's apparel shops, as well as to friends and neighbors.

For further information:

Traditional Patchwork Patterns: Full-Size Cut-Outs and Instructions for 12 Quilts,

Carol Belanger-Grafton. New York, Dover, 1974.

Vogue Guide to Patchwork and Quilting, Vogue Editors, ed. New York, Stein and Day, 1974.

THE BRIDAL GOWN GAME

After a few years of being out of vogue, weddings are again becoming popular as a means of expressing devotion between a man and a woman.

Cash in on this reemerging trend by custom designing and creating wedding gowns, bridesmaids' gowns, flower girl outfits, and related apparel. Needless to say, this work is a specialty of a high order, with flawlessness a must.

Start by creating outfits for friends, neighbors, and relatives. Also try to work through established bridal registries and department stores. Advertise in the wedding section of your local newspaper and in the Yellow Pages.

BATCHES OF PATCHES

Humorous, witty, sexy, and even obscene patches are popular nowadays. Patches are sewed onto clothing over every conceivable part of the body—and over some that are inconceivable!

The trick is to come up with some catchy wording. If you can't think of anything yourself, perhaps you could "cheat" just a bit and refer to joke books found in libraries and bookstores. Distribute your patches to souvenir and novelty shops, and to variety stores.

For further information:

Appliqué Stitchery, Jean Laury. New York, Van Nostrand, 1966.

EXOTIC EMBROIDERED NECKTIES

Have a creative flair with embroidery? Well, here's one area where you can express your most far-out fantasies.

Ever since the hippie invasion of 1967 men's neckties have been getting progressively more outrageous. Make up some colorful ties and sell them to menswear and department stores. Leave them on consignment if you can't sell them outright. Don't be afraid to ask top prices (assuming your work is good). Unique handmade wearing apparel always commands a premium.

For further information:

> *Embroidery Design,* Enid Mason. Newton Center, Massachusetts, Charles T. Branford, 1969.

> *Design in Embroidery,* Kay Whyte. Newton Center, Massachusetts, Charles T. Branford, 1969.

DOLLING UP DOLLS

This enterprise offers two ways to make money by creating clothes for dolls. Both, if promoted properly, can be financially rewarding.

One way is to make clothing to fit standard sizes of dolls sold in toy shops. The other is to have customers bring their dolls to you to be custom-fitted. Types of clothes might include hats, dresses, coats, shoes, bathing suits, and lingerie.

Get started by making up some samples to be displayed in toy and children's apparel shops. Also spread word among friends and neighbors. Advertise in the Yellow Pages.

For further information:

> *Fashions for Dolls,* Barbara Drew. New York, Drake, 1972.

> *Sewing for Twentieth Century Dolls.* Johana Anderton. Riverdale, Maryland, Hobby House Press, 1972.

QUILT KITS

Any form of quilting is a tiresome and time-consuming process. But you can make this task a lot easier for quilters by providing them with kits containing precut squares of

material and enough lining, needles, and thread to finish the job properly.

Make your kits available in twin, full, queen, and king sizes, and sell them through craft shops and department stores.

MAKE BUTTONHOLES?

It's unlikely that you'll accumulate your first million by making buttonholes. But if you think that some people aren't making a good living at it, you've got another guess coming.

What you probably don't realize is that making a buttonhole is not an easy task, even for an experienced seamstress. For this reason tailors and seamstresses can ask, and get, one dollar and up per hole. So, as you can see, the income from just four garments per day, each requiring five holes, can buy your bed and board.

To promote your buttonhole business spread word to local retail fabric shops, leave notices up on supermarket bulletin boards, and advertise in the newspaper classifieds.

GOLD FROM GLOVES

Ladies' gloves, men's gloves, children's gloves and mittens, work gloves, ski gloves, golfers' gloves—when you think about it, the glove market is a large one.

Make your own patterns by cutting up old gloves, which you can find in secondhand stores and thrift shops. Get your raw materials from leather suppliers, handicraft shops, and garment manufacturers.

Sell your work through men's and ladies' apparel shops, and department and sporting goods stores.

REWARDS FROM REWEAVING

In contrast to conventional methods of sewing and patching holes and burns in fabric, reweaving is a method whereby the patching material is taken from the inside of the damaged garment itself and then skillfully woven into the damaged area. The repair work is almost invisible. There is a special technique involved and, because of this, a good reweaving job commands a higher fee than would ordinary mending.

The Fabricon Company, 2019 West Montrose Avenue, Chicago, Illinois 60618, sells a course on the subject. Write them for free literature.

HAMMOCKS

Who doesn't love to lie in a hammock on a warm afternoon, sipping a Cuba libre or mint julep?

Help promote the leisurely life by creating your own attractive versions of these age-old suspended sacs. They can be made of canvas, woven netting, or leather. The material can be dyed various colors or, in the case of leather, distinctive designs can be tooled into it.

Sell your creations to gift shops, hardware and variety stores, and department and sporting goods stores. Mail order is likewise a good outlet for this product.

For further information:

How to Make Your Own Hammock and Lie in It, Denison Andrews. New York, Workman, 1973.

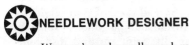

NEEDLEWORK DESIGNER

Women's and needlework magazines, as well as needlework wholesalers, are constantly seeking fresh design ideas to use in promoting their products—and they'll pay handsomely for them!

Submit your designs by sending a color transparency or color print of your work. If they like your idea they'll ask you to send the finished piece.

Find suitable magazine markets for your designs by noting magazines at your newsstand which feature needlework designs. *Thomas Register of American Manufacturers,* at your library, will list needlework wholesalers.

For further information:

Creative Needlework, Jo Springer and Solweig Hedin. New York, Arco, 1969.

Designing in Stitching and Appliqué, Nancy Belfer. New York, Sterling, 1973.

SLIPCOVERS AND DRAPERIES

Here, too, you'll be putting your creativity to work—this time designing and sewing slipcovers and draperies.

Obtain your samples from fabric manufacturers, who supply them free to professionals.

To get started, let friends and neighbors know you're in business. You'll also want to canvass new housing developments in your area or, better yet, try to contract with a local builder to supply all of his new homes with draperies.

For further information:

How to Make Lampshades and Draperies, Pier Montagna. Bridgeport, Connecticut, Key Books (order through Associated Booksellers, Bridgeport).

Complete Guide to Curtains, Slipcovers, and Upholstery, Marguerite Maddox and Miriam Paake. New York, Pocket Books, 1963.

Streamlined Curtains and Covers, Renee Robinson and Julian Robinson. New York, St. Martin's, 1968.

PROFITS FROM PILLOWS

If you've got a healthy imagination you should be able to come up with all sorts of interesting—and salable—ideas for pillows.

You can embroider designs on them. You can sew witty sayings or ribbons onto them. You can make throw pillows, bed pillows, or "monster" pillows—those huge bean or Styrofoam-filled things that can be used in a living room or recreation room as lounge chairs.

Sell your creations to gift, variety, and department stores. Once you get rolling, you'll find that this is a pretty "soft" way to make a living.

INSIGNIAS AND MONOGRAMS

Local sports associations — Little Leagues, bowling and softball groups, high school and college baseball, football, basketball, and track teams—all require that insignias and numbers be embroidered on their uniforms. You can get sample books of the insignias, as well as the insignias themselves, from manufacturers who specialize in this line.

In addition, a good portion of your business will come from individuals who desire monogramming of such items as shirts, bed pillows, and handkerchiefs.

For the above, you'll need a sewing machine equipped to do zigzag stitching. To get team business, simply contact the specific organizations. To get individual customers, leave notices in clothing and department stores.

For further information:

Introducing Machine Embroidery, J. Lillow. Plainfield, New Jersey, Textile Book Service, 1969.

BARBECUE APRONS

Worn mainly by hosts and hostesses of barbecue dinners, these aprons will feature clever designs and witty sayings calculated to raise a chuckle or two from their guests.

Or, your aprons might just feature outlandish (even outrageous) designs or risqué (or downright obscene) illustrations.

Market your products through novelty and gift shops, hardware and variety stores.

CASH FROM COSTUMES

Who needs costumes? They're popular at children's parties, masquerade parties, store and company promotions, fairs, carnivals, and other festive occasions—and people buy them as well as rent them.

After you've created a batch of various types such as clowns, hobos, witches, rabbits, ducks, pirates, bears, and, of course, Santa Claus outfits, promote your products through department stores, children's clothing, and novelty shops. Keep your eyes open for upcoming parties, conventions, and store promotions, and be sure to get your enterprise into the local newspaper as a feature article.

For further information:

Costume Patterns and Designs, Max Tilke. New York, Hastings House, 1974.

Costume Design and Making, Mary Fernald. New York, Theatre Arts Books, 1967.

ALTERATIONS AND MENDING

This business is frequently called "the big little business." While the idea of your directing an international cartel of alteration and mending corporations is somewhat farfetched, it's nevertheless possible for you to successfully run a full-time enterprise of this type.

To get started you'll need a sewing machine, some sewing materials, and a few clothes racks. Spread word of your service to friends, relatives, and neighbors. You can also economically print up and distribute handbills in nearby suburban shopping centers.

For further information:

Garment Altering and Repairing and Tailor Shop Management, Clarence Poulin. Penacook, New Hampshire, Clarence J. Poulin, 1967.

Tailoring Manual, Gertrude Strickland. Corvallis, Oregon, Oregon State University Book Stores, 1972.

18
Offbeat: Preposterous Possibilities for Producing Profits

Do you have a penchant for the preposterous? A leaning toward the ludicrous? A bent for the bizarre? If you like to step to the beat of a different drum, this chapter will, most certainly, provide the rhythm.

Engaging in many of the following enterprises may indeed cause you to be thought of as somewhat weird by friends and strangers alike. Enjoy it. Not only will you be out of the rat race of a conventional occupation but, in operating your bizarre business, you'll find yourself the subject of much curiosity, interest, perhaps controversy but, above all, publicity—much of it free.

So wander now into the wacky world of weird work, and step to any drumbeat your fancy dictates.

Strange Services

 **PROMOTE THE GOAT!**

Besides providing you with milk, these affectionate, intelligent creatures can provide you with a livelihood. How? You can go door-to-door in the suburbs, offering to loan one of your goats every week or two as a quiet, effortless alternative to the lawnmower. As a bonus, lawnowners will get free organic fertilizer.

After you've successfully booked up your goats for the summer, use your time to approach county and state road departments with your expanding herd. Explain that they are far cheaper and more efficient than those clumsy mechanical roadside mowers. Arrange a fat contract for your organic, ecological mowers.

When your herd numbers in the thousands, you're ready for the big time. Federal forests and recreation areas are over-ripe for your highly effective firebreak browsers. You can keep down the undergrowth in such fuel breaks at a fraction of the cost of human work crews. Such a plan is already underway in Cleveland National Forest. However, if your suggestion is rejected, don't let it get your goat. Keep on milking your charges for what it's worth.

For further information:

Starting Right with Milk Goats, Helen Walsh. Charlotte, Vermont, Garden Way, 1972.

ODD OBJECT OUTLET

If you like playing detective and dealing in strange and unique objects, set up an agency to dredge up hard-to-find items for your clients.

A shrunken head, a moon rock, an 1804 silver dollar and a hen's tooth are a few examples. Track down your goods through the Yellow Pages, *Thomas Register of American Manufacturers*, importers, foreign manufacturers and suppliers, and any other sources your ingenuity will lead you to.

WEALTH FROM WAR WORRIES

Do you own a large tract of idle land in a remote area? You don't have to wait decades for the land to appreciate before you can realize a big profit on it. Here's how to cash in on it *now*. Set up an A-frame prefab. Stock it with a few cots and a large supply of staples that keep indefinitely, such as government-issued Multi-Purpose Food, available through Meals for Millions Foundation, 1800 Olympic Blvd., P. O. Box 1666, Santa Monica, California 90406. Make sure plenty of water is available from a well or spring.

Now advertise discreetly in well-heeled circles the existence of an exclusive survival camp in a wilderness area, a safe refuge during a nuclear war or other national disaster. For an initial fee of $2,000, plus $500 a year maintenance, your clients have the right to pitch their tent on the property and share water and food there.

This may sound like a crazy, unworkable idea, but it's been done in Northern California—and very profitably.

PIE-IN-THE-PUSS SERVICE

Recently a company has leaped into national prominence by offering a most unusual service. For a fee, its operatives will agree to plunge a pie into the face of anyone the customer fingers. Naturally, throwing a pie into the face of Robert Redford, Raquel Welch, or the President of the United States would involve a proportionately higher fee than usual.

Start your own pie-throwing firm by putting ads in the local paper. As your business builds you can branch out into cakes, puddings, rotten tomatoes—even bacon fat and molasses!

Get to know a good attorney beforehand.

IMPORT-A-WIFE

Unfortunately, many men in our society are long on money and short on good wife material. Solve this problem for them by arranging to import willing women from countries like Germany and Sweden.

After contracting with your male clients, and collecting a partial fee, your job will be to advertise for the women in foreign newspapers, then make all arrangements for transportation and immigration.

This business has been worked successfully in the past, with clients paying the "broker" as much as $500 for his services. Come to think of it, there are probably many American women who would pay to have men imported from the Continent.

EMPLOYEES FOR FIRE?

To our way of thinking this ranks among collection agencies and auto repossessors as one of the more abominable ways of making a living. Nevertheless, here it is.

Many merchants have the serious problem of employee theft in their business. To help merchants combat this, you'll supply an actor or actress who will be hired, work along with the employees for a while, then get "caught" stealing. The individual will be publicly chastized by the proprietor, led out the door by him, and supposedly taken to the police station for booking.

Naturally, the whole thing is a "setup" in

order to frighten the employees into refraining from stealing from the boss. See what we mean by abominable?

RENT-A-HIPPIE

Many times people in the more conventional suburban areas want to throw a party and endow it with "atmosphere" by inviting hippies, bohemians, beatniks, or other colorful types. By running a party-staffing service you could profit by providing party throwers with hippies, blacks, fiery-eyed radicals —even psychiatrists and nuclear physicists!

First you'll need to build up a stable of these various types. Base your fees to the party thrower on the demand for the type of person selected to attend the party, and take a commission of the fee for yourself.

MATERNITY AND BIRTH PHOTOGRAPHER

As a maternity and birth photographer you make an agreement with a pregnant woman and her husband as follows: Beginning in about the fourth month of pregnancy, you drop by their house once a month and take a few pictures of the prospective mother. The main purpose, of course, is to show the woman in various stages of pregnancy.

Just prior to the time of birth, you are called. Donning surgical garb, you enter the delivery room with the mother to record the baby's delivery on film: a priceless family record for all time. Be sure, however, to obtain permission from both the doctor and the hospital, in writing, before you even start the project. Also, you must have a pretty strong stomach.

To get started, contact local maternity shops and obstetricians, making them aware of your specialty.

BIKE SKIING

We've all heard of a ski run, but how about a bike run? If you have some property in a hilly area, create several long, paved, curved, sloping trails to be used as bike runs. Each trail will have a different degree of curve and slope—a different element of danger. You'll also need some sort of "bike lift" to haul the bicycle and its rider back up to the top of the hill for another run.

Naturally, you'll want to secure a good liability insurance policy before starting this enterprise.

UPHOLSTER WALLS?

It seems that a new home-decorating trend is beginning to emerge on the West Coast. Apparently tired of the harshness of inside walls, California residents are having their walls "upholstered" with carpeting or furniture material. Why not start a trend like this in your community? Then cash in on the fad as a "wall-upholstery expert."

A good way to start would be to upholster your own walls in some outlandish fashion. Then invite a photographer and writer from the local newspaper into your home for an interview, which will give you valuable free publicity.

DEMONSTRATORS UNLIMITED

This might be the name you'd select for an enterprise in which you'd supply sign-carrying demonstrators for any cause. Naturally, you'd be responsible for matching the demonstrators to the cause, making up the signs, and seeing to it that your personnel arrive at their demonstration on time (and get out alive!).

Accumulate a stable of various types by advertising in the classifieds. Then contact organizations in your community for possible jobs. Have a good insurance policy for your demonstrators.

MANUFACTURE HANG GLIDERS

Hang gliding is rapidly becoming the rage among daredevil enthusiasts across the country. Strapping himself into the harness of a huge winged kite, the "pilot" can become airborne by jumping off a cliff or by being towed behind a motorboat or automobile.

The manufacture of hang-glider kits, which sell for anywhere from $50 to $1,000, is becoming big business. If you're interested in jumping into the fray, your best bet is to go to California, where most of the action is.

For further information:

United States Hang Gliding Association, Box 66306, Los Angeles, California 90066. You can get Dan Poynter's *Hang Gliding* through this organization. For a five-dollar membership fee they will send you a copy of their directory listing manufacturers, clubs, schools, and flying sites.

HANG GLIDER CLUB

Here you'll need to own or lease mountaintop or cliffside property. Then a shed and a supply of hang gliders should be enough to put you in business. Make your money by charging for rental, instruction, and use of your "takeoff facilities."

Usually, it takes time to get a business of this type off the ground. So just hang in there—soon your profits will soar!

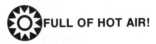

TALK IS CHEAP

Many people are hesitant to burden their friends with their problems, yet need *someone* to tell their troubles to. A San Francisco firm solves this problem by selling conversations!

This agency has carpeted cubicles in which an individual can sit and converse with a sympathetic staff member. Fees are about ten dollars per hour.

Can your city use a service like this?

FULL OF HOT AIR!

Telling you how to acquire, construct, or operate a hot-air balloon is beyond the scope of this book. But if you can figure out a way to do it, you can get top dollar by using your balloon in advertising promotions for large corporations.

After all, if Goodyear considers operating a blimp a good promotional activity, your hot-air balloon should be every bit as valuable to publicity-minded firms.

For further information:

Hot Air Ballooning, Christine Turnbull. New York, Sports Car Press (order through Crown).

OFFBEAT TRAVEL GUIDE

Tourist guidebooks, of course, are available for most foreign countries with a high tourist trade. But you'll write and publish a guide which will give information to the reader that he would have difficulty finding elsewhere, such as where to buy merchandise at a discount; where to rent bicycles and motorcycles; and preferred spots for meeting people of the opposite sex. You might even include a section on gay bars and houses of ill-repute!

SKYSCRAPER WINDOW-CLEANING SERVICE

If you don't suffer from vertigo you can make some good money doing something that a lot of others wouldn't attempt: cleaning the windows of large buildings—both inside and out.

Do this work on a contractual basis. You'll need a crew of men and one or more "swinging stages"—electrically operated platforms on which the cleaning crews stand.

To start, contact managers of large office buildings and department stores in your area, offering your aerial adeptness, your towering talents, and your cleaning capabilities.

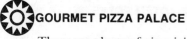

GOURMET PIZZA PALACE

There are plenty of pizza joints around, a testimonial to the popularity of this dish.

Turn this fact to your advantage by opening your own establishment catering to gourmet tastes (and pocketbooks).

Of course, it's possible to eke out a living making and selling standard dishes of this kind. But since you're interested in bigger-than-average profits, you'll want to open your establishment in the more posh section of town, featuring such unheard-of dishes as lobster, caviar, and ground venison pizzas. To get the community talking, you might even offer a peanut butter and jelly pizza. Good luck!

For further information:

Goldberg's Pizza Book, Larry Goldberg and Leonore Fleischer. New York, Random House, 1971.

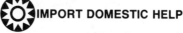

IMPORT DOMESTIC HELP

Well-to-do U. S. citizens have continual difficulty in getting and keeping dependable maids, cooks, governesses, and other domestic help. You can profit greatly here by working through European and Scandinavian agencies in recruiting suitable help for your clients. Your job will be to make the necessary arrangements with immigration authorities, as well as to arrange for transportation of the domestics.

To get started, contact embassies in Washington, D. C., for names and addresses of overseas agencies specializing in this field. You'll also need to get up-to-date information from immigration authorities.

In addition to paying your fee, your clients will be responsible for paying all transportation costs and incidental expenses.

TEACH YOGA

If you're not already trained in this ancient Indian discipline study with a guru until you feel confident enough to teach others. Then hold classes in your home, at the Y, in an evening adult school—even on television.

For further information:

The Complete Illustrated Book of Yoga,

Swami Vishnudevananda. New York, Pocket Books, 1972.

Introduction to Yoga, Annie Besant. Wheaton, Illinois, Theosophical Publishing House.

Fundamentals of Yoga: A Handbook of Theory, Practice and Application, Rammurti Mishra. Garden City, New York, Doubleday, 1974.

HOME EXCHANGE AGENCY

People all over the world will be interested in this service, which involves individuals or families exchanging homes with one another for a specified time. Think of it! Exchanging your home in Lynchburg, South Carolina, for one in Freeport, Nova Scotia, for a month, or temporarily trading your residence in Waterville, Washington, for one in Waterproof, Louisiana.

Your firm would act as a go-between, or clearinghouse, for parties desirous of an exchange. Find prospects by advertising in American and foreign travel magazines.

Absurd Art

BE A TOILET ARTIST

Decorating toilets may very well bring you your first artistic flush of success!

Using gaily colored enamel paints, there are an infinite number of patterns, portraits, and printed signs that you could apply to these very necessary fixtures.

The first step would be to paint your own toilet in some outrageous manner. Then show it off to friends, neighbors, the press —anyone who might spread the word about your unique talent. Also leave brochures in mod boutiques.

CHIMP ART

If you lean a little to the crazy side buy yourself a chimpanzee and put him to work as your artist. These animals have a reputation for being fine abstract painters, but even if yours turns out to be so-so, who wouldn't go ape over a genuine chimp masterpiece?

Set up your studio and gallery in a busy section of town. Let the animal work in the window where he can be seen. Frame his creations nicely and charge well for his services.

AUTO ART

One *does* get tired of seeing cars painted in only one plain color. You can help brighten up our roads by putting your artistic ability to work repainting cars. Stripes, polka dots, flowers, fruit, even nudes—they'll all appeal to one person or another.

Ply your trade initially around college campuses, expanding into the rest of the community as your idea catches on.

COLD CASH

As an "ice sculptor" you'll carve such novel items as animals, Christmas figures, religious symbols—even punch bowls and vases—for cocktail parties, weddings, baby showers, and other social events.

Your job will entail donning winter clothing and working inside an ice plant with mallet and chisel until each creation is finished. Then if you thaw out in time, you'll deliver it to the customer just prior to the event.

Start by donating a few of your creations to cocktail parties around town. If you're good, word will spread and soon you'll have more business than you can chisel.

For further information:

Snow Sculpture and Ice Carving, James Haskins. New York, Macmillan, 1974.

Ice Carving Made Easy, J. Amendola. New York, Corner Book Shop, 1970.

CARVE TOTEM POLES

There is a man in Arizona who specializes in hand-carved Indian totem poles. These are used to decorate the lawns, even the living rooms, of some of his town's more affluent residents.

Start by reading up on Indian lore to get to know your product. Illustrations of this primitive art form can also be found in the book below.

Make up samples, displaying some in your front yard, loaning some to restaurants and shopping centers, and taking some smaller ones door to door for sale.

For further information:

Wolf and the Raven: Totem Poles of Southeastern Alaska, Viola Garfield and Linn Forrest. Seattle, University of Washington Press, 1961.

BE A MELON CARVER

If you're a frustrated sculptor you might try relieving your frustrations by carving large pumpkins, rutabagas, squash, and watermelons into the shape of animals, flowers, buildings—even into caricatures of your customers and of famous personalities.

These masterpieces can then be used as attention-getting displays for food and department stores, in fairs and carnivals, and in the window of any small store that needs a promotional gimmick.

Make up a few small samples and take them around to the above-mentioned prospects to get orders for your work.

Products That May Never Sell

REVERSE MOUTHWASH

TV and magazine ads imploring us to make our breath "kissing sweet" by using mouthwash may indeed enable us to make friends of acquaintances, lovers of friends, and spouses of lovers. But how about that obnoxious individual you simply *can't stand?* The one who leers at you in the office every day. Or the blind date that you've just discov-

ered has two heads—and nothing in either one of them!

The authors have an unconventional but simple solution for these predicaments: mouthwash that smells like a mountain of camel dung, a barrelful of garlic, or the carcass of a long-dead elephant.

Where can you market this unique creation? Anywhere—except in local perfume shops!

TIPSY TOOTHPASTE

Let's face it, brushing one's teeth after every meal, as dentists suggest, is indeed a chore that most people would rather avoid. However, for those who like the taste of alcohol, liquor-flavored toothpaste would turn this chore into a delightful activity. Varieties of toothpaste flavored with Scotch, bourbon, rum, brandy, and even beer ought to sell to such folk.

The authors haven't the vaguest idea regarding a formula for this novel product. Nevertheless, we do remember having seen it successfully marketed some years back.

Sell your tipsy toothpaste to novelty shops and to any outlet where more conventional types of toothpastes are sold. In addition, this would make an exceptionally good mail-order item.

PHOILET SEATS

The above is not a typographical error, nor is there anything wrong with your eyesight. This is the authors' term for toilet seat covers on which photographs have been printed.

Here the helpful photo sensitizer comes to our aid. The customer will send in his favorite photo with the order. Then, using the photo sensitizer, either you or a lab will copy and print the photo onto the seat cover. The finished product, along with the original photograph, is then shipped to the customer.

Photo sensitizing material can be purchased at any large photographic supply outfit or ordered from Rockland Colloid Corp., 599 River Road, Piermont, New York 10968.

Naturally, your price will have to include the cost of the (ahem) raw materials as well as any labor involved.

CRAZY HIGH CHAIRS

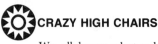

We all know what a baby's high chair looks like. But can you imagine a swaying version, so-called because it's attached to one wide, flexible leg anchored to the floor? You've heard of a water bed, but how about a "water high chair"? Or, better yet, a "self-feeding" high chair? But don't ask the authors how to construct these ingenious devices—that's your problem.

All we know is that these and other unique models would be a hit with parents seeking the bizarre. Sell them to department and furniture stores, children's shops, and restaurants.

BAKE MONSTER CAKES

If you have a good-sized oven and don't mind "baking away" your days, you can make good money by specializing in "theme" cakes that serve 500, 1,000, 2,000 people.

Cakes may be made in any shape. Automobiles, boats, houses, churches, castles, animals—anything is fair game.

How to start? Bake one—at your own expense, if necessary. The ensuing rush of publicity will start the orders rolling in.

For further information:

Your Book of Cake Making and Decorating, Patsy Kumm. Levittown, New York, Transatlantic Arts, 1974.

A BONANZA ON THE BEACH

Believe it or not, millions of dollars' worth of coins and valuables are lost on our public beaches every year. All you need do to start recovering this lost loot, this abandoned booty, these retrievable riches, is to purchase a metal detector and start searching! You'll find coins, watches, rings, bracelets—plus a lot of bottle caps and beer cans.

Metal detection equipment sells for fifty dollars on up into the hundreds, depending on the quality. Just be sure to get one that'll do the job. Find suppliers in the Yellow Pages.

BE AN INVENTOR

One of the best ways to escape from the rat race is to invent a better mousetrap!

Potential ideas are all around us. That can opener or pencil sharpener can be improved upon. How about a toaster that automatically butters our toast for us? Or, better yet, a marketable substitute for the internal combustion engine? You can get a lot of good ideas from publications such as *Popular Science* and *Popular Mechanics.*

Think about it.

For further information:

How to Become a Successful Inventor: Design a Gadget in Your Spare Time and Strike It Rich!, James Schwenck and Eric McNair. New York, Hastings House.

How to Invent, Forrest Gilmore. Houston, Texas, Gulf Publishing, 1959.

Successful Inventor's Guide, Kenneth Kessler and Carlisle Kessler, Englewood Cliffs, New Jersey, Prentice-Hall, 1964.

TOILET HUMOR

"Be the first on your block to provide gag toilet tissue for your guests." So your ads might read for this new twist on an age-old item.

Make up some witty sayings or cartoons, consulting joke books if necessary. Then get together with a toilet paper manufacturer and arrange for "publishing."

Distribute your novel product to outlets where the plain version of this product is normally sold. In addition, sell to novelty shops and through mail order.

AUTO BOUTIQUE

We've got ladies' wear boutiques, wig boutiques, gift boutiques—even children's boutiques. Why not an auto boutique?

Locating your exclusive shop in the best section of town, you'll provide such extravagances as mink steering wheel covers, custom-made hood ornaments, ivory dash knobs, and sterling silver gas caps.

In keeping with your intended image of exquisiteness and elegance, you'll want to open your business with a "grand premiere" (grand openings are for *ordinary* stores), employing searchlights, celebrities, entertainment and, of course, champagne and caviar.

FLOWER FRANNIE

This is (or was) the name of a sweet old lady who used to peddle her homemade corsages to tourists around the French Quarter of New Orleans a few years back. As she carried a small tray through the night, gardenias, orchids, and a ready smile were old Frannie's stock in trade.

We can't guarantee that you'll get rich doing this—or even that you'll make a decent living—but one thing is certain: You'll be your own boss and make many friends at the same time.

For the Sexy Set . . .

SEDUCTIVE MEN'S APPAREL

In Hollywood, California, there is an outfit doing big business in items such as see-through brassieres, flimsy lingerie, and crotchless underwear for ladies. But why should women have all the fun? Why not manufacture and sell seductive apparel for men?

What types of items could you offer? Hmm. You could start with a jaunty nightcap (with the hanging part shaped like a phallus, of course), progress to bullfighter-style pajamas (including cape, but *not* sword), then go on to a see-through G-string.

Piney Woods, Mississippi, would definitely be the *wrong* place for this business. But opening a store in San Francisco or New York, and dealing in mail order, just might turn the trick for you.

THE BARE FACTS

They never advertise openly, but there are hundreds of resorts around the country catering to the nudist set, and most of them are prospering.

If you have country property, perhaps a wooded area with a lake or swimming pool, why not open up a resort of this type? You'll need a fence or wall to keep out the curiosity seekers, and be sure to get a business license (if required) *before* you start.

A HAIR-RAISING OCCUPATION

We don't know how it all started, but in our society an abundant shock of hair on a man's chest is taken as a pretty sure sign of masculinity. As a result, it's no wonder that a man possessing a barren chest is made to feel somewhat effeminate on the beach or in the bedroom.

What can you do about this sad state of affairs? Specialize in providing these bald-breasted bucks with a new, profuse batch of chest hair through the use of "chest wigs."

First, contact wig manufacturers who already produce, or who can come up with, this item. Find them in the *Thomas Register of American Manufacturers,* at your library. Then open a shop in a large city and promote your product heavily, stressing custom-fit as well as a choice of colors and textures.

CHASTITY BELTS

It's a fact that in the Middle Ages, before a married warrior went off to battle he'd guarantee his spouse's faithfulness by locking her organs into a chastity belt before he left, entrusting the key to his manservant just in case he didn't return.

Eventually, however, chastity belts fell upon disuse, hastened, no doubt, by the questionable loyalties of the servants involved.

Today, in San Francisco, a man works full time custom-making these devices for his customers. He doesn't ask them any questions.

Neither should you if you decide to enter this very unconventional field.

EROTIC JEWELRY

In San Francisco there is a jeweler who specializes in creating custom-made erotic jewelry of all kinds. Taking orders for everything from cuff links to chessmen, he'll fashion anything within or without the bounds of social acceptability. Needless to say, his well-heeled clients have nothing more important to spend their money on.

Naturally, you wouldn't want to start a business of this type if you lived in a place like Pigeon Forge, Tennessee. But if you're a cosmopolite, give it a try.

FANCY UNDERWEAR

Here, again, we apply a new idea to an old product and, presto! We have a potential money-maker.

Using your imagination and creative abilities, you can probably come up with dozens of designs, illustrations, and appropriate sayings that can be sewed, embroidered, or silk-screened onto *all* types of underclothing.

Make up some samples of your better work and take them around to local department and clothing stores. If you have some really unique products, try marketing them through mail order.

NUDIE BEACH

Many individuals like to escape this life of crowded cities and imposing social restrictions temporarily by casting off their clothes for a day and running nude under the sun.

If you own or can lease a long stretch of isolated beachfront property, you can earn your living simply by charging admission to it. No advertising is necessary. You'll soon get plenty of free publicity—good and bad!

Creature Corner

PESTS' PESTS

You may think we're a little flea-brained to suggest this scheme, but here goes. Catch yourself a nice assortment of garden spiders—you'll probably get a good windfall in any fallow field or vacant lot. Market your spiders in see-through jars with ventilated lids through garden shops all over town. Spiders can go for some time without food, but a few drops of water should be put in their container every day. Since garden spiders are the natural enemies of destructive garden pests, you can honestly bill your spiders as organic pesticides.

The hardest part about this deal will be to convince the garden shop owner of the salability of your product. But believe us, the spiders will work hard for the buyer's money. Their life depends on it.

When your spider market is glutted, you can try marketing other organic pesticides such as lady bugs, praying mantises, toads, and lizards.

CANINE COSMETICS

Believe it or not, a New York firm does big business by selling such items as lipstick, eye shadow, false eye lashes, toenail polish, and perfume for—you guessed it—dogs.

Their customers include not only local residents but loads of mail-order clients from around the world. If you dig earning your daily bread by contributing to the glamorization of our canine friends, jump into the fray. To beat the competition, though, perhaps you should come up with some new product ideas such as bubble bath, wigs, and underpaw deodorant.

FOR PIOUS POOCHES

Here we go from the ridiculous to the sublime: Crosses, rosary beads, Jewish yarmulkes and prayer shawls—for dogs! These are the types of items a New Orleans outfit specializes in.

I doubt if there would be room for another shop of this type in New Orleans, but any other large city should be fair game. These items would also sell especially well through mail order.

RATTLESNAKE HUNTING AND BREEDING

If you've got a stout heart you might just consider rattlesnakes as a source of profit. Zoos regularly buy snakes for their collections. The venom can be sold to laboratories for use as an ingredient in snake-bite serum. The meat can be supplied to canneries, which can sell it as a delicacy. Skins are always in demand by shoe, belt, and handbag manufacturers. Heads are mounted and sold as novelties. Even the rattles are used for various purposes.

You could elect either to breed the snakes or to hunt them during the season. Rattlesnakes are usually found in desert and mountainous areas and are best caught during the early spring, when they begin to emerge from hibernation.

If you know nothing about the animal or potential markets, your best bet is to get first-hand information by attending one of the many "rattlesnake derbies" held in various parts of the country each year. These local events serve the dual purpose of ridding the surrounding area of dangerous animals and providing a tourist attraction for the town. A partial listing of these annual events follows—write to the chambers of commerce involved for exact dates.

- Whigham Rattlesnake Roundup, Whigham, Georgia—January.

- Waurika Annual Rattlesnake Hunt, Waurika, Oklahoma—April.

- Mangum Annual Rattlesnake Derby, Mangum, Oklahoma—April.

- Okeene Annual Rattlesnake Hunt, Okeene, Oklahoma—April.

- Waynoka Annual Rattlesnake Hunt, Waynoka, Oklahoma—April.

- Rattlesnake Festival and Gopher Race, San Antonio, Florida—October.

GRAVE MARKERS FOR PETS

If you're at all good at lettering, buy yourself an inexpensive wood-burning or chiseling set and some short slabs of wood from a local lumber company. Then put some classified ads in your newspaper advertising custom-made grave markers for deceased pets. You might also get permission from local pet store owners to put a notice up on their wall; be sure to let veterinarians and grooming salons know about your service as well.

In addition to marking the slabs, you could also paint them and decorate them with plastic flowers.

MONKEY BUSINESS

Barnum went to great extremes to promote his enterprises, and so should you, if necessary.

From a pet shop get yourself a friendly (some aren't so lovable) monkey. Train him to jump up on children's shoulders on command. Then get permission from a zoo, amusement park, shopping center—anywhere children congregate—to station yourself on their property, shooting the kids with the monkey on their shoulder. Use a Polaroid.

For further information:

How to Make Better Polaroid Instant Pictures: Complete Guide to Successful Use of the Polaroid Land Camera, Paul Giambarba. Garden City, New York, Doubleday, 1970.

Polaroid Photography, Kalton Lahue. Los Angeles, Petersen, 1974.

CANINE COOKBOOK

Write a cookbook specializing in recipes for the barking set. Dishes might include

Chow mein, Spaniel stew, and Great Danish pastry. Naturally, you'll want your recipes to be nutritious as well as novel. You might also include recipes for cats, rabbits, hamsters, birds, goldfish, and two-toed sloths.

To start, write query letters to book editors, whose names you can find in the *Writer's Market,* at your library.

PRECOCIOUS PARAKEETS

This is a great idea for someone who wants to have fun and make money at the same time.

Buy a number of parakeets—they sell for under ten dollars each at most pet shops. Then, using a tape recorder, teach the birds a few simple phrases such as "Good morning," "Welcome to my store," and "Son of a gun."

When you've got these feathered fellows talking up a storm, take them around to small stores, offering to sell the owner a package consisting of a bird, an inexpensive cage, and some feed for fifty dollars. It'll be a great promotional idea for the store—and a real money-maker for you.

PET HOTEL

Pet owners lavish millions of dollars a year on their pets—so why not start a luxury pet "hotel"?

Endow your establishment with human characteristics. For instance, have "suites" instead of pens, china plates instead of feeding bowls, filet mignon instead of dog chow—you get the general idea. Personalized attention such as daily grooming and walks are also important.

You needn't restrict your services to dogs. Cats, birds, rabbits, guinea pigs, and fish are all possible candidates for your hotel.

Charge five dollars per day and up.

DOG TOGS

If you're a frustrated fashion designer, why not break into the field by designing and custom-making clothing for dogs? Sweaters, vests, jackets, knitted collars, even fur coats are possibilities in this lucrative field.

To get started, let pet shops, veterinarians, and grooming salons know about your services. You could also promote your business by holding a dog fashion show in a department store, letting the pooches model your wares. Be sure to let the media know beforehand so that you can capitalize on some free publicity.

WOOL FROM WOOFER

You won't find "dog wool" in the dictionary, but it's simply fiber from long-haired dogs such as Samoyeds, poodles, collies, and malamutes.

In this unique business customers will bring fibers to you from their own dogs for spinning and/or weaving. Then you'll sew or knit articles from the material, such as sweaters, hats, mittens, socks, scarves—even a stuffed replica of the animal from which the material came!

For further information:

Spinning and Weaving, Glen Pownall. New York, Drake, 1973.

Creative Spinning, Weaving, and Plant-Dyeing, Beryl Anderson. New York, International Publications, 1971.

PET CEMETERY

If you have a little land outside of town you could offer a complete burial service for pets. Make available the same services that a human funeral home provides. This would include caskets, grave markers, and burial. If you wanted to get even more entrenched in the business you could offer cremations, urns, and vaults. However, be sure not to bury yourself in details!

To get started, let veterinarians and pet shops know about your service. Once you get going, you can probably get some free publicity by calling your local newspaper and TV station. A venture of this type has news value and they will probably be more than happy to find out about it.

Show Biz

☼ BE A VENDING MACHINE

A resourceful San Francisco street artist has proven that it's possible to make a living with no more than a large cast-off cardboard carton from an appliance dealer and a dubious ability to play a trumpet. Dubbing himself "The Human Jukebox," he opens a trap door from inside the box and belts out a tune whenever coin or currency is pushed through a hole by an expectant tourist. Perpetual crowds seem to keep this man's coffer well filled.

Even if you can't play a trumpet or other instrument, you can still use this gimmick to your advantage. How? By singing, dancing, or performing a magic trick.

☼ TEACH BELLY DANCING

You say it's even difficult for you to dance out of bed in the morning, much less teach belly dancing?

C'mon now. Anybody from six to sixty can learn this ancient Egyptian art, and once you learn, you can profit by teaching this stomach squirming, this tummy twisting, this paunch parading to others.

Hold classes at the local Y, an evening adult school, a recreational center, or on television. To attract attention, take on some male students, or put on an exhibition. Another way to ply your trade would be to work as a nightclub act.

For further information:

The Secrets of Bellydancing, Roman and Sula Balladine. Milbrae, California, Celestial Arts, 1972.

The Serena Technique of Belly Dancing, Serena Wilson and Alan Wilson. New York, Pocket Books, 1974.

☼ WHAT ARE YOU—A COMEDIAN?

You'll be able to answer this question in the affirmative if you have a natural ability to make people laugh—and if you promote that ability.

Start out by performing your routines at cocktail parties, lodge meetings, nightclubs, resorts, and fairs. There's no limit to how far you can go if you've got what it takes.

We'll be watching for you on TV!

For further information:

How to Be a Comedian for Fun or Profit, Harry King and Ann Lee Laufer. Studio City, California, Laufking, 1972.

Comedian's Gag File, Robert Orben. Hackensack, New Jersey, Wehman, 1974.

☼ FRANTIC OVER PHRENOLOGY

This science, which developed around the beginning of the nineteenth century, supposedly allowed the phrenologist to determine mental ability and character by feeling the shape of an individual's skull. Although modern neurology has long since debunked phrenological theories, you can use phrenology as a gag at festivals, fairs, carnivals, flea markets, and company picnics.

After getting permission to ply your unique trade, dress yourself up in a robe and turban. Have a gaily decorated tent for your "readings." A French accent would likewise be an asset.

For further information:

How to Read Character: A New Illustrated Handbook of Phrenology and Physiognomy, Samuel Wells. Rutland, Vermont, C. E. Tuttle, 1971.

Phrenology, Sybil Leek. New York, Macmillan, 1971.

☼ BE A FORTUNE-TELLER

Using a crystal ball, palmistry, or Tarot cards, you'll hire yourself out as a fortune-teller at fairs, carnivals, parties, company picnics, and other celebrations.

After getting permission from the people in charge of these events, set yourself up in an ominous-looking booth or tent. Dress like a gypsy, replete with golden earrings. It would likewise help your image to cultivate, for the event, a thick European accent.

For further information:

> *Your Practical Guide to Fortune Telling,* Rod Davies. New York, Pinnacle, 1974.
>
> *Sybil Leek Book of Fortune Telling,* Sybil Leek. New York, Macmillan, 1969.

 YOU—AN ASTROLOGER?

Don't kid yourself. Anybody can learn astrology and any good businessperson can make money at it.

If you're not familiar with the subject there are scads of books that can be consulted. Then, after you've sharpened up your astrological abilities, start doing horoscopes for your friends. Work out a fund-raising plan with organizations whereby they get 25 percent of your fee for each member that becomes your client. Appear on a TV talk show and discuss your field. Write a book. Offer to do the mayor's horoscope, free. Write a newspaper column.

For further information:

> *Astrology for All,* Bhawani Mishra. Thompson, Connecticut, InterCulture Associates, 1974.
>
> *Astrology and Foretelling the Future: A Concise Guide,* Thomas Aylesworth. New York, Franklin Watts, 1973.

 CLOWNIN' AROUND

You can buy or rent a clown's getup at any costume supply company. Give yourself an appropriate name, such as Bingo the Clown, and learn a few simple magic tricks in order to amuse the children. It might also help to get yourself a funny-looking bicycle or small car to ride around in.

Get started by advertising your availability for children's parties, shopping center promotions, parades, fairs, conventions, and church bazaars, and by contacting the people in charge of these events. Charge an hourly fee.

For further information:

> *The Amateur Magician's Handbook,* Henry Hay. New York, Thomas Y. Crowell, 1972.
>
> *Magic Tricks for Amateurs,* W. Dexter. Hackensack, New Jersey, Wehman.
>
> *Professional Magic for Amateurs,* Walter B. Gibson. New York, Dover, 1974.

 TEA LEAVES TALK

It's said that the patterns formed by tea leaves after the tea has been drunk tell many tales—past, present, and future—of the drinker.

Make an arrangement with a high-class supper club or tearoom to read customers' tea leaves each evening. Charge each customer a few dollars. If you're a good judge of character and can give entertaining readings, you'll be an asset to the business, and you shouldn't have to split any of your earnings with the boss.

Naturally, you'll want to don gypsy attire, as well as affecting a convincing European accent.

For further information:

> *Art of Tea Cup Fortune Telling,* Minetta. Hackensack, New Jersey, Wehman, 1964.

RUN A TALENT AGENCY

Seek out singers, dancers, musicians, magicians, and novelty acts in your area. You can find them by placing ads in the paper or by making the rounds of local nightspots featuring live entertainment.

After you've got a stable of performers lined up you'll act as agent, booking them for parties, weddings, bar mitzvahs, and so on.

As agent, you'll collect 10–20 percent of the performers' fee.

YOU—A VENTRILOQUIST?

Sure! With a lot of practice you can be putting your words in someone else's mouth—and getting paid for it! Naturally, in addition to training, you'll need a ready wit and the ability to entertain audiences.

Once you've developed the necessary skills, rent your act out to children's parties, store openings, fairs, carnivals, conventions—anywhere people expect to be entertained. You might also register with a booking agency and approach the program directors of local TV stations about the possibility of having your own show.

For further information:

Ventriloquism for Beginners, Douglas Houlden. Cranbury, New Jersey, A. S. Barnes, 1967.

You Can Be a Ventriloquist, Robert Hill. Chicago, Moody Press, 1974.

COSTUME BRIGADE

This unique idea involves making, renting, or buying from two to six costumes. One might be a long-eared rabbit; another, a large mouse or friendly-looking bear.

Hire some friends or college students to don the costumes. Then make a deal with an amusement park, department store, shopping center, or airport to entertain their customers by having your friends prance around in the costumes a few days every week. Charge a set fee. In addition, you might want to bring along a Polaroid camera and sell pictures of the children posed with the various animals.

For further information:

Costume Patterns and Designs, Max Tilke. New York, Hastings House, 1974.

Basic Pattern Drafting for the Theatrical Costume Designer, William H. Shaw. New York, Drama Book Specialists, 1974.

BE A GRAPHOLOGIST

Graphology, or the science of analyzing handwriting, can be profitably sold as a service through classified ads in national magazines of general interest. Concentrating especially on fan and women's magazines, you'll offer a complete analysis for a few dollars. A long analysis isn't necessary—a paragraph or two will be fine.

You can also earn money with this ability at fairs, carnivals, shopping centers, beaches —anywhere people congregate.

For further information:

How to Analyze Handwriting, Hal Falcon. New York, Trident, 1971.

A Manual of Graphology, Eric Singer. New York, Hippocrene, 1974.

GO-GO AGENT

This idea won't work so well in a place like Horse Branch, Kentucky. But if you live in sin-filled San Francisco or naughty New York, you might consider acquiring a stable of go-go girls and then persuading nightclub owners to hire them.

The girls needn't be professional dancers—or dancers at all, for that matter. As long as they're young, curvaceous, and able to gyrate with the music, they'll do fine. Take 15 percent of their wages as your commission.

Bibliography

The following publications will provide general information on starting and operating a small business:

How to Organize and Operate a Small Business, Clifford Baumback, Kenneth Lawyer, and Pearce Kelley. Englewood Cliffs, New Jersey, Prentice-Hall, 1973.

How to Run a Small Business, J. K. Lasser Tax Institute. New York, McGraw-Hill, 1974.

You, Inc., P. Weaver. Garden City, New York, Doubleday, 1973.

Up Your Own Organization!, Donald Dible. Santa Clara, California, Entrepreneur Press, 1971.

How to Start Your Own Small Business on a Shoestring and Make Over $100,000 a Year, T. Hicks. Englewood Cliffs, New Jersey, Prentice-Hall, 1968.

Starting and Succeeding in Your Own Small Business, Louis Allen. New York, Grosset & Dunlap, 1968.

Starting and Managing a Small Business of Your Own, Small Business Administration. Washington, D. C., Superintendent of Documents, U. S. Government Printing Office.

Problems in Managing a Family-Owned Business, Management Aid #208. Available from any Small Business Administration Field Office, or write Small Business Administration, Washington, D. C. 20416.

The following three publications will provide valuable ideas and advice for the small businessperson:

- *The Franklin Letter*, P. O. Box 95, Demarest, New Jersey 07627 (monthly).

- *Income Opportunities*, 229 Park Avenue South, New York, New York 10003 (monthly).

- *Guide to Earning Extra Income*, 363 Seventh Avenue, New York, New York 10001 (published every two months).